Managing as a
Performing Art

Managing as a Performing Art

New Ideas
for a World
of Chaotic Change

Peter B. Vaill

89-984

Jossey-Bass Publishers
San Francisco • London • 1989

MANAGING AS A PERFORMING ART
New Ideas for a World of Chaotic Change
by Peter B. Vaill

Copyright © 1989 by: Jossey-Bass Inc., Publishers
350 Sansome Street
San Francisco, California 94104
&
Jossey-Bass Limited
28 Banner Street
London EC1Y 8QE

The excerpt reprinted on pp. 175-176 is from *Tao Te Ching* by Lao Tsu,
translated by Gia-fu Feng and Jane English. Copyright © 1972 by Gia-fu Fe
and Jane English. Reprinted by permission of Alfred A. Knopf, Inc.

Library of Congress Cataloging-in-Publication Data

Vaill, Peter B.
    Managing as a performing art.

    (The Jossey-Bass management series)
    Bibliography: p.
    Includes index.
    1. Management. I. Title. II. series.
HD38.V23 1989   658.4   88-32842
ISBN 1-55542-140-7 (alk. paper)

Manufactured in the United States of America

The paper in this book meets the guidelines for
permanence and durability of the Committee on
Production Guidelines for Book Longevity of the
Council on Library Resources.

JACKET DESIGN BY WILLI BAUM

FIRST EDITION
    First printing: January 1989
    Second printing: June 1989

Code 8913

The Jossey-Bass
Management Series

Contents

Preface

Managing as a Performing Art is about leadership and management in modern organizations. The book is personal and reflective; through it I try to convey my love for the subject and for the people who act as leaders and managers as well as to provide straightforward information. This is also an impassioned book because I am very worried about our present capacities to understand the organizational world in which we live and work and to perform the appropriate actions to fulfill the needs of this world. Events are outrunning understanding in all sectors of society. The men and women about whom I have written in this book live and work in the midst of constantly changing events—in many cases they create new events. To the extent that the imperatives of action are disconnected from the musings of thought, we are in considerable peril.

I don't know if there is a "muse of management," but there ought to be one. The nine muses of Greek mythology were the patron goddesses of the arts and sciences. Management is widely believed to be an art, a *performing art* if you agree with what I have written in Chapter Eight of this book. Certainly managers are constantly in need of the clarity, competence, and courage that an attentive muse could provide. But the Greek muses were shrouded in mist, and they came and went unpredictably. Any manager extrapolating about the fickleness of the muse of management is allowed to mutter, "You've got THAT right! Tell me about it." What I do in this book is write about the sorts of ideas we have available for coping with the organizational worlds of the present and future. I critique those ideas, play with them, turn them around, pun on them, and sometimes work hard to puncture them. This book can perform no higher service than to stimulate readers to do these same things.

The Manager's Point of View

Every organization is a small universe containing receding galaxies of specialized knowledge and interests. The practical manager trying to get something accomplished provides the chief "gravity" in these little universes. The manager's interests and energies hold things together.

The gravity created by organizational leaders and managers turns some people off, but it has been my principal preoccupation for the past twenty-five years. A glimpse into the situation of a leader or manager who is trying to help things happen in one way rather than another in an organization is what I got out of six memorable years at the Harvard Business School. At Harvard they called this situation the *administrative point of view,* and it was a concept of tantalizing vagueness to most of us there. I can almost pinpoint the exact moment when I "got it," when I saw what it means to be in this crucible.

My wife and I once watched a BBC production of Jean Anouilh's modern rendering of *Antigone.* Creon, the king, leaves Polynices's body to rot in the open as a symbol of what will happen to revolutionaries. Antigone entreats the king to let her give her brother a decent burial. In their drawn-out, emotional exchanges, all the tragic dilemmas of action, responsibility, the right thing versus the expedient thing, and power versus morality are displayed with an aching poignancy. It becomes abundantly clear that Antigone is absolutely right within her moral frame of decency and love (which we all cherish), but Creon is also juggling moral frames: his responsibilities to Antigone, to Polynices, to the people and the state, to himself, and to the gods.

He is caught in the classic, tragic "vise" of conflicting values and responsibilities. The crunch Creon is in requires what the faculty at Harvard Business School called an *administrative point of view,* and what we would now call a *managerial point of view.* It is a mentality and posture that requires one to juggle, balance, and reconcile conflicting values and priorities, all in relation to objectives and constraints. It does not involve the luxury of a single-minded zealousness for just one value or goal.

In the end, there are no perfect solutions to leadership and management problems; and frequently there aren't even any good solutions. But because the essence of leadership is action and responsibility, one cannot *not* act. If you are a manager/leader in an organization, *to be is to act and to live with the consequences of your actions.* Leaders and managers aren't talking enough about these issues among themselves. In this book I try to point to the territory that needs further exploration.

Who Should Read This Book

My intended audience is the many men and women with different roles in our society who are finding that they need to take a fresh look at organizations and how to manage them. *Managing as a Performing Art* is a book of ideas, not of how-to-do-it prescriptions. The primary audience for this book will be organizational managers and leaders and specialists in organization development (OD) and human resources (HR) management. Other readers will be academics seeking new theories and consultants seeking new ways to be helpful. My fondest hope, however, is that regular, down-to-earth, practicing managers will find these ideas interesting and relevant. Too many of the recent books for practicing managers have been how-to-do-it checklists. This book takes the real situation and concerns of the practicing manager much more seriously.

The Main Themes and the Contents of the Book

Two themes recur throughout this book, and they are introduced in its title. Both of these themes are explored thoroughly in Chapter One. The first theme, the performing arts metaphor, expresses the dynamism, fluidity, extraordinary complexity, and fundamental personalness of all organizational action. The second theme is that of chaotic change. In using that term I am not just being colorful. I am using the word *chaotic* in the sense that Gleick (1987) suggests—that is, to describe a system that is *unstable at every point.* Ackoff (1974) called the same phenomenon a *mess*—that is, a system of problems or instabilities. The present environment of chaotic change requires a response so different from the traditional managerial approach of diagnose-plan-implement-evaluate that perhaps I should not even use the simple word *change* to refer to the kinds of events contemporary managers are facing. The main image used in Chapter One is permanent white water, and with it I intend to capture the pace, complexity, novelty, danger, and nonstop challenge of the modern environment.

Chapter Two is a discussion of managerial competencies. I'm a little suspicious of these competency approaches because I don't think we've thought enough about the real texture of managing. In order to determine competencies, you have to be very simplistic about managing, I think; and in Chapter Two I discuss in detail some of the disturbing consequences of being so simplistic.

Chapter Three is about my favorite topic—excellence and high performance. My main focus is on the enormously important role of clarity of purpose, but I also described a couple of twists to which I don't think we've paid enough attention. First, excellence is in the eye of the beholder (as the chapter's title suggests), and second, you're *never* done with *purposing*—by which I mean the ongoing process of getting clear and staying clear on the purpose of the organization.

Chapter Four peers into the dark side of excellence and discusses some of the things we may have overlooked about people and organizations in our fascination with high performance. As I point out in this chapter, my worst fears are that the pursuit of excellence will become just another fad in management; that our illusions will be followed by disillusionment; and that this subject, which is at the core of what managing and leading are all about, will lose its significance among practicing managers.

Chapter Five exposes some of the basic puzzles managers deal with daily. Managers usually try to make improbable events and achievements more likely, but in so doing they are confronted with paradox and contradiction. In Chapter Five I try to help managers feel more "friendly to paradox." In the process I offer a new view of the attached, involved manager, whose understanding of what is possible and of effective management grows from unfolding experience within the organization instead of from external forces.

Chapter Six describes the way in which managers think about things and introduces the mentality of the "technoholic," the person who is hooked on techniques, cookbooks, lists, and methods. Through Chapter Six I hope to help free the technoholic from these compulsions, for in the world of permanent white water nothing ever quite works as it is intended to or expected to.

In Chapter Seven I focus on a particular aspect of the highly technical world we live in—that is, the problem of communication in a room full of people who don't understand each other's expertise, but among whom collaboration and synergy are somehow supposed to emerge. The chapter title, "Satchmo's Paradox," refers to Louis Armstrong's famous remark: "If you have to ask what jazz is, you'll never know." Satchmo and his indescribable specialty—jazz—become metaphors for the soup we are all swimming in.

In Chapter Eight I describe managing as a performing art, a metaphor I first fashioned for a commencement address I gave to the graduates of the George Washington University School of Government and Business Administration in 1974. It is an enormously liberating idea, and it invokes new thoughts about leading and managing in any setting.

Chapter Nine explores and develops a notion I have heard from dozens of managers over the years—that is, that the possibilities of excellence in any organization ultimately depend on the people and how managers work with them. But Chapter Nine poses a tough challenge, too, for in it I argue that if we are serious about the significance of people, we had better honestly consider our ideas about human nature.

In Chapter Ten I introduce a new way of thinking about

organizational culture and suggest that it is valuable to understand culture because the world of permanent white water may destroy it! Like the preceding chapter, Chapter Ten is a call to arms to managers and leaders.

Chapter Eleven, "What Should the Top Team Be Talking About?," asks what, to me, is one of the most important questions for managers and offers some tentative answers. Along the way some new thoughts are offered about strategic management and top management development.

In Chapter Twelve I look to the Far East and explore how the fascinating philosophy of Taoism may apply to Western managerial situations. As in earlier chapters, my mood is reflective and speculative as I look at some promising ideas that may help managers and leaders cope with the incredible instability of their world.

In Chapter Thirteen I try something different: I fantasize a conversation among five of the great shapers of the industrial age. In this conversation I ask about the role faith plays in our acceptance of the theories developed by these great innovators. Managers live more in a world of faith than they like to acknowledge, and this chapter is a playful attempt to make that acknowledgment a little easier.

The final chapter, on spirituality in organizational life, presents a crucial piece of the whole puzzle, even though I consider myself only a beginner on the whole subject. At some deep level, however, I think *executive development IS spiritual development*. It is on this note that the book draws to a close.

Thus the book combines a deep, rich, personal view of what good management is all about with what I hope is an unflinching look at the nature of the world in which we live today. A former football coach turned top manager said to me recently, "Management is just one big broken play where we're all making it up as we go along." And a theater director, who knew something about management, told me he thought managing and leading are more like *street theater* than anything else. Just so from these two friends of this book. Good advice to be borne in mind as we proceed.

Style, Tone, and Mood

One of the most popular of the psychological tests managers are learning from these days is the Myers-Briggs Type Indicator (MBTI) (Briggs, 1980; Kroeger and Thuesen, 1988). One can be either an Extrovert (E) or an Introvert (I); a speculating, dreaming Intuiter (N) or a hands-on, data-oriented Sensate (S); a logical, clear-headed Thinker (T) or a subjective, people-oriented Feeling (F) type of person; and one can prefer one's ability to Perceive (P) the world (N or S) or one's ability to Judge (J) the world (T or F). These four dimensions and two possible types of each give us sixteen possible types. I am one of the less common types, the INFP: an Introverted, Intuitive, Feeling, Perceiver.

I am not sure myself how much significance the MBTI has. On the one hand, I don't think one's behavior can possibly be determined by one's psychological type; but on the other hand, it is quite natural for an INFP to harbor such doubts. Nevertheless, I do think that this is a book that only an INFP would write or, for that matter, *could* write. The chapters are full of ideas, many of which are fairly new and different. They come from the nonstop spinning of my mind, which is a hallmark of the Intuitive (N). If you know how strong N's operate, you will not be surprised to learn that a good half or more of the ideas in this book emerged as I wrote it. My Feeling (F) side makes a lot of subjective judgments with which I am actually quite comfortable, even though I know they're just the result of my personal point of view and, therefore, highly debatable. A lot of the writing is very personalized, too, which is another sign of the F.

Perceivers (P) love montages. This book is more a montage than it is a single linear argument. A set of concerns about organizations and managing is expressed here, and these concerns lend themselves to a variety of literary methods. I have tried to be mindful of order and linear logic in the flow of my discussions, but I realize that the overall organization is elusive. That is why it is important to keep in mind while reading this book the two broad themes mentioned earlier.

MBTI theory says that if you are an Introvert (I) and you show the world a relaxed, somewhat disorganized Perceiver (P) attitude, then you probably have a strong Judger (J) inside that is keeping careful track of what is important. That is true of me: My Judger is quite strong regarding the quality of ideas about management. For many years there has been this little perfectionist bean counter in me that won't let first drafts and sketches be seen by others until they're cleaned up, organized, and pulled together. I have copied and collated a lot of pages of my writings over the years, all the while telling the little perfectionist inside not to worry, it's only an informal handout and no big deal. This book is published, therefore, against my better "Judger-ment." (I had to say this to make its issuance possible.)

Through it all, the Introvert (I) in me just floats along in its bubble, enjoying the ideas and feelings that come along. Introversion permits me to blithely declare a lot of "truths" in this book with which others might disagree. I have removed a lot of "from my point of view" and "it seems to me" qualifiers, and the copyeditor has removed more. I want readers to know, especially the Sensates (S) who like facts and the Thinkers (T) who like logic, that I know how subjective and impressionistic this book is. Rather than throw it against the wall when my NFing becomes too much, lie down for a while in a dark room and muster facts that support or refute what I've written. Then, please stay in touch.

Thanks

INFP's aren't easy to have as colleagues: I certainly wouldn't load up on them myself. It is especially important to me to say how much I appreciate the support I have received from everyone with whom I have ever been associated professionally. The list of people who have supported my NFing over the years with cries of "Keep it up" is long and diverse. In the OD Network, the Organizational Behavior Teaching Society, the NTL Institute, the Army Organizational Effectiveness Program, the MetaNetwork, the universities where I have worked, and the dozens of companies and agencies for which I have worked, there are hundreds of people I wish I could thank personally for encouraging me in my style of thinking and working.

Out of this large group there are three colleagues I want to thank publicly: Robert Tannenbaum, formerly at UCLA, and Jerry Harvey, my colleague at George Washington University, can take a lot of the credit for the quality of the ideas contained in this book. Despite all the moaning and groaning these days about the loss of community and the decline of "connectedness," the readiness of each of these men, in all his loving toughmindedness, to be my friend proves to me beyond any doubt that there is still hope for me, for us, and for this world. William Hicks, my Jossey-Bass editor, did what no one else has ever been able to do: He coaxed my Introverted Judger (IJ) to let go of its little hoard of half-baked ideas and allow them to be printed and bound between hard covers. For helping me over my qualms, he has my undying gratitude.

Finally, to my wife, Debbie, I want to express my thanks and love for sharing the word processor and herself.

Johns Creek   Peter B. Vaill
Lusby, Maryland
January 1989

To my parents,
Stanley T. Vaill and Elizabeth B. Vaill,
with love

The Author

Peter B. Vaill is professor of human systems at George Washington University's School of Government and Business Administration in Washington, D.C. From 1973 to 1978, he was dean of this school. Before joining the faculty of George Washington University, he served on the faculties of the University of Connecticut School of Business Administration and the UCLA Graduate School of Management. In 1980, he was visiting professor of organizational behavior at the Graduate School of Business, Stanford University. He holds a B.A. degree (1958) in psychology from the University of Minnesota and M.B.A. (1960) and D.B.A. (1964) degrees from the Harvard Business School.

Vaill's special fields of interest are strategic management, organization development, and the philosophy of social science. In 1972, he created a theory of high-performing systems, and he is widely known as a pioneer contributor in the field of organizational excellence.

Vaill is a well-known consultant and lecturer to management groups. He was editor of the American Management Association's journal, *Organizational Dynamics,* from 1985 to 1988. He is active in the Organizational Behavior Teaching Society, the OD Network, and the NTL Institute.

Managing as a
Performing Art

Chapter 1

Permanent White Water

How much change, uncertainty, and turbulence can the modern manager handle? Everyone these days seems to be talking about the need to handle substantial amounts of change, uncertainty, and turbulence, but seldom do we find people talking about the possibility that we may be approaching some kind of red line of the psyche, some state where it is all just too much to cope with. We don't like to think about this possibility, and the managerial culture that has shaped our thinking gives us little help. As a manager in a major pharmaceutical company said to me some months back, "We aren't so much on the red line as we're in the red *zone*." I thought that this was a little lame, and I could tell that he did, too; but his impulse was to evade the crunching thought behind the red-line (boiler gauge) metaphor, and so was mine. He sought in the notion of a red *zone* yet a little more slack to get him through the next few crises in his company. He had to tell himself that he could still work a little smarter or at least a little harder to get over the foreseeable humps of his managerial life. He didn't want to think that maybe hump-getting-over under essentially impossible conditions is and will be managerial life for the foreseeable future. And neither did I.

A manager who attended a seminar I was conducting—
a more realistic sort than my red-zone-seeking friend—supplied
me with the metaphor that in various ways runs all through this
book. It is the metaphor of "permanent white water." "Most
managers are taught to think of themselves as paddling their
canoes on calm, still lakes," he said. "They're led to believe
that they should be pretty much able to go where they want,
when they want, using means that are under their control. Sure
there will be temporary disruptions during changes of various
sorts—periods when they'll have to shoot the rapids in their
canoes—but the disruptions will be temporary, and when things
settle back down, they'll be back in the calm, still lake mode.
But it has been my experience," he concluded, "that you never
get out of the rapids! No sooner do you begin to digest one
change than another one comes along to keep things unstuck.
In fact, there are usually lots of changes going on at once. The
feeling is one of continuous upset and chaos."

He offered this metaphor in response to one that I had
suggested, that today's leaders and managers are in the position of stepping into the dark with most of the initiatives they
propose. They don't know what's going to happen next. That
actually makes the step-into-the-dark metaphor not quite right,
I had just said, because when you step into the dark, you still
make the assumption that your foot is going to come down on
something solid, even if you don't know what it is going to be.
Today's executive can't even make that assumption. That was
when this manager suggested that we live in a world of permanent white water.

I like this metaphor. It has a strong visual appeal. It
vividly conveys a sense of energy and movement. Things are
only very partially under control, yet the effective navigator of
the rapids is not behaving randomly or aimlessly. Intelligence,
experience, and skill are being exercised, albeit in ways that we
hardly know how to perceive, let alone describe.

Yet this is precisely what I shall be trying to do in these
chapters. I think the revolution we are in is first and foremost
a revolution of the total situation. It is not just new kinds of
problems and opportunities that we are facing, but whole new

contexts within which these problems and opportunities reside. Twenty years ago, Emery and Trist said that in turbulent environments, "the ground itself is moving" (Emery, 1969, p. 249). This image captures the change of context; indeed, it suggests that contexts themselves have destabilized to the point where we can no longer assume that the basic structure of the context surrounding a situation will hold still long enough to make a planned course of action feasible. At least that's the way it *feels:* more and more, executives cannot count on the presence of markets; the availability of technologies; the likely actions of competitors, foreign and domestic, and of legislators and regulatory bodies; or the reactions of employees, of their families, and, indeed, of their own bodies and minds to the kinds of actions they are contemplating. This is what I mean by a destabilized context: things one used to be able to take for granted, treat as relatively given, can no longer be viewed that way. In a destabilized context, you cannot know exactly what your problems are!

Perhaps even the metaphor of permanent white water is not adequate: we are not talking merely about a wild river; we are talking about an unpredictable wild river.

Ralph Siu has captured the problem of a continuously changing context in the idea of what he calls "Chinese baseball" (Siu, 1980). The mythical game of Chinese baseball is just like American baseball in all respects save one: in Chinese baseball, whenever the ball is in the air, anyone is allowed to pick up any base and move it—anywhere! I don't know whether anyone has actually tried to play such a game, but the image certainly captures the feeling of not being able to count on anything as one attempts to score runs or make outs. Or, indeed, *would* we be attempting to do these things in quite the same way as in "regular" baseball? Maybe we would find that run scoring and out making themselves change as the context unfolds (that is, as the bases move around unpredictably) and that one actually needs a completely different concept of what playing "well" means. One might discover that there is a kind of correlation between existing contexts and the goals that can be reasonably sought. Under certain sets of conditions, one doesn't even try to score runs or make outs, whereas other conditions are more propitious for run scoring and out making. Learning to tell the difference then becomes absolutely crucial. It is fascinating to consider how one actually would play Chinese baseball. The game would make an interesting recreational activity for an off-site executive development meeting.

Steps into the dark, permanent and unpredictable white water, Chinese baseball—these are the images we carry with us into this series of discussions of the lives of leaders and managers in the present and future organizational world. These comments about shifting contexts only set the stage, however, for what I want to talk about in more detail in the pages that follow. Many writers have written forcefully and colorfully about the pace of change and the turbulence of the world we live in. The preceding discussion should serve as a reminder of many of the things people such as Alvin Toffler, John Naisbett, Daniel Yankelovitch, and others have been saying. My focus in what follows is a bit different. I want to talk at some length about three things that are profoundly affected by the rise of a world of shifting contexts: (1) how the job of the leader-manager has been changing in relation to these changing contexts; (2) how the process of learning the job and developing within it is also changing; and (3) how the combination of these first two leads to the need for new philosophies of what life and effective action taking in organizations really are. Particularly in this third category, I am going to talk about some deeper matters than practicing executives are usually confronted with. The only question in my mind at the outset is whether I will be able to talk deeply *enough* to match the challenge. Following Siu's suggestion, we are talking about a game that no one knows how to play. That means that we must be prepared to look in some strange places for our ideas, and it means perhaps that some of our more cherished ideas are not good maps for the courses of action that executives are trying to follow. ''In the midst of an earthquake, the last thing I want is an overly detailed map,'' says Ed Speedling, director of organization development (OD) at New York's Mount Sinai Medical Center. We have to question some of the maps that we have, and we have to question the ways that we learned these maps. I am going to suggest some new values and priorities that are becoming important to mapping this game that no one knows how to play.

One of the phrases we have been hearing a lot lately is ''working smarter.'' It is offered as the main line of defense against the turbulence and threatening chaos. The need to work smarter has almost become a cliché. I want to push what we mean by this phrase—rather hard, in fact, for in some ways I heartily agree that we have to work smarter. But I think that some of the common connotations of the phrase aren't so smart anymore. In fact, some meanings are rapidly becoming obsolete. Let's take a minute to review these familiar meanings of what it is to work smarter. Later on, I will describe a more forward-looking concept of working smarter.

One approach that we all understand and use frequently is to put more stuff to read into our attaché cases (perhaps even add a second attaché case), mentally cross off what we had been planning for the evening or the weekend, and decide that a burst of reading and writing will crush some issue that either has become a crisis or has been kicking around our in basket for weeks. In other words, working ''smarter'' often really means working *harder*. Another variation on the theme of increased effort is that we decide that we are going to schedule ourselves more tightly: we figure out how to kill more birds with one stone on our trips and at our meetings. Tighter scheduling is not necessarily smarter scheduling except in the sense of filling up available time. However, I suspect that most readers of these words have already been around this smarter = harder track about as many times as they want to go. Even though we still may be trying to squeeze in additional things, in our heart we know that the bucket is getting pretty full and that when we really look at it, we aren't ''tightly'' scheduled: we're *over*scheduled.

A second meaning of ''working smarter'' does have to do with becoming smarter. Relentless, nonstop pursuit of more and more knowledge about the job has become part of the managerial landscape: advanced degrees, conferences, workshops, briefings, self-study. Any airport bookstand is a testimony to the existence of a vast market for more knowledge about management

and leadership. Once again, this very familiar strategy for coping is not wrong; rather, it is inadequate. We are all studying
about as hard as we can study, and we still find ourselves dealing daily with issues that go beyond our knowledge and experience. The theories and models we have been studying were not
formulated for the actual world of permanent white water, even
those that purport to handle "uncertainty." The uncertainty
that they handle is the uncertainty the creator was able to imagine. That is uncertainty within a specific frame, for all these
models and techniques make assumptions.

For example, consider a financial forecasting formula we
might study. It assumes that we have the data; it assumes that
no other forces will contaminate its approach; it assumes that
its objective is the objective we actually want to achieve. Furthermore, it assumes that the technical approach taken will be *per-
ceived* to be appropriate, not just by the person who is "cranking
the data" but by those who must supply the data, understand
and live with the results, support the approach in meetings, and
so on. The *political* meaning of technical approaches to organizational problems is not often given much weight by those who
advocate the techniques. This is the problem with all technical
knowledge: it doesn't know what it doesn't know (see Chapter
Seven). Yet the person who would use a technique is embedded
in a live situation and has to take the consequences for what
people think of the technique. Perhaps this is why techniques
enjoy such faddishness. Once a particular approach achieves
"credibility," one can almost hear a collective sigh of relief in
the organization, for at last people think they know what they
are talking about. Some management consultants know this
yearning well and market aggressively to it. Yet the white waters
keep lapping at the edges of the problem and of our confidence.

The third meaning of "working smarter" is one that has
become very popular in the 1980s. It is working more shrewdly,
more cleverly, more politically. It is the smartness that knows
where the power is, that knows how to walk and talk, that sniffs
changes in the power winds before others do. It is the world
of the fast track and of looking out for number one, of not getting mad but getting even, of knowing that those who have the

gold rule, and that when the going gets tough, the tough get going. It is simply the only way to be in many of our organizations, an ethos that Kelly (1987, 1988) nailed in his memorable portrayal of the "destructive achiever." In terms of personal survival, it does seem smart to be aggressive. Yet I think we know that in the longer run, such individuals develop reputations as untrustworthy. What seems to save them is that they keep moving on. They leave the corrosive effects of their operations for others to clean up.

These three kinds of working smarter—working harder, working technically smarter, and working politically smarter—are not, I repeat, wrong. They are inadequate. We already know how to practice them, and we are practicing them about as fully as they can be practiced. Even though there is still a lot of talk about doing each of these even better, and we all receive junk mail by the pound each day inviting us to enroll in yet one more workshop to upgrade our skills or buy a set of "can't miss" cassette tapes that will tell us everything there is to tell about, say, strategic management, in some deeper part of ourselves I think we know that there isn't much juice left in these solutions.

We have to understand the new managerial jobs if we want to cope more effectively with the world of permanent white water. We have to talk about what has been happening to the jobs of managers and other sorts of leaders. We have to take a look at the actual forms of thinking and acting that these jobs now invite and discourage. I don't mean so much that we have to look at the functions performed—such as strategic management or management information systems (MIS) development—as that we have to look at the content of the positions themselves and the organizational milieu that these jobs exist in. We have to ask what kind of a world it is we are trying to be smart *in*. This is the next question.

The Manager's Job—Myths and Realities

The questionnaire in Exhibit 1 will be our entrée into this new world of what managers and leaders are actually doing these days in organizations. I have titled it, with intentional casualness,

"A Manager's Job." I have administered it to close to 500 M.B.A. students and young managers, about equally divided between men and women and for the most part between the ages of twenty-three and thirty-three. About 20 percent of the respondents have been from countries other than the United States. To experienced managers, the items on this questionnaire are familiar territory, and they will have to think about it a little differently from the way that I encourage beginning managers to approach it; but I think I can still make my point, regardless of one's level of experience. I suggest that readers fill out and score the questionnaire now, before reading on.

Exhibit 1. A Manager's Job.

Listed below are some statements a thirty-seven-year-old manager made about his job at a large and successful corporation. If your job had these characteristics, how would you react to them? After each statement are five letters, A to E. Circle the letter that best describes how you think you would react according to the following scale:

A I would enjoy this very much; it's completely acceptable.
B This would be enjoyable and acceptable most of the time.
C I'd have no reaction to this feature one way or another, or it would be about equally enjoyable and unpleasant.
D This feature would be somewhat unpleasant for me.
E This feature would be very unpleasant for me.

1. I regularly spend 30–40 percent of my time in meetings. A B C D E
2. A year and a half ago, my job did not exist, and I have been essentially inventing it as I go along. A B C D E
3. The responsibilities I either assume or am assigned consistently exceed the authority I have for discharging them. A B C D E
4. At any given moment in my job, I have on the average about a dozen phone calls to be returned. A B C D E
5. There seems to be very little relation in my job between the quality of my performance and my actual pay and fringe benefits. A B C D E
6. About two weeks a year of formal management training is needed in my job just to stay current. A B C D E
7. Because we have very effective equal employment opportunity (EEO) in my company and because it is thoroughly multinational, my job consistently brings me into close working contact at a professional level with people of many races, ethnic groups, and nationalities and of both sexes. A B C D E
8. There is no objective way to measure my effectiveness. A B C D E
9. I report to three different bosses for different aspects of my job, and each has an equal say in my performance appraisal. A B C D E
10. On average, about a third of my time is spent dealing with unexpected emergencies that force all scheduled work to be postponed. A B C D E
11. When I have to have a meeting of the people who report to me, it takes

Exhibit 1. A Manager's Job, Con't.

---

my secretary most of a day to find a time when we are all available, and even then, I have yet to have a meeting where everyone is present for the entire meeting. A B C D E

12. The college degree I earned in preparation for this type of work is now obsolete, and I probably should go back for another degree. A B C D E

13. My job requires that I absorb 100–200 pages per week of technical material. A B C D E

14. I am out of town overnight at least one night per week. A B C D E

15. My department is so interdependent with several other departments in the company that all distinctions about which departments are responsible for which tasks are quite arbitrary. A B C D E

16. I will probably get a promotion in about a year to a job in another division that has most of these same characteristics. A B C D E

17. During the period of my employment here, either the entire company or the division I worked in has been reorganized every year or so. A B C D E

18. While there are several possible promotions I can see ahead of me, I have no real career path in an objective sense. A B C D E

19. While there are several possible promotions I can see ahead of me, I think I have no realistic chance of getting to the top levels of the company. A B C D E

20. While I have many ideas about how to make things work better, I have no direct influence on either the business policies or the personnel policies that govern my division. A B C D E

21. My company has recently put in an "assessment center" where I and all other managers will be required to go through an extensive battery of psychological tests to assess our potential. A B C D E

22. My company is a defendant in an antitrust suit, and if the case comes to trial, I will probably have to testify about some decisions that were made a few years ago. A B C D E

23. Advanced computer and other electronic office technology is continually being introduced into my division, necessitating constant learning on my part. A B C D E

24. The computer terminal and screen I have in my office can be monitored in my bosses' offices without my knowledge. A B C D E

Scoring: 4 points for each A, 3 for each B, 2 for each C, 1 for each D, 0 for each E. Compute the total, divide by 24, and round to one decimal place.

The point is a simple one: We aren't prepared for the sort of world this questionnaire portrays. The "culture" doesn't prepare us: our management classrooms and textbooks don't prepare us; even the commentators on how turbulent the world is becoming tend not to get as concrete as this questionnaire does about what life in these organizations is actually like. Experienced managers, however, consistently report that this questionnaire mirrors their work environment very well. As one person commented, "We're supposed to assume that all or most of these things are true of *one* job, right? Because they're all true of mine!" "How did you know what my job is like?" asked another.

If we take this degree of "upset" and unpredictability seriously, I think it changes everything. This is *real* Chinese baseball, and our calm statements about managers being planners and goal seekers and strategy formulators and implementors mean little if anything in this world. When the context is destabilized, as is that portrayed in this questionnaire, it changes everything.

How do respondents "do" on my questionnaire? Well, the scoring is the same as we all learned for calculating our grade point average in college. One who would "enjoy very much" and find "completely acceptable" each of the items on this questionnaire will end up with a 4.0 average. One who finds each of the items "very unpleasant for me" ends up with a zero. You get an *A* if you like these things, and you flunk if you don't. The results are remarkably stable. The range is narrow, and no particular subpopulation of age, sex, experience, or nationality seems to do better or worse than any other subpopulation. The average score is between 1.5 and 1.6—a *D+/C−* sort of grade. The range is between about 1.0 and about 2.2. There are few outliers, and the highest score ever achieved, 3.2, was that of a woman from the Dominican Republic who was just out of college and who had been admitted to both the Harvard and the Wharton business schools but had chosen to attend my university in Washington.

These results are not intended to be more than suggestive, for I believe that that is all one can ever ask of any attempt to quantify human actions and thoughts. There doubtless are flaws of validity and reliability in the questionnaire, and I am not recommending that anyone found their doctoral dissertation on it. But the results are interesting. They seem to bear out the idea that we aren't really ready for the world that today's managers are actually living in.

The job characteristics portrayed on the questionnaire are of course not "bad" in any absolute sense. A "good job" is totally in the eye of the beholder. The young people—M.B.A. candidates and relatively new managers—who filled out the questionnaire obviously don't find these characteristics very attractive. But why? Not for "psychological" reasons in the first instance, although qualities such as "tolerance for ambiguity" and "risk-taking ability" may enter into the evaluations of some of them. Regardless of psychological factors, it seems to me that these results are telling us that young people are unprepared for life in such organizational worlds. They think that management and leadership are something different from this. What do they think they are? What mythology of the managerial job do they hold?

I hypothesize that there are some "myths of management" that are operating to produce the negative feelings the questionnaire has captured. By *myths* I do not mean "useless and inaccurate belief systems." Without some shared stories to tell ourselves about the world around us, human beings cannot know what they collectively believe, and hence all but the most elementary communications are severely limited. However, as the environment and organization members change, it becomes necessary for myths and myth systems to change. If they are prevented from changing, either by ignorance and inattention or, worse yet, by the dogmatic imposition of a party line, myths can become very harmful by impairing a person's capacity to understand the surrounding world. What are these myths of management that may presently be impairing our capacity to understand the manager's world? There are at least seven that operate powerfully in our cultural consciousness and that have not yet been overturned by the world of permanent white water. A brief sketch of the seven follows; it must be borne in mind that they operate not as a list but as a system:

1. *The myth of a single person called "the manager" or "the leader."* This myth implies that there is a coherent, whole function or role to be performed. It is a very old idea that received enormous reinforcement in the twentieth century with the Harvard Business School's adoption in the 1920s of "the administrator" and later "the general manager" as the primary focus of its mission as a school (Copeland, 1958, p. 151). It is a vast

abstraction, of course, for all kinds of people without the title or the power have opportunities for management and leadership in the modern organization. The myth, though, obscures these possibilities. It also grounds new research about the competencies of this abstract "manager," a body of work the next chapter will question quite sharply.

2. *The myth that what the leader leads and the manager manages is a single, freestanding organization.* This myth is very much the legacy of the economists of the nineteenth century with their concept of "the firm" and the sociologists with their notion of a "bureaucracy." Once again, one must make an enormous simplification to abstract a collection of people and physical objects out of the total flow and call it "an organization." Our notion of the organization is a *mixture* of a physical differentiation and a conceptual differentiation. We have done it so thoroughly and so profoundly that the myriad of interconnections between the organization and its environment is obscured. This makes it difficult for us to understand the organization's sensitivity to its environment. Furthermore, the thorough reification of the idea of "organization" dulls our sensitivity to all the different ways the organization can appear, depending on the point of view of the observer.

3. *The myth of control through a pyramidal chain of command.* Hierarchy, the idea of having someone to report to, is another image that is deep in the culture's psyche. It is almost synonymous with "being organized"—the idea that someone is in charge (Peters, 1987, p. 395). Thus, the very common phenomenon of multiple power centers in the modern organization exists as an aberration, as something that should not be. Yet there it is in the form of networks, matrix structures, project groups, and other interfunctional bodies. Furthermore, while modern managers rail against their operating structures—have you ever heard anyone say they *love* their matrix?—no one wants to go back to a pyramid and a singular chain of command. Once authority is out of the bottle and has seeped through the organization, people do not want to return to the old days of drops of authority from a single, tightly regulated spigot.

4. *The myth of the organization as pure instrument for the attainment of official objectives.* Various of us, particularly those concerned

with the "human side" of the organization, have been struggling with this story for many years. It was demolished technically by Roethlisberger and Dickson (1939) with their concept of "informal organization," and various attempts have continued over the years to harmonize the needs of people with the needs of the organization (Argyris, 1957; McGregor, 1960; Blake and Mouton, 1964). But the myth keeps resurfacing whenever the going gets tough and we seem to think that some kind of stripping down of the organization to its bare essentials is the way to ensure its survival. I address this problem in more detail in Chapter Three. For the moment, let it simply be said that narrow and instrumental definitions of what an organization is are a little like holding to a narrow definition of what "real" baseball is, even though the rules change recommended by Siu has already been officially adopted!

5. *The myth of the irrelevance of culture.* More than with most of these myths, there is probably at least intellectual agreement that the myth of the irrelevance of culture has got to go. At the "gut" level, though, it is as strong as or stronger than any on the list, the gut level being the flash conviction and feelings we have that our own way of operating in the organization is the only right one or that the "American way" of running an organization is the only right one. As anthropologist Edward T. Hall noted, too often we Americans have "assumed a naively evolutionary view which classified most foreigners as 'underdeveloped Americans'" (Hall, 1973, p. 24). This is ethnocentrism. It operates on many levels of awareness and out of many different kinds of cultural coagulations—ethnic, racial, and national; professional, tribal, and organizational, to name a few. With all this going on, it is hard to understand why we keep talking as if there were not cultural forces invisibly influencing *all* thought and action in organizations. Maybe it would just make life too complicated to contemplate the truth. One might not be able to assume that anything could get *done.* Later on, I shall have a good deal more to say about culture. For the moment, it is sufficient to say that pretending it isn't there is foolish.

6. *The myth of a product as the organization's primary output.* As we move further and further into a service economy, it is becoming more and more clear that we can't think of "service"

in the same terms as we have always thought of products. Services aren't standardized little packages. Service is a human interaction that unfolds in real time. To really think of oneself in the service business changes the way one thinks of the business entirely. Especially, it changes what we think the "bottom line" is. What a struggle it is, though, to get out of the units-of-output frame and stay out of it. Even fields that have always been service businesses, such as hospitals and universities, are finding themselves increasingly pressured to standardize their services for purposes of cost control and easier long-range planning.

7. *The myth of rational analysis as the chief means of understanding and directing the organization.* This is the assumption we have been making in U.S. management for most of the twentieth century—that effective action is a process of rationally figuring out what needs to be done, and then rationally doing it. We may be reaching the limits of this model, though, in the world of permanent white water and games that no one knows how to play. Another mentality and style might be more appropriate—for some kinds of projects, anyway. Even though more and more research is confirming its importance, *intuition* is still pretty suspect, and *mystery* positively makes most of us nervous. We aren't comfortable letting things happen, adopting, as I will be describing later, the Chinese notion of "wu-wei" (no-action). But amid the complex turbulences and contingencies of the present world, our impulse to crush a problem with rational analysis isn't serving us so well either, so perhaps at least some questions need to be raised.

These seven myths certainly don't exhaust the frame of mind that underlies the low scores on my questionnaire in Exhibit 1. But they are an attempt to get behind the mirror to understand what the ideas are that we half-consciously carry with us into organizational life. My main point is that at the same time our culture is rapidly evolving a turbulent new society and collection of organizations, old ways of talking about these new forms hang on and cloud our thinking, depress our energies, cause us to view with alarm and prepare for the worst. We are like the Frank Burns character in the TV series "M*A*S*H" when confronted with the freewheeling style of Hawkeye: "Pierce

can't be right. Army life and medical life weren't supposed
to be like this. Nobody *told* me I'd be having to work with
such outrageous people under such impossible conditions.'' I
wonder whether we are as ridiculously funny at times as Frank
is. It gives pause as you sit in a meeting and think about what
you might say next or muse about why things seem to be so
screwed up.

These seven myths could as easily be called ''principles'';
in fact, that is what they *are* called in management courses. Viewing them as principles, learners over the years have come to
attach much more truth and reality to these ideas than they war-
rant. This is how they get so deeply implanted in our minds:
we think they are the last word on the matter in question, when
in fact they are at best a statement of current consensus; at worst
they are ideas that have become irrelevant, but the most vocal
participants in the consensus—let us be blunt, ''the professors''—
don't know it, because they haven't looked lately and/or don't
know how to look at the changes that have been occurring.

We are possibly moving out of a principles-driven world
entirely, at least in the sense of automatic reliance on principles.
But even if we aren't, the principles embodied in these seven
myths need a much closer look than they have been getting.
To keep turning these myths over and over to see what they
really are made of is a principal occupation of this book.

Old stories don't just die by themselves. They die when
more apt stories come along, stories that fit people's feelings
and experience better, stories that take account of more going
on around us, stories that ring true. This whole book is about
these new stories, but perhaps it is a good idea to say here, near
the beginning, what the new characteristics are that are in need
of new stories, new interpretations. Basically, I want to try to
formalize a little bit the various tasks and experiences that are
described in Exhibit 1.

First, we need new stories about *results and accountability*.
It isn't just that today's manager is the quintessential goal
achiever. That is pretty well understood and has been true for
a long time. What we are seeing today is more and more emphasis on accountability and results at the same time that the

"achievability" of results and the "assignability" of accountability are becoming more and more uncertain and problematic. Some might say that all the current emphasis on "pay for performance" and "competency attainment" is little more than wishing for calm waters. In this chapter I try to describe more fully how today's managerial job is going to defeat attempts to make it "operational" and "clear." The attainment of results and the bearing of responsibility in a world of continuous unpredictable change are among the toughest questions we face. We are talking about taking responsibility and acting vigorously even though you're not sure what you're doing. It is not a game of pursuing known, fixed objectives with tried-and-true methods.

This situation has produced what might be called "the Grand Paradox of Management," for to be a manager in the modern world is to take responsibility for controlling what is less and less controllable. As the world becomes less stable and predictable, the paradox intensifies. Strategically, it is resolved by declaring that today's executives must be *leaders*. The precedence of leadership over management has never been more imperative than it is today. One can't simply "manage an existing system," for the unstable environment continually threatens to render any given structure and set of policies out of sync with its demands and opportunities. Under these conditions, a leadership model is far more appropriate than a managerial model. The leader constantly invents strategies that are intended to improve the system's adaptation to its present and future environment. Strategies that are consciously intended to improve adaptation and that are chosen reflectively with an eye on their futurity are the strategies that a leader or manager can take responsibility for. This process of leading the organization in an unfolding adaptation is the real meaning of "keeping one's options open," and it is no surprise that this phrase has had an intuitive appeal to thousands of leaders. Leaders and managers *feel* the riskiness of this white water world. The need is to go forward with a heightened awareness of what the risks are and what it is necessary to have faith in. I develop this idea further in Chapter Thirteen.

The need to be an effective member of the leadership *team* is a third characteristic of the new management job. "What should the top team be talking about?" is another question, dealt with in Chapter Eleven. While we talk teamwork constantly in management, and while there are thousands of published pages about the nature of effective teamwork, it remains a very fragile idea—one that seems hardest to practice just when it is needed most. The main incentive to being an effective team member is that all other styles so obviously detract from getting the work done in the highly interdependent networks of the modern organization. But there are many disincentives, including reward systems that focus on individual brilliance rather than team achievements, the pressure for results and the need for leadership just noted, and the individualistic bias of North American culture (Hofstede, 1980), to name just a few. An additional disincentive existing at a deeper level is the lack of what are called "group process skills" among so many organization members. Teamwork doesn't happen automatically, and it doesn't result just from the exhortations of a single leader. It results from members paying attention to how they are working together, identifying issues that block teamwork and working them through, and consciously developing patterns of working together that all members find challenging and satisfying. Team members have to *talk* to each other about how they are working as a team; they have to *process* their group actions. This calls for a collective self-awareness, openness, and maturity that are still not widely found in very many teams in our culture.

All three of these characteristics—emphasis on results, more leadership and risk taking, and more teamwork—involve the modern executive intensely with other people in the organization. Books could be written about the checkered history of the question of the importance of people in organizational effectiveness. We do seem to be in a period where more and more executives would agree with what the director of strategic planning of a large high-tech manufacturer said to me recently: "I have become convinced that the number-one strategic issue facing our company over the next five to ten years is the people factor." To that, thousands of human resources executives will mutter "At last!" and "Amen." However, to declare that the modern managerial job is *people management* through and through is only the beginning of the adventure. As those who have consciously tried to incorporate this "people factor" know, the task of leadership and management only becomes more complicated as a result. I try to develop some of these subtleties in Chapter Nine. Basically, we are talking about one of the new kinds of "working smarter"—working *collectively* smarter.

Earlier I said that the myth of control of operations through a pyramidal chain of command is in need of substantial modification for the organizational worlds we actually live in. The characteristic we have to come to terms with is *ambiguous authority*. The ambiguity can cut in several different directions for a person: you can have authority for some issues in your job but not for others. You can share authority with one or more others for most issues—so-called committee management. You can have authority that goes with the position but find it subservient to technical expertise that resides in other positions, lower in the official hierarchy. The form and degree of authority you possess can be undergoing change as a result of changes in technology, markets, or other surrounding factors. The form and degree of authority can be relatively well understood and accepted by others, or, at the other extreme, they can be a matter of confusion and contention. It is even possible that none of these features exists and that instead there is simply a maddening vagueness and fuzziness concerning who has authority to do what. As I noted earlier, we still think that such blurring of "unity of command" is absolutely bad. We still look back on organizational events, with the clarity of 20–20 hindsight, to how things might have been different if someone had been more definitely in charge. Before we evolve true comfort with ambiguities of authority, we need to become comfortable with our interdependence in the organization, with our fundamental relatedness, for psychologically the wish for clear authority is a wish for immunity from contingency and the unpredictability of others. The new images and stories we need are of joint action, of the whole being greater than the sum of its parts, of the interdependence of leaders and followers.

One of the less widely noted characteristics of the executives that Peters and his colleagues have been describing is the utter individuality of most of them (Peters and Waterman, 1982; Peters and Austin, 1985; Peters, 1987). It is not only Peters's data that display this *individuality*. The idea is all through the current literature on executive effectiveness. If we are going to say that this modern executive has to be effective with people in all sorts of circumstances, we must face the fact that each person is going to practice this effectiveness in his or her own way. It cannot be a matter of cookbooks or formulas. The thing that the highest-performing executives have discovered is that their greatest assets are their own passions for the organization and its mission and their own common sense when it comes to getting the most out of the people they have. Their unwillingness to turn themselves inside out to conform to some behavioral scientist's theory is remarkable. In both Chapters Two and Eight, I give some further attention to the artistic side of a manager's effectiveness, for I think it is in that realm that the real secret lies. It is not that there are no concepts one can use to enrich one's thinking and action. Rather, the problem is the *kinds* of ideas we have been relying on for the past several decades. We have thought that management and leadership could be informed and enriched primarily by scientific research, or at least by a particular kind of scientific research—what I call in Chapter Eight the "list of functions" approach. I think that this assumption is proving to be a mistake and that we need to rethink the sources and nature of the knowledge we would presume to "apply." Some of our best leaders and managers have long since concluded that their own intuitions are the best guides to action. I think we should understand that, celebrate it, and see what we can learn from it.

Not only does the new executive role call for individuality, it calls for *the whole person*. Less and less does it make sense to think of these positions as delimited functions that can be described in traditional "duties and responsibilities" terms. Today's executive is learning that everything he or she has ever done counts in the job. Not only all the "business subjects" are relevant, but so too are all the liberal arts one ever studied.

The more one knows about other cultures, the better. The more one knows about ethics and morals, the better. The more one knows about the nature of science and what its limits are, the better. The more different kinds of organizations one understands, the better, for sooner or later the modern manager has to do business with nearly every kind of organization there is—public and private, profit and nonprofit. The more one knows about physical and mental health and human development, the better, and particularly the more one knows about oneself, the better. And so on. My point is that in principle this list is virtually without limit. In the world of permanent white water, one cannot know where the next opportunity or threat is going to come from. Yet when it comes, a great deal depends on possessing or being able rapidly to acquire a useful way of thinking about it so that courses of action one has under way will not be shattered. This job that calls for the whole person is enormously absorbing. I have tried to capture this phenomenon, especially its two-edged quality of potential self-fulfillment and potential burnout, in my discussions of leadership as "time, feeling, and focus" (Chapter Eleven).

The characteristics that I have mentioned so far mean that the modern executive role is extremely *stressful*. It is probably more stressful than those who are doing it realize, for in the same way that an overweight person cannot feel the extra poundage, the highly stressed person develops mechanisms to block the impact of the stress on his or her basic ability to function. There is a large and still growing literature on the medical and psychological aspects of executive stress. Important as all this material is, there is an aspect of stress that is not getting the attention it should. In Chapter Fourteen, I try to develop another approach to the stress of life in modern organizations, an approach that interprets stress in different terms from those that all the medical and psychological research tends to use. I argue that a fuller view of the causes of stress is needed if we are to understand the nature of the malaise that so many millions of us feel.

In the last few paragraphs, I have said that the new executive positions are much more personal, more absorbing, and more stressful than many realize. Furthermore, these jobs are personal, absorbing, and stressful in a particular *way* that is relatively new: The modern leader-manager is required to be able to reflect and philosophize to a degree that sometimes astonishes (and infuriates) the down-to-earth, no-nonsense, let's-get-on-with-it sorts of men and women who have traditionally held these jobs. The job has become more intellectual and scholarly, in the best sense of these words. It requires an ability to work with theory, interpret research results, identify and reconsider underlying assumptions, communicate at length with others both inside and outside the organization (as opposed to just being "briefed"), read critically, and write forcefully and concisely. All this is a direct though not often mentioned expression of the information age. Very few, even if they possess Ph.D. degrees, are as well equipped as they need to be to live in this world of concepts and ideas that is yet a world of action and commitment. Indeed, this is perhaps a better way to put the point: The organizational world of permanent white water has evolved requirements for the leader-manager for *higher-quality thought and action* than ever before. It is not merely the action capacity of the traditional can-do problem solver. And it is not merely the intellectual capacity of the traditional inhabitant of the ivory tower. It is a genuine new mix, a mix that has been theorized about over the centuries by political philosophers as they contemplated what truly wise rulers needed to be like. We seem to have backed into a situation in the postindustrial society where we need thousands and thousands of such individuals in all sectors of society. My fear is that we don't realize it for the most part, and even those who do realize it have not yet cracked the problem of how we are going to foster the development of such individuals. This question weaves all through the chapters that follow.

Here then are nine characteristics of the modern jobs of managerial leaders in organizations:

1. More accountability
2. More need for leadership
3. More emphasis on teamwork

4.   More intense involvement with people
5.   Greater ambiguity of authority
6.   Greater emphasis on one's individuality
7.   More involvement of the whole person
8.   More stress
9.   A new mix of an intellectual and an action orientation

The first three of these characteristics are already subject matter for management development programs and are generally accepted as realities by most observers. There is more debate as to whether the other items are crystallized and important enough to be foundations for new education and training. Some people will have no problem with any of the items on the list, whereas others will have trouble accepting the need to do something about one or more of the characteristics. For example, on the question of ambiguous authority, some might say that it is today's younger managers' personal problems with authority that are really the issue. They allegedly need to have things spelled out for them more than earlier managers did. They are less comfortable with ambiguity, they are more insecure. The problem isn't so much an absolute increase in the ambiguity, this thesis would argue, as it is a decrease in the current generation's ability to tolerate less than perfect clarity.

There is some merit in such a critique, for indeed job characteristics and personal experience always interact and become entangled, particularly in managerial jobs, where personal style plays such a large role. Rather than force ourselves to choose, though, let us assume that indeed there may be twin processes going on: job characteristics are changing, and personal awareness, expectations, and aspirations are also changing, though not necessarily in a way that fits with changing job requirements. In the next section, I discuss the kinds of personal learning needed by men and women who want to exercise managerial leadership effectively. I then again take up the question of the relation between job requirements and personal abilities.

Another Look at "Working Smarter"

In the world of permanent white water, where change itself is changing, what are we like? How do we act, and how does it feel to be in the midst of such situations? What would it be like to actually try to play Chinese baseball, especially if one already has a self-image of knowing how to play regular baseball, "real" baseball? This question goes to the heart of how we are doing in modern organizations and of whether we will be able to give them the quality membership and leadership that they need. In this section, I want to consider how we typically respond to permanent white-water conditions and then discuss some new ways of "working smarter" that I think have rapidly evolved from luxuries to imperatives of learning.

One of the most obvious things about us when we try to play a game we have never played before is that we don't know exactly what we are trying to accomplish. We may tend to be unrealistic about goals, setting them either too high or too low, or indeed misstating them entirely. An example of this last might be a neophyte teacher-trainer facing a first class and unconsciously assuming that the main goal is to have enough material to keep the trainees occupied for the whole time. That, of course, is not the "real" goal, and on reflection, the beginner knows it, too. But in the midst of the uncertain new situation, the operative goal may be to avoid embarrassing silences or pauses.

Our motivation is fragile, too, in new situations, oscillating between eagerness and discouragement as various facets of the new game present themselves and we try to practice the skills the game entails. In fact, even as it isn't easy to say what the goals ought to be, it is also unclear how to think and feel about the activity. Various feelings are triggered in the learning process, and the question as one feeling or another courses through us is "Is this it? Is this what being good at this feels like?" or a negative feeling, "Why can't I get it right?" These questions often aren't sharply in awareness. They linger just offstage but are very much a part of the experiences of learning. We want feedback under such conditions. We want to know how we are doing, whether we are making the beginning moves that will lead eventually to competence. But since we are in a learning mode and know we don't exactly know what we are doing, we don't want the feedback to be more judgmental of us than our level of competence warrants. We want to be treated not as a pro, but rather as a learner. We're a little touchy about this, because the culture says that when giving feedback to people who know what they are doing, you are not to pull your punches. Call it as you see it. The culture has less to say to those, such as parents and schoolteachers, who are in a coaching role. How do you give feedback to a learner who wants to know but who feels incompetent, has fragile motivation, and can hardly even imagine what competent performance is?

Learners themselves, of course, are likely to be relatively forgiving of their mistakes. After all, the feeling is, "I'm new at this." It is less clear whether learners are more likely to be forgiving of other learners' mistakes in games they have never played before. It depends a lot on how much stress coaches and other authority figures are injecting. Tragically, teams of learners can easily be driven apart and into destructive competition as each scrambles to survive and learn to play this game that no one knows how to play. It would seem that a manager would want to avoid such a situation if possible.

An experimental frame of mind is another aspect of one's attitude in a new game, particularly one of any complexity. We try various approaches and attitudes and often are quite deliberately experimenting. To experiment requires quite a bit of freedom, of course, and if pressure for performance is put on, it will drive out experimentation; it will also probably lower motivation. Sometimes a person will react to imposed controls and constraints by going to the other extreme from experimentalism and adopting the mood and mode of the rote learner. The attitude becomes "Have it your way. Tell me exactly what to do and I'll do it. I'm putting myself in your [the boss's, the teacher's] hands."

The boss or the teacher is presumed in our culture to know how to do whatever it is the learner is learning. That's why he or she is the boss or teacher. But in the world of permanent white water, the leader too is playing a new game. The knowledge and skills that earned the promotion to leadership are eroded, sometimes quite rapidly, by the pace of change, or indeed rendered obsolete all at once by changes in technology, markets, legal judgments, or new organizational structures. This puts the leader in a painful, paradoxical position: One would *like* to be a learner with everyone else, but the culture says that leadership responsibility demands that one already have the competence in order to help others acquire it and evaluate their performance. Yet where is one to acquire it? What is an efficient way to learn it oneself? It is a game no one has played before, and no one knows exactly how to play it. This is the vise that grips the leader-manager in the world of permanent white water. A great deal of midnight oil and an incredible number of workshop hours in hotel conference rooms are being consumed these days as these people try to stay up to date technically while continuing to exercise their leader-manager function. If ever there was a need to know how to "work smarter," it is in relation to this condition.

There are three additional impulses that bosses or teachers might have regarding the learners in their charge. These three impulses aren't so much in service of the learner's needs as they are attempts to help the boss manage the painful paradox I have just described. For one thing, it is common to want the learner to make a relatively long-term commitment to the activity, whatever it is. We want the student to make a commitment for the entire degree program. We want the trainee to agree to stay with the company for a certain number of years after the training has been completed. Indeed, early resignations of new employees before the training dollars have been "recovered" is one of the more vexing current problems in the management of training. The learner, of course, feels in no position to make a long-term commitment and doesn't even think that it makes sense to demand one. The learner accedes reluctantly to "the policy," but it hardly builds the learner's loyalty to be forced to commit oneself to what is essentially a mystery—that is, what things are going to be like in the future.

In another form that this pressure for commitment takes,

higher-level managers act as if they don't even realize that employees are being required to play a game they have never played
before. Rather, the message is that "there are some new challenges," "the new strategy is going to call for sacrifices," and
so on, but there is never an open recognition of the degree to
which fundamental change is occurring and that the attitudes
and actions that formerly were keys to effectiveness are now inappropriate or obsolete. This is a curious collusion—that of not
quite facing how much change we are trying to absorb in modern
organizations. It is probaby another coping mechanism we use
when we're not sure of what we're doing—to pretend that it
isn't as different from what we know as it seems. Neither the
boss nor the employee, the trainer nor the trainee, is probably
eager to contemplate the true amount of uncertainty and mystery
that the learning tasks of the modern world entail.

The second and third impulses that leaders may yield to
in the turbulence of nonstop change are to seek stability through
routinization and to seek stability through *inspiration*. Regarding
routinization, Leavitt (1962) long ago observed that it is very
common for human beings to convert novel situations into routine ones. Fluidity, contingency, and uncertainty are fine in
measured amounts, but one should not have to constantly be
starting anew. Leavitt's point was that we make organizations
"unhuman" by our very human habit of reducing the novel
to the routine. An unhuman organization is one where there
is no more novelty to reduce. In the world of permanent white
water, though, this urge may have another cost. It may tend
to blind us to the fact that we are making little if any progress
in reducing novelty, no matter how much time we spend reor-
ganizing, spelling out new job descriptions, developing scenarios
of desired modes of functioning, and producing long-range plans
and scheduling events on program evaluation and review technique (PERT) charts. The absurdity of this Sisyphean situation is not lost on employees. As one said to me recently, "All
the time we spend organizing does not result in our being better organized!"

Inspiration is a more fashionable strategy these days for
trying to cope with permanent white water. Organization after

organization is trying to inspire people to cope with the uncertainty and turbulence, often by bringing in outside speakers and
consultants who will help people achieve ''peak performance''
(see Chapter Four). Doubtless the writings of Peters and his colleagues and the many in-company presentations he has made are
the impetus for this movement, although it has been around the
edges of American management thought for many years. The
tent-revival style has been used in American sales meetings for
decades. Regardless of whether Peters is right or wrong about the
importance of inspiration to high levels of performance, there is
one thing his research on excellence as well as my own makes
abundantly clear: leadership and management that inspire are
themselves inspired! Too many managements have brought in
inspirational, charismatic speakers and consultants from outside
but have not themselves been sufficiently inspired to build on the
energy that the outsider stirs up. The truly excellent organizations
have leaders who are themselves inspired in the first instance and
who are communicating this inspiration directly and concretely
to organization members (see Chapter Eleven). I mean no criticism of those management groups that have been unable to gel
an inspirational message that they can communicate directly and
concretely. In fact, I have great sympathy for those managements
that have so far failed: in the world of permanent white water,
inspiration is battered and negated by the turbulence and change.
At what point in, say, the first five years of the AT&T divestiture
process are things settled enough to formulate an inspirational
message? In the midst of growth rates such as those experienced
in the 1970s by Apple Computer or Nike Shoes, what inspirational message besides ''Hang on!'' will make any sense? What
of an inspirational kind could commanding officers in Vietnam
have said? Or managers involved in the Bhopal disaster? Quite
possibly in all these situations, people did reach deeply into
values and feelings and find ways of talking that had an inspiring effect. What I am calling attention to, though, is how difficult it can be, and how little abstract management technique
has to do with such anguished searching. The whole question
of vision in the midst of constant turbulence and confusion is
a matter that the final chapter in this book must take up again.

In the last few paragraphs, I have been talking about some typical ways in which we respond to situations of great ambiguity and fluidity, situations where we find ourselves having to play a game that we have not played before. Most of these responses, I have suggested, are not adequate to the true challenge that is posed, and in particular they are not adequate as strategies for playing a game that will continue indefinitely to be a new game. This is the characteristic of the modern environment that we keep underestimating: Things are *not* going to settle down. New values are *not* going to become "established" to replace old values. Technologies are *not* going to "shake down." We are *not* going to descend on the learning curve to a mode where we are smoothly performing whatever the new activity is. Wherever we look, we see managerial leaders trying to cope with continuous change of a fundamental sort. Since the central feature of this game that I am talking about is the fact that it changes its own rules and terms of effectiveness as it proceeds, we clearly need some kind of guidance system for playing it that might be equally flexible, or at least have the potential of becoming equally flexible. Manager-leaders can't look where they have looked before—in managerial principles and in organizational policies and procedures—for these are the very things that keep being rendered out of date and inapplicable to emerging situations. The rules and policies can only be temporary and ad hoc themselves; they can't be the timeless benchmarks that they have been in the past.

The greatest asset we have for these conditions is our own consciousness, our own awareness, provided that we can permit its virtually infinite flexibility to operate, and provided that we can maintain communication among our various awarenesses as the world unfolds around us. These two tasks—maintaining flexibility of consciousness and communication among consciousnesses—are discussed in various ways throughout this book. "Managerial consciousness" I take to be the single most underexplored phenomenon in organizational life, yet it is challenged at every turn by the modern environment. We cannot take our understanding as given, nor, more importantly, can we take our *capacity* to understand (to learn) as given. Another way to understand this point is to imagine what the world would be like and how we would feel about it if consciousness were fixed and immutable, incapable of changing its priorities and perceiving things in new ways. Clearly, we would experience chaos if this were what consciousness was like. We do change, we do adapt—even the most rigid and dogmatic of us are constantly adapting to emerging conditions. I am interested in better understanding how we do this, and I am interested in helping leaders and managers do it better.

Earlier, we took a look at three common approaches to "working smarter" that are widely practiced in the organizational world: working harder and harder—the workaholic strategy; studying harder and harder—what in Chapter Six I call the "technoholic" strategy; and trying to be more clever and politically astute in the organization—a "powerholic" approach. I use the *-holic* suffix deliberately to call attention to the habitual, even compulsive quality of each of these three approaches. Because they are so deeply implanted in our culture and so widely practiced, we do not probably think of them as compulsions, that is, as courses of action we feel we *must* engage in. Each of us has to consider for ourselves the extent to which one or more of these has its hooks into us. For myself, I have felt all three, but the workaholic response in particular is one that has a special hold on me.

To the extent that these three, singly or in combination, operate as habits or compulsions, we are not free to consider afresh what "smarter" can mean in one of these permanent white water situations. Our understanding of "working smarter" needs to be expanded to cover the variety of situations we are being presented with. If we are to liberate ourselves from these compulsions, I think there are three dimensions that have to be woven into our attempts to be smarter. They do not necessarily negate the three that we already understand and practice so thoroughly, but I think that they possibly transform them. These three dimensions are (1) working collectively smarter, (2) working reflectively smarter, and (3) working spiritually smarter.

The problem for consciousness in a world of permanent white water is to stay sufficiently open yet sufficiently centered to handle the surprises, puzzles, contradictions, and absurdities that the modern world presents. The three kinds of working smarter I have just named function to keep consciousness open to the variety and complexity it is immersed in without casting it loose completely from its moorings of familiar thoughts, feelings, and values. To work collectively smarter is to remain in touch with those around us, both with their ideas and with their energy. In the hurly-burly and pressure of organizational life, we know how easy it is to rush from meeting to meeting and from project to project, without connecting in any but the most superficial way with those we meet in the process. Other people become "human resources" to us and lose their fullness as people. Even with those we call our friends, too often we find ourselves saying "we must get together and catch up" while the weeks and months go by without it happening. And even when "catching up" does happen, it is an abstracted, once-removed kind of process, more reportage than actually sharing ideas and feelings that are real in the here and now. Working collectively smarter, on the other hand, should give us access to others' support and them access to ours. The sense that one is embedded in a support system can be a crucial comfort—not a luxury—in the permanent white water. The modern organization has lagged tragically in fashioning support systems that will help people bear the stresses of the job. We talk a lot about "networking," but I wonder how seriously we take it. And do those who need it most—those who do not know how to work smart collectively—take it seriously at all?

Reflection, the second new approach to working smarter, is the capacity to reconsider what the world is presenting to us, to examine the grounds on which an idea rests and the assumptions that must hold true if a proposal is to work as intended. Reflection is the capacity to "notice oneself noticing"; that is, to step back and see one's mind working in relation to its projects. In philosophical language, it is a "phenomenological reduction" (Zaner, 1970), but we don't need such elaborate phraseology to name something that is as familiar as reflection. Reflection is the principal means to resolve "Satchmo's Paradox" described in Chapter Seven. Satchmo's Paradox poses the problem of how we can ever unlock ourselves from the strictures of our own expertise in order to see the world through other eyes, and to see our own expertise through the eyes of one who does not possess it. Reflection's greatest enemies are dogma and pressure, and neither is in short supply in the contemporary organization. Authoritarian systems, which modern organizations still tend to be, do not want too much free thinking going on. The truth is that not *enough* free thinking is going on. Reflection, singly and in groups, is an absolutely crucial resource for understanding the nature of whatever white water is presently coursing through the system. Chapters Five and Six continue the discussion of reflection; Chapter Five applies it to the phenomenon of "paradox," and Chapter Six discusses it in relation to technology.

Finally, I raise the somewhat risky idea that we need to work *spiritually* smarter. It is risky because of all the baggage so many of us bring to the discussion. In a sense, we are all experts on this subject, because matters of spirit, faith, and religion and their psychological consequences have played such a large role in most of our lives. Many of us are blessed, or plagued, with unforgettable experiences in these realms. For some of us, the subject is so precious that we can hardly bear to consider it in such a secular context as a management book; for others, the subject is ridiculous and does not merit passing mention. In Chapters Thirteen and Fourteen, I argue that it is meaningful to talk about the needs and opportunities for spiritual leadership in today's organizations. I try to show that we already rely on a larger measure of faith than we realize, and that the question is therefore not so much faith versus facts as it is faith in *what* and *why*. To work spiritually smarter is to pay more attention to one's own spiritual qualities, feelings, insights, and yearnings. It is to reach more deeply into oneself for that which is unquestionably authentic. It is to attune oneself to those truths one considers timeless and unassailable, the deepest principles one knows. It is not easy in the modern organization to maintain this attunement; it has to be worked at, yet I don't think we hear enough talk about what working at it involves. I want to put such talk back on the agenda.

Doubtless, "working smarter" will always have strong connotations of increased effort, increased technical knowledge, and increased power. In the preceding paragraphs, though, I have been saying that we need new attention to the three dimensions of working collectively, reflectively, and spiritually smarter. Otherwise, our tried and true reliance on increased effort, knowledge, and power is not sufficient for the white water world. In the chapters that follow, these questions will come up again and again. I have a montage of ideas about them, not a unified thesis. Perhaps that is the nature of the white water problem: it doesn't yield to a comprehensive theory. I think sorties can be mounted from various angles, though. I hope with the chapters that follow to conduct some successful sorties myself, but almost more I hope that the mood and style of these raids will inspire readers to lead expeditions of their own.

Let us begin with an exploration of one of the hottest topics in the management field these days—the search for precise models of what managers do in the hope that if we can ever figure out exactly what it is managers are up to, we will be able to teach these competencies to learners.

Chapter 2

The Theory of Managing in the Managerial Competency Movement

What do managers really do? How do they acquire the skill and competence to do what they do? What can educators and trainers do to improve the process by which managers acquire this skill and competence?

These, it seems to me, are the three fundamental questions behind the so-called competency movement (CM) that is currently receiving so much attention in management education, particularly in that sector of management education that is concerned with helping managers improve their skills with people. While I cannot say that I have studied this movement exhaustively, I did contribute in the mid-seventies to the exploratory studies on the subject by the American Assembly of Collegiate Schools of Business. I have not remained involved with the effort, but I have since heard several briefings on the work. Furthermore, I, like other management educators, have continued to hear criticism about graduating B.B.A's and M.B.A.'s— that they can't manage, aren't interested in managing, think

This chapter was first published in *EXCHANGE: The Organizational Behavior Teaching Journal,* 1983, *8* (2), 50–56. The journal is now called *The Organizational Behavior Teaching Review.* Reprinted with permission.

"management" is essentially a process of rationally analyzing "problems" and deciding on "optimal solutions" and are generally insensitive to the nuances of organizational cultures and the deep human dilemmas that lie just below the surface of the apparently well-managed organization.

I am very uneasy about the competency movement in management education. It is not that I am against "competency," and not that I do not accept responsibility for contributing to the competency of the students I see in class and the managers I see in various workshops and consulting relationships. But the work I see being done on the subject of understanding managerial competency and the efforts to contribute to it in education and training are not very consistent with what I think the managerial job is, and are not very consistent with what I think is going on when a learner is attaining competency. In this chapter, I raise some of the concerns I have about the CM as I understand it. My intent, like everyone else's, is to contribute to the improvement both of managing and of teaching about managing.

The Competency Movement as a Theory of Managing

I don't think there has been enough discussion of the theory of managing implicit in the studies of competency that have been conducted. The studies I have seen seem to start with the questions posed at the beginning of this chapter. The primary cognitive strategy that has been employed is what might be called a "factorial" or "dimensional" approach. In other words, the question "What do managers do?" has tended to turn into the question "What are the main factors in the manager's job?" The researcher has then differentiated a list of factors out of the job wholes of a population of subjects. These lists have been subjected to further tests of reliability. Sample sizes have received careful attention. Validation of the lists has been more tricky, but researchers apparently have satisfied themselves that these lists do include factors that can be found in managerial jobs.

But do managers experience their jobs as lists? Does anyone have any evidence on this question? The transformation of the job whole into a list of factors is a fateful step, in that it will influence subsequent criterion-attainment research, teaching and training designs, and ultimately the careers and personal success of live men and women in the real world. I know that I don't experience action roles, be they managing, teaching, parenting, consulting, or anything else, as a list of factors. My clincial sense is that other managers similarly experience their job wholes in a variety of ways other than lists, but I can't prove it, and of course, with my own cognitive tendencies, I may be a biased perceiver.

Some years ago, I wrote an essay about OD consulting whose premise was that we should not tell change agents how to act without paying a lot of attention to how the change project looks from the actor's point of view (Vaill, 1974). I tried in that essay to speculate about the actor's "practice theory," by which I meant something very close to Argyris's "theory-in-use." I defined an actor's practice theory as "the models of situations and his relation to them which the actor develops in his mind. His practice theory is, literally, a personal theory guiding his practice, bearing some relation to public, objective theories about organizational situations, but in no sense identical with them" (p. 72). I did not then and do not now draw Argyris's conclusion—that managers must be shown how ill founded their subjective theories-in-use or practice theories are. Rather, my conviction is that there is far more wisdom in practice theories than academic theory has yet begun to tap. With regard to competency, my hypothesis is that the study of managing from a manager's point of view will reveal many subtle modes and mixes of competency. These are likely to be more valid expressions of what is really going on than an externally generated list of factors can possibly be.

There is more to the theory of managing embedded in the CM than merely its assumption of the listlike nature of competency. Below, I present some propositions about managing and the manager's environment that must hold true in order for the CM's strategy to be effective. After each proposition, I have sketched some reasons why the proposition might *not* be true. In other words, I think the CM is presuming a world that does not exist, or that is at least quite improbable.

1. *Competencies in managing are relatively independent of each other. Attainment or nonattainment of one type of competency does not affect the probability of attainment of other types.* This is the metaphysical claim on whose truth rests the strategy of making lists of key factors in the manager's job. (*Metaphysical* is used here in a purely descriptive sense; no pejorative overtones are intended. All research strategies rest on metaphysical assumptions.) It seems more likely to me, as in fact some competency studies recognize, that the competencies do "cluster." "Interpersonal competency," for instance, is a general phrase that covers a considerable variety of individual competencies. The more clustering there is in the manager's job, the more questionable it is that distinct competencies can be identified and teaching and training strategies developed to produce them.

2. *The manager's job has identifiable outputs that result from the exercise of various competencies.* This proposition may have validity for an individualized task with physical products as outputs. But neither is managing individualistic, nor does the activity typically have physical outputs. "Competency" is the capacity to produce an intended, identifiable consequence. If managing is a highly interactive, flowing process, rather than a neat structure of cause and effect, does the idea of competency in the sense of capacity to produce effects have any meaning at all? I suggest that just below the surface in the CM is the very kind of linear cause-effect thinking that we criticize in managers!

Another variety of this cause-effect thinking in the CM may actually be a logical fallacy. This is the assumption that if we identify the competencies possessed by effective managers, and then teach them to learners, these learners will become effective managers. Bayesian statistics refutes this assumption. If I see it raining, I can predict that I will see people with umbrellas. But if I see people with umbrellas, can I predict with equal probability that it will rain? No. Those who die of lung cancer tend to have been smokers. Those who smoke, however, have a much lower probability of dying of lung cancer. The probability that the mother of a child who is born blind had German measles during pregnancy is much higher than the probability that a pregnant woman with German measles will have a blind child. Probabilities are not symmetrical in many cause-effect situations, yet I see no one in the CM seriously considering this phenomenon in the study of managerial competencies.

3. *Managerial competency is a high-leverage variable in the attainment of increased organizational effectiveness.* Every manager knows that a very large number of things influence organizational effectiveness. The more complex the organization and the more turbulent its environment, the more of these things there are and the more complex their interdependence and joint action and, therefore, the more interactive and fluid managing becomes. The question must be asked whether the CM presumes a "managerial world" that is a great deal more stable and predictable than the modern world of managing really is.

4. *Related to 3. above: Given the ambiguity and fluidity of all organizational situations, stability and control are introduced and maintained in the person of the "manager." The manager is a creator and restorer of order.* Managers are also innovators, leaders, fundamentally creators of *dis*order. The 1980s are seeing renewed emphasis on these modes of managing. One wonders whether the competencies that go with creating change might be even less unitlike and easily understood than the competencies that go with equilibrium maintenance. Certainly the research on planned change underlines how much one's personal style and "touch" influence how a process of change goes. Possibly, the CM will unconsciously underemphasize the competencies that go with innovation and disorder and end up fostering a regulative at the expense of an innovative view of managing.

Another way to make this point is to say that any specification of requisite managerial competencies assumes that we know the future, that we know what the requisite competencies will be. Yet, at the same time that we flirt with the CM, we are speculating about a world of "transformation," of "postindustrialism," of a "third wave," of an "information age." Under conditions of possibly radical transformation, why do most lists of competencies omit what may be the most strategic competency of all: "capacity to shelve one's competence in favor of an openness to the new"? Nearly twenty years ago, California consultant Will McWhinney coined the term "pedamorphosis"—the

capacity to change back to a more childlike frame of mind—
to capture this need for openness to the new among managers.
The CM seems to be ignoring this point.

5. *Exercise of a competency is relatively unaffected by the real-
time, here-and-now perceptions of the manager. To possess a competency
is to know when and how to use it.* Most lists of competencies I have
seen do contain an item that might be called generically ''freedom from perceptual distortion.'' Perhaps that does take care
of it, but I am left feeling uneasy. All my experience with action
roles, including those for which I know I possess high competence, teaches me the extraordinary variety and subtlety of
perceptual distortions. One of the chief sources of distortion,
in fact, is my own conviction of competence in a situation. The
time to be most careful is that moment when ''This job is a piece
of cake'' flits through one's mind.

Perception, in me at least, is not a stop-action photograph
that I take of a situation in order that I may determine what
sort of competence is required in it. Perceiving is an act occurring continuously in parallel with my action in situations. Situations unfold before me, partly as a result of my effects and partly
as a result of other factors. But perceiving what I am doing and
what is happening, and what I *am* doing and what *is* happening, are inextricably interwoven. The metaphor of parallelism
is only a very loose approximation. Thus, perceptual ability cannot be merely another item on the competency list. The exercise of my competencies and the understanding of their effects
are perceptions through and through.

If the exercise of all competencies is interwoven with perception, and if perception itself is of a fundamentally different
order, more deeply rooted in my character and personality, what
bet are we making when we teach competencies without dealing with this deeper phenomenon?

6. *Competencies can be attained and exercised across a wide range
of action contexts.* The oft-mentioned but lightly regarded ''artistic''
dimension of managing is the defense that is made to those who
say, as I have, that managing is highly contextual, fluid, interactive, not a list of skills, and so on. But what do we mean by
an artistic dimension? If we took managerial artistry more seri-

ously, would we describe requisite skills with lists? Would we assert the kind of cause-effect relationships I criticize in proposition 2? System theory would certainly answer these questions with a resounding no!

Managerial artistry blends such contextual factors as the following: the degree of geographical dispersion among participants; the extent to which the situation is "high stakes"; the sheer number of people involved; the time available for the exercise of a competency; the endemic stress level among participants; and the presence of norms in the situation about the manager's competence itself. Obviously, there are many more such factors, and of course they do not exist or present themselves to the actor as a list either. None of the competency lists I have seen has "artistry" as a list item itself, and properly so. But if it is not a list item, what is it? What *is* its relation to the operational competencies we are trying to inculcate? It seems to me that the CM, while not denying the importance of artistry, tends to leave it as a personal quality or factor that will somehow enliven, enrich, and individualize a person's exercise of the competencies. The CM further assumes that the existence of a phenomenon of artistry does not by itself invalidate the search for competencies and the development of teaching and training methods to inculcate them.

There is, however, another way of thinking about artistry, which leads me to the conclusion that the CM is wrong in regarding artistry in the way that it does. Consider the relation between the phenomenon "managing" and the phenomenon "artistry." The artist, of whatever sort, tends to possess extraordinary competency with respect to such things as the nature of his or her materials, the history of the particular art, the ways the artistic product is likely to be experienced by others, methods of working, and the like. But all these unitary competencies are subordinate to something else: *the expressiveness of the artist,* whether we call this expressiveness "creativity" or "insight" or "inspiration" or whatever. I define an "art" as the attempt to wrest coherence and meaning out of more reality than we ordinarily try to deal with. The artist is after this "something more," determined to find coherence and meaning embedded more subtly and deeply in experience than the rest of us see. The artist is after a theme, a dimension, an aspect of existence that no one else seems to see in quite the same way. From the very beginning of training, the artist is reminded daily that if the enterprise is nothing else, it is a celebration of one's specialness.

In a book of advice to aspiring writers, Sidney Cox once remarked, ''What you mean is never quite what anyone else means, exactly. And the only thing that makes you more than a drop in the common bucket, a particle of sand in the universal hourglass, is the interplay of your specialness with your commonness'' (Cox, 1962, p. 19). In teaching managing, what interplay of specialness and commonness do we seek to foster in learners? This is a question that few tend to ask. Interest in the question is certainly not very evident in the CM. I think, however, that leading and working with people in purposeful situations require a greater sense of this interplay and capacity to perform it oneself than practically any other sphere of activity. That *is* what managing is, in my opinion. The whole history of the organizational behavior movement in management education can be understood as a groping for this interplay, as an expression of the profound value we place on *all* the people in an organizational situation—on the managers and the managees. The CM, to the contrary, vastly overemphasizes the commonness dimension of managing at the direct and possibly irretrievable expense of the specialness dimension.

7. *Exercise of a competency is possible irrespective of the morals, motives, and competencies of those toward whom a competency is directed. For instance, a competent negotiator can negotiate regardless of whether the other party is equally sincere.* The word *interaction* rolls off our professional tongues so smoothly that it is easy to forget what the word is saying: that in social behavior, there are always at least two purposeful consciousnesses operating, and that in choosing actions, each is taking account of itself and of the other in real time. To be sure, the CM includes ''interpersonal competence'' on its lists of factors (the phrase itself is virtually a cliché), but I am a little nervous about what the CM thinks such competence is. Will it be defined as ''knowledge of theory and research about human behavior and ability to apply it in

situations''? Will the CM drift toward equating such competence with a quasi-scientific deduction about what is needed in a particular situation?

In our litanies about the "situational" nature of management, we often forget that no scientific law can ever explain an individual case, nor can the law by itself ever produce valid and unequivocal guidance on what should be done in a situation. The law always contains a *ceteris paribus,* and the individual case never does. The individual case contains both the phenomena the law is concerned with and all the other things the law leaves out or assumes equal.

To the extent that "interpersonal competence" does involve use of theories and research findings, what then can it possibly be? It most certainly is *not* the reduction of a particular case to a general law, for, as noted above, this "case" has the marvelous capacity as an intentional consciousness itself to both anticipate and react to the way that "it" is being treated. It does not experience itself as an "it," while the assumption that some law applies rests on the other person holding still as precisely this—an "it."

Therefore, one does not possess an attribute called "interpersonal competence" conceived as an ability to work skillfully with people across a variety of situations. Such an image of oneself is an incorrect and dysfunctional starting assumption, and it becomes more incorrect and dysfunctional as the situation gets more and more complex and unique. What sort of a competence is one that is best forgotten in the here and now, or best not even conceived of in the first place? Not one, certainly, that lends itself easily to operational specification on a list of key competencies!

8. *No deleterious system effects are introduced by the possession and exercise of a competency by a manager, or, if such effects do arise, competency to deal with them can be developed by the same process as that by which the original competencies were developed.* The intent of the CM is constructive. It wants to contribute to organizational effectiveness. However, to the extent that this proposition describes the CM's underlying assumption, it places the CM in a dangerous position. If deleterious effects do arise from the correct

exercise of a competency, the CM will tend to conclude that it must have misdefined that competency or that its training methods must be incorrect in some way, or both. This will lead proponents of the CM to new research and new teaching and training designs that are aimed at avoiding the negative effects.

In addition to all the questions I have raised above, one final issue emerges from the likelihood that deleterious effects will occur from time to time: The CM, it seems to me, cannot help but foster and contribute to specialization in managing. As competencies become more and more precise and supposedly operational, while available teaching and training hours stay relatively constant, we will unquestionably divide and subdivide the field of management further and further. There already is a trend under way over the past couple of decades away from general management training and toward more specific "majors" and "fields of concentration." The CM will accelerate this trend.

Of course, the cynic in me observes that such a development will be a boon to the assessment center devotees and the career path planners. This chapter is not about those two related fields, but they intertwine philosophically and practically with the CM. I will leave it at this: The more we specialize, standardize, and career program the young men and women who want to learn managing, the more rigidities we introduce into the system, and the more we alienate these very people on whom organizational futures depend.

In this section, I have tried to state and criticize some key aspects of the theory of managing on which the CM is based. I have tried to show that to the extent to which my eight propositions are faulty, the CM is faulty. Behind the questions I have raised, of course, lies an alternative theory of what managing is. The men and women we are training are entering a mode of living I call being-in-the-world-with-responsibility. What this phrase means to me is only hinted at in the above remarks, and, in fact, it presently exists in my mind only as a series of hints, glimmers, and mental excursions. Somehow, though, I think we have to cling to what it means to be a whole person with purposes in a situation with others who have their own purposes.

The wholeness of oneself in relation to the wholeness of others is not presently apparent in the CM's approach to managing and to its improvement.

Some Concerns

Dear Peter:

As usual, you have written a provocative paper that raises some crucial questions about the "competency movement." I have some concerns, however, in your position. It feels as a wholesale indictment that admits of no benefits to this approach. The worry I have is that the reader will write off your entire argument thereby missing many of the valuable observations.

In a sense, I think you fall into a similar trap as you accuse those in the competency movement of doing. Namely, both of you have a non sequitur in your reasoning (although yours starts at the opposite point).

As I understand your critique of the logic underlying those advocating the teaching of managerial competencies, it is as follows:

1. If we can find effective managers, then we can study what competencies they use.
2. If we know those competencies, then we can teach them to future managers.
3. And, if thse competencies are learned, the students will become effective managers.

As you point out, the first two statements may be correct without the third necessarily following.

But I think your reasoning also requires a logical leap of faith between your first two propositions and the conclusion. As I understand it, you are saying:

1. A manager's job is more than a bunch of competencies.
2. True managerial effectiveness comes from learning the complexities, artistry, and interactive properties in behavior.

3.   Since the second can't be learned from the first, there is
     no value in the first.

Let me use some analogies from learning how to ski
(where I have some effectiveness) and learning how to play the
violin (where I have none) to show that even though your first
two propositions are correct, the third does not follow.

In any sport or artistic endeavor, much effort is spent
learning the basic component parts. I spend much time on the
practice slopes working on how to weight the skis and how to
shift the weight, and as I hear my neighbor's son, much time—
too much time—is spent on similar basic skills learning the
violin. You are correct that becoming a competent skier or a
quality violinist, at some point, requires forgetting all the component parts and responding to the whole. But the latter can
best be done when the first have been well ingrained.

One of the major problems I see with students and managers in their effort to achieve excellence, is that they don't have
the basic skills that are needed. If they knew how to confront
others nondestructively, give feedback, lead meetings, build
teams, negotiate well, build collaborative relationships, then it
would be far easier for me to help them learn when to do this
(and when not) and how to integrate these separate skills that
will always be needed—I don't worry about their being outdated.

Where I think you are on target is the danger if we, as
educators, assume that knowing these and other competencies
are sufficient to attain excellence. While necessary, they require
a point where we say to the student "Now that you know all
of that, forget it and put yourself in the situation of an actual
manager in an actual situation and perform!" Students are likely
to resist that ambiguity and perhaps seek the safety of learning
set skills. But isn't that what the challenge of education is all
about?

Best,

David L. Bradford
Graduate School of Business,
Stanford University

Dear David:

Thanks for your commentary. You too are provocative and you have helped me focus my thinking substantially, as I hope to display in the next few lines. I want to do two things below: First, I see that I have to question the CM's logic at a more fundamental level than I did in the paper you are reacting to. Second, and related, your comments on learning skiing lead me to raise some questions for all of us about how much we really know of the process of competency acquisition. In general, these two efforts will show how deeply my thinking is divided from what I see in the CM. Contrary to your worry, perhaps it *is* necessary that the tack I am on be entertained or flatly rejected in a rather wholesale way. The problem as I see it exists at the level of basic philosophies of inquiry. I am trying to take big bites out of the CM, not just nibble at its edges.

To my first task: The CM makes a basic assumption which it does not question, and which it probably is not even aware of as an assumption (or presupposition). It is this: *Competencies exist.* The fundamental question then is, what is the basis for assuming that competencies exist or, as the philosophers would say, what is the ontological status of the idea of a competency? So you see, I think that even the first proposition which you attribute to the CM ("If we can find effective managers, then we can study what competencies they use") is of very doubtful validity. The debate should be occurring at the level of this proposition before we proceed with all the research and subsequent designing of teaching/training programs and evaluating "criterion attainment" of learners. The *whole* argument you summarize is of at least doubtful validity; and of course my personal opinion is that the argument is thoroughly faulty.

The CM commits what Alfred North Whitehead called the "fallacy of misplaced concreteness" (Whitehead, [1925] 1967). The CM is on the way to forgetting that those lists of factors I was talking about are abstractions. And they are abstractions of a very tricky sort for they involve splitting action from consciousness. Managing of any sort, let alone highly effective managing, is a very personal intertwining of consciousness and action. The CM's idea of what definitely *exists* is an abstracted statement of visible action-capability; in fact the CM's idea of what is real is an abstraction twice-removed for in its creation of a competency it has aggregated the visible action-capabilities of many actors, smoothing out the differences of energy-level, personal style, and cultural attunement which individual actors manifest.

> The disadvantage of exclusive attention to a group of abstractions [says Whitehead], however well-founded, is that, by the nature of the case, you have abstracted from the remainder of things. In so far as the excluded things are important in your experience, your modes of thought are not fitted to deal with them. You cannot think without abstractions; accordingly it is of utmost importance to be vigilant in critically revising your *modes* of abstraction. It is here that philosophy finds its niche as essential to the healthy progress of society. It is the critic of abstractions [Whitehead, [1925] 1967, p. 59].

Speaking of Whitehead's fallacy, Abraham Kaplan says, "The fallacy lies in thinking that the *one* is as concrete as the *many* from which it is constructed" (Kaplan, 1977, p. 293). Closer perhaps to the Organizational Behavior tradition is General Semantics' idea of confusing the word with the thing, mistaking the map for the territory. The dangers of "reification" aren't discussed in the social science literature as much as they should be. Reification also pertains to the sort of confusion I think the CM is stuck in.

The CM assumes that an individual trainee will be able to reunite the newly learned behavior with consciousness, and that no real violation of the personal intertwining I spoke of has been committed by the abstraction. But I am doubtful. I am doubtful empirically because of all the struggles I have watched over the years as learners tried to figure what such things as "openness," "giving feedback," "being participative," etc., *mean for them personally* in their own ways of thinking and acting in relation to others. More importantly though, I am doubtful on logical grounds (for maybe I have been cursed with particularly cloddish learners, though, I don't think so). You *can't* split consciousness and action. The empirical competencies we are talking about have assumptions woven all through them about the nature of the consciousness which is going to implement them. Perceptive learners see this right away when they see that the practice of these actions involves changes in values, shifts in the focus of one's attention, re-inspection of one's past experience with people. They realize that we are messing with their heads as well as their "hands," as it were. We have all been confronted by such learners. The most honest and effective teachers and trainers realize the inextricability of consciousness and action and try to work caringly with both. The CM is going to drive these folks out of the classroom.

Which brings me to my second main point. What I am talking about does not just apply to the interpersonal and organizational sensitivities we associate with the teaching of Organizational Behavior. It applies to all processes of competency acquisition. It applies to learning auditing, and market research, and planning, to computing breakeven points and learning programming. It applies to all learning. Yes, it applies to learning to ski.

To learn to ski involves, as you say, paying attention to the various actions which go to make up "skiing." But to think about how one learned skiing is to pay attention to something else. It is to pay attention *to one's processes of attention* while one was practicing the requisite actions. Now, I haven't been on a pair of skis since I was fourteen, though I practically lived on them in my childhood as a Minnesota kid. But let me make some guesses about what the books and/or instructors said to your *head* as well as to your body. I'll bet they said things like:

> "Don't be embarrassed that you're on an easy practice slope."
> "Don't worry about looking funny."
> "Don't cut corners with cheap or ill-fitting equipment."
> "Make it a family project."

"Figure it will take you about X-hours of practice to become reasonably confident and competent."

"If you let yourself fall this way (a statement to your body), you won't get hurt (a statement to your mind)."

. . . and so forth

Or maybe they didn't, in which case many of the actions seemed pointless. You didn't feel like you were getting anywhere (notice consciousness continuing to burble, even though the instructor wasn't paying any attention to it?). This is why computer programming is so hard for some people: the instructors don't realize they are tinkering with the tips of consciousness as well as with the tips of the fingers. It is why so many kids quit piano lessons. It is why business school is so almighty boring to so many of our students. They get no feel for the romance of managing, which is just a colorful way of saying that the faculty is not helping them feel like managing will be something they will enjoy.

We don't turn off our minds while we are learning actions. We *can't*. Some demonic ideologues of past and present realize this, by the way, and undertake to control attention and awareness concomitant with their control of actions-to-be-learned. It is perhaps appropriate that we are asking ourselves these questions as nineteen eighty-four dawns, for those of us who seek to liberate the human spirit through education are in a race of rather sobering importance. I don't see demonic ideologues in the CM for managing, but I see some impoverished ideas about the nature of the human spirit. Masters and Johnson have not succeeded in killing love with their competency studies of the sex act (sic), although they and the porno crowd have managed to confuse a lot of people. I hope the CM does no better with learners of managing. Meanwhile, those of us who see the defects have a lot of work to do.

My very best,

Peter

Chapter 3

Winning Is Only the Thing
You Think Winning Is

The question is: Is the idea in this title sour grapes? Surely we prefer to believe that the definition of success, of effectiveness—winning, if you will—is fixed, known, not a matter of negotiation or a sliding scale. Yet the intent of this chapter is to explore precisely the opposite idea, namely, that this title is literally correct, and that our understanding of our goals and priorities is no more a fixed element of the situation than anything else. In the world of permanent white water, the definition of winning slides around and has to be constantly tended.

We don't like it when people seem to be playing with the definition of success. The suspicion is that it can't help but be self-serving: success will be defined in such a way as to make its attainment easy. Our culture frowns on such tinkering: You're supposed to play by the rules everybody understands, not make up your own.

Yet we are conscious that victory isn't always *victory*, as evidenced in such phrases as "hollow victory," "Pyrrhic victory," "win the battle and lose the war," "dodged a bullet," "lucked out," and so forth. Victory can be an accident; it can be luck, it can be achieved at too high a cost. Indeed, the possibility that victory really may not be *victory* is always present on the edge of our awareness. The trouble is that we have a hard time thinking about it directly. Instead, the assumption is that goal setting is essentially a rational process that, once performed, does not need to be performed again during the life of the activity and that certainly should not have to be performed *continuously* over the life of the activity. Yet the opposite is precisely the contention of this chapter. ''Goal setting''—which, of course, creates the meaning of "winning" for any activity—is part of the ongoing process of the activity. It is not front-end activity only, or even primarily.

What the group or organization thinks winning is drives action on a minute-to-minute basis. A former college basketball coach once told me that one of the coach's key problems is to get all the players to define "winning" in the same way. For some, winning can mean always being willing to play hurt; for others, it can mean never playing hurt. Where one player may believe in starting fast and hanging on, another will take it easy early in the game and go all out at the end. For one, each game can be an individual freestanding challenge; for another, the challenge is a series of games, or even a whole season. Some players regard all opponents equally; for others, some opponents are much more important than other opponents, and winning against one of the others isn't really "winning."

We don't often think of the psychological nuances of winning, yet these differences are clearly real. It is not too hard to see how much effort a coach might need to invest in getting everybody on the same wave length regarding what winning is going to mean for the team and keeping them there. This action by the coach—it is really leadership I am describing—goes on continuously, and particularly it goes on in the emerging game situation when things aren't going as expected. In other words, the definition of winning is *open:* open to the effects of what has happened so far, and open to the unfolding possibilities and constraints that were not foreseen at the beginning. In their actions, the players may be seen to be pursuing the goal as they understand it, but what each understands the goal to be may differ, as it may also differ from the coach's version or from a fan's. When we can't understand another person's behavior, it is often because we don't understand what that person thinks the goal is.

At this point, a skeptic may want to ask whether I am really saying that "winning the game," defined as having more points on the board at the end than one's opponent, is a matter of subjective perception. Am I really saying that there can be disagreement about who actually, finally "won"?

Yes. Even where there is both an operational definition of winning (more points on the board) and agreement about it among those concerned, there can still be disagreements about whether some outcome was a "win," "success," "effective," or what have you. Record books are full of asterisks—it is as simple as that. But I am not really as concerned with the situation where there is an agreed-to operational definition as I am with the process by which agreed-to, operational definitions are created in the first place and maintained over the life of the activity.

If the definition of winning can slide around in the minds of the members of a sports team, this is nothing compared to the diversity of thinking one can find in a typical work organization. Every manager has encountered the astonishing differences of understanding that can exist in a work force. Differences can exist regarding the importance of quantity versus quality, the long term versus the short term, the needs of line versus those of staff, headquarters versus field, management versus labor, profits versus service to the customer, winning at any cost versus more lofty principles, and so forth.

The trouble is that these differences are often not seen as competing definitions of success, effectiveness, or winning. Instead, the title of this chapter is ignored, and the speaker, especially if a high-ranking person, treats differences such as these as departures from "the truth." "Truth," of course, is the official purpose or objective if one exists; if not, "truth" becomes whatever the speaker perceives as truth. This interesting capacity to individually define truth while ignoring the fact that everyone else may do so also is what has led me to define an organization as a place where everyone is right, and everyone is wrong!

The Key Process of "Purposing"

Some years ago, I made up the word *purposing* and defined it as "that continuous stream of actions by an organization's formal leadership that has the effect of inducing clarity, consensus, and commitment regarding the organization's basic purposes" (Vaill, 1982, p. 29). The key thing here is the continuity of effort. This is what is so often forgotten, and it is especially important to think in terms of continuity when one is in a world of permanent white water, a world of unpredictable opportunities and constraints, a world of surprises.

As this is written, the management of Ashland Oil is struggling with the technical and the public relations problems that accompany a huge spill of diesel fuel into the Monongahela River near Pittsburgh, Pennsylvania. It is the surprise—no, the *shock*—of such an event that I am trying to relate to the question of what "winning," or effectiveness, means. The management of Johnson & Johnson faced the same thing with the Tylenol poisoning disaster, and the Union Carbide management was similarly shocked by the Bhopal tragedy.

But we don't need such extreme examples to make the point: Surprises call into question what you're trying to do. Surprises force organization members to integrate the actions they were taking before the surprise with the actions the surprise itself requires *and still* stay on course regarding the main purposes. When we say that an organization has "grown like Topsy," what we mean is that the shape it has taken is the result of twists and turns of adaptation to the unfolding world around it, that it had no real direction of its own apart from just "staying alive" in its environment.

We have barely begun to grasp what a world of continuous surprise means for planning, for structuring the organization, for devising and administering reward systems, for operating career development systems, and so forth. The great bulk of what we think sound management is rests on an unstated assumption of either "no surprises" or, at worst, "infrequent and manageable surprises." The consequences of this much more turbulent world that we have are concretely present but conceptually mysterious. That's why we need to consider how this most fundamental of all management categories—the definition of the main objective—is affected by the world of permanent white water. In a very real sense, all the chapters in this book are concerned in one way or another with this question of how a sense of purpose is created and maintained in an organization when there is such a large and powerful range of forces that would defeat the effort.

The Nature of Organizational Values

Recently, I asked a group of members of the senior executive service of the federal government to describe the grounds for decisions that they routinely heard within their agencies. I have subsequently asked the same question of several groups of senior corporate executives. The grounds for a decision, I reasoned, are really the values that are being used to make the decision. I was concerned not with the substantive content of a decision but with the "reasons why" that are offered. An interesting list resulting from these queries captures the competing definitions of "winning" or "success" or "effectiveness" that are at stake in any given decision-making process:

1. Because the law requires it
2. Because "So-and-so" personally ordered us to do it
3. Because this approach won out in competition with others
4. Because another organization does it this way
5. Because it was for the good of the company (team, agency)
6. Because it was the scientifically correct thing to do
7. Because it makes the best use of our resources
8. Because it is the best way to reach the objective
9. Because it was the easiest, most expedient approach
10. Because we just knew this was right
11. Because we had to compromise, and this was the result
12. Because doing something was better than doing nothing
13. Because we wanted to call attention to ourselves
14. Because of basically divine revelation
15. Because this was the result of careful sustained dialogue
16. Because our survival was at stake
17. Because our specific ideology (beliefs) dictated it

These responses never present themselves as a coherent list of options; rather, they appear as an utter jumble of noisily advocated alternatives. It is easy to forget that values have an emotional charge. Values mean something to people. They are the family jewels and are not juggled about casually. When one's values are vindicated, the feelings are of elation and triumph. When one's values are ignored or denied, it hurts.

These are commonplace ideas, in a sense, but they gain a sobering significance when we consider how constantly and profoundly and thoroughly the modern organizational world constitutes a nonstop challenge to any given value system. When Peters declares that the modern excellent company is a "values-driven" enterprise (Peters and Waterman, 1982), I can heartily agree with him, but I must insist as well that the modern corporation is also a "values-muddled" place—indeed, a "values-anguished" place—in which the search is just precisely for that sense of focus and forward movement that a well-articulated and widely supported value system provides.

We cannot merely go "back to the basics" of values that we once held but have drifted away from. Our traditional values are not "wrong" so much as they are not formulated in relation to the problems we have today and will have tomorrow. We should squeeze our traditional values for every ounce of wisdom and sustenance that we can, but we must also recognize that we may have to go "forth to basics" as much as back to them, forth to new criteria and to new meanings of old criteria, forth to new ways of talking about values and new forums and new learnings about the sorting out of various values. I am suggesting that modes of discourse are called for that no one ever told us would become "business as usual" in organizational life. The kind of "values clarification" I am talking about has always been the respected and cherished activity of the wisest philosophers and critics. I am suggesting that in the fast-moving world of the present and the faster-moving world of the future, we have to bring these capabilities out of the libraries, the seminaries, and the mountaintop retreats, and directly to the decision points we all confront daily.

Principles of Values Clarification

Some readers will connect the phrase "values clarification" with pioneering work done by Sidney Simon in the 1960s (Raths, Harrison, and Simon, 1966; Simon, Howe, and Kirschenbaum, 1972). He did indeed perceive, in connection with the profound social change of the sixties, that individuals were moving apart at the level of basic values. Simon's contributions are underappreciated, I think, and in particular his emphasis on *methods* of sorting out value differences is an important contribution.

Leadership and management in the turbulent modern organization are values clarification. If indeed "winning is only the thing one thinks winning is," then the real question is "What is the process by which clarity about effectiveness (winning) is developed and maintained?" "Leadership" is the articulation of new values and the energetic presentation of them to those whose actions are affected by them. As much as anything else, it is a teaching and coaching process in which the object is to help people embrace and experiment with values that they might not otherwise consider. "Management" is the discovery of value conflicts and the invention of processes for working them through. Managers work for greater harmony among the elements that are already present in the situation. Leaders change the elements. Each kind of organizational action is indispensable to the other.

Beyond these general remarks about values clarification, there are ten principles to be kept in mind as one is going about the process. They apply equally whether one is functioning in a leadership or a management role. First, the most important step of all is to learn to hear values being articulated amid the content of all communication. The seventeen values I listed above are not often advanced discussed as ends in themselves. They are inserted parenthetically, sometimes humorously or even apologetically. They tend to be cast in familiar-sounding phrases, sometimes in aphorisms or quotations from famous people. It is sometimes a major achievement just to hear what grounds (values) are actually being advanced in a memo or a meeting.

Second, and apropos of the problem just mentioned, is the need to be able to state and restate values evenhandedly. Nothing will divert a values clarification process into an argument more quickly than restating some of the values in question in more favorable terms than others. It is important to say that the ability fairly to state a position one personally disagrees with is difficult but learnable. It is the cornerstone skill of Carl Rogers's famous conflict resolution technique where each party must restate the other's last point to the other's satisfaction before proceeding with his or her own next comment (Rogers, 1961, p. 332).

Third is the sticky problem of the relativity of most or all values. If you are seriously going to try to intrigue people with new values or reconcile conflicts among existing values, you can't be constantly getting hung up on whether one value or another deserves "full and fair" consideration. The best principle is that all values deserve consideration, even though not all values will turn out to be appropriate and applicable to a given situation. This is itself a value judgment—basically rooted in the democratic tradition (Lombard, 1971).

Fourth, Peter Drucker calls this the doctrine of "no final victories" (Drucker, 1981, p. 87). He was speaking of Japanese managers' belief that one should never crush an opponent even if one is able to, for by such restraint one earns the right to be treated the same way when the positions are reversed.

As a fifth idea, it is important to remember that values are displayed in our *actions*. It is what we do and don't do, say and don't say, react to and don't react to that reveals our values. And it will be in these modes that we work through our value problems with others, too. Every manager knows how hard it is just to get the parties in the same room and listening to each other. That is often the main achievement—far more important to the values clarification process than the exact content of what is said. People come to share values when they can collaborate *in action* with others. Give the parties something to do together, and then be prepared for them to struggle through to important discoveries about each other. Furthermore, activity is a better indicator of how much real energy people are willing to exert for their values, as opposed to merely paying them lip service.

Sixth, Weisbord observed some years ago that successful change processes usually are accompanied by various "helpful mechanisms" (Weisbord, 1978, p. 44). This powerful idea is deceptively simple. Helpful mechanisms are noticed neither in their presence nor in their absence: if they are present, they are taken for granted, and if they are absent, they are not missed. But when some such mechanism—some practice or device or attitude—is present, things go more smoothly. It is likely that effective value clarification processes are permeated with helpful mechanisms that help people get over their suspicion and awkwardness. It is a little hollow, of course, to sing the praises of helpful mechanisms while being unable to say how or why they arise in some specific situation. Nevertheless, it is valuable to know about their role, so that when a helpful mechanism is spontaneously invented, it will be seen and valued for what it is.

A seventh principle is to pay particular attention to so-called core values that various people hold. These are values that are involved with enhancing a person's sense of self in the world as he or she wants to think of it. Values establish identity, in other words, but identity is in the eye of the beholder, and it is always problematic, always potentially in question. It is important to know when one is treading in this tender area. As the OD profession has learned over and over again, resistance to change can pop up in the most unexpected places and in the most surprisingly intense ways. It is not the logical but the psychological we are dealing with when we are trying to understand why people are resisting some idea or initiative. In terms of goals and effectiveness and "winning," I am suggesting that "resistance to change" can frequently mean simply that the resister doesn't understand or agree with the values that he or she is being asked to act on.

Eighth, if one doesn't like a person's actions, there is always the temptation to try to suppress them. However, suppression of a person's actions is also a symbolic suppression and denial of the person's values. Values, being inner, feeling-laden attitudes, refuse to be suppressed and denied. They simply find another activity for their outlet. Send the child to her room, and she continues being noisy there. Discipline the employee for lateness, and he finds another irritating way to express his individuality. It is easy to say, as McGregor (1960) did, that managers should find ways for employees to pursue their own goals through acting for the company's goals. But if the company's goals are unclear or are sufficiently inconsistent or in conflict with the employee's, it is going to take a lot of hard work to find and sustain an accommodation between the employee's values and the organization's. And it must always be remembered that, in the longer run, suppression doesn't work. The best argument for participative management is that since suppression doesn't work, values clarification and value conflict resolution must still somehow go on.

As a ninth observation, the "value of values clarification" is itself in continual question. The closer the process can be kept to the work of the organization, the more the superordinate value of organizational survival and effectiveness can support the process and allay the natural impatience that some feel with repeated discussion of values and priorities. If whether the organization itself ought to exist and prosper is in question, then this question has to be dealt with prior to clarification of other values. Otherwise, people will see no point in such discussion. Many organizations in both the public and private sectors are in jeopardy at this very basic level: it isn't very clear that they should exist at all, and, this being unclear, people have little energy for more detailed discussion of *how* they should exist. Much writing in the strategic planning field declares that basic mission and purpose have to be set first; but less often do writers consider what happens when this is not possible, or when attempts to do it keep failing.

Finally, it is important to remember that all values are ultimately nonlogical. I do not mean *illogical,* which implies that values are antirational and that logic cannot be used to develop and critique them. *Nonlogical* means that, at the core, the meaning to a person of a particular value is not decided by logic and reason. *Translogical* or *supralogical* might actually be a better word, for these words capture the notion that the meaning of values is beyond logic. The nonlogical quality of values brings us back to the title of this chapter: what is important is what we decide is important.

Five Frontiers of Organizational Values

I have been stressing in various ways how management and leadership in organizational contexts may be viewed as a process of ongoing values clarification. That *is* the most important business. That *is* the key job that needs doing, and that *is* the job whose significance we keep underestimating.

It remains to consider just who we are talking about in this values clarification process. Think of any complex organization. What are the values that need to be shared by everyone, and what are the values that need have intense meaning only in various subparts of the organization? Beyond the organization's boundaries, what are the values that the organization and its key constituents need to share? To what extent can we keep values that are incompatible from colliding with each other? How do we communicate to all the parties involved that the process of values clarification is one that is going to receive high priority? In some ways, the current "excellence literature" and the "teamwork literature" before it have simplified the game by tending to stick with relatively small organizations where there is considerable built-in homogeneity of background and interests. The question is whether there is a point beyond which values clarification is not really possible, and a leader or manager will be wiser to revert to strategies that don't involve people communicating effectively with each other and working to integrate interests. This is really the question of systemwide change.

The larger and more heterogeneous the system, the more one who would lead in values clarification needs a way of thinking about all the various *kinds* of values that can be operating. The world of permanent white water has demolished the monolithic models of "capitalist enterprise" or "bureaucracy" or "hospital" or "university" that we have inherited. These models define each organization's core values. But what today's organization *is* is in question. The identity of its constituents and its obligations to them are open and evolving. What is needed is a scheme that forecasts for an organization's leadership what sorts of value issues it can expect to confront.

There are five categories of values that a human system of any size has to come to terms with. To the extent that values

are confused or absent in any of these categories, the values
clarification job is only partially understood. "Winning," in
other words, is a five-dimensional thing, not a one-dimensional
thing. It is still "only the thing you think winning is," but to
the extent that you try to define winning more narrowly or lop-
sidedly than these five categories, you can expect that voices
that you are overlooking or trying to ignore will find ways of
making themselves heard.

   Am I suddenly saying that there are some "absolutes"
in the values clarification process? To say that there are five
categories that you have to come to terms with sounds like I
am arguing that there is an objective truth about values after
all. I don't think that I am saying this, though. Instead, I am
talking about who the "you" is in the expression "only the thing
you think winning is." I am suggesting that those who have a
stake in the organization—its "stakeholders," as they are called—
can be expected to want a piece of the definition of "winning";
that is, a piece of the question of the organization's priorities.
Traditionally, it has been "management" that owns the definition of priorities. The postwar era, though, has seen a dramatic
change on this score. Priorities are now the business of all kinds
of individuals and groups that formerly were supposed to wait
passively for whatever benefits the top management chose to
toss their way.

   This change is not yet one that most organizational leaders
and managers accept and have in their bones. It will take at least
a couple of more generations for this to happen. (It is important to note, by the way, that what we are really thinking about
here is a major change in the meaning of "private property"
and "management prerogatives.") But meanwhile, let us see
whether we can't just say simply what these categories are within
which, like it or not, the values clarification process will be going on.

   Let us call the first values clarification category the *Economic*. This is the question of where gross revenue is going to
come from and of what the "bottom line" is going to be. The
income statement from top to bottom is a set of value judgments.
Ironically, the expression "bottom line" is itself maddeningly
imprecise: as every accountant knows, there are multiple "bot-

tom lines" between "revenue" and "retained earnings," multiple opportunities to decide whether one is going to spend (or distribute) funds or hang on to them, and in either case, why. It is not often noted that "overhead" is really a series of value judgments. Somebody decides how much is going to be spent on office furniture, the company picnic, the telephone system, and so on. The kind, degree, and form of cost control are all value judgments, and if some costs are going uncontrolled, that too is a value judgment.

The second major category of values clarification is the *Technological*. How is the organization going to do whatever it does? What are its choices of method? How close to the state of the art does it want to operate? Cost of various options comes up in the first category; here the question is of efficacy, of doing the job to some decided level of quality and quantity.

Third is what I call the *Communal* category. What kind of a community does the organization want to be? What does it want its members to feel and to receive as a result of being associated with this organization? The values in this category are more recently formulated and more debatable, because formal work organizations were not originally created 200 years ago for the benefit of their employees. Nevertheless, the OD profession and others have shown, convincingly, I think, that values in this category cannot be ignored. The organization does not have the luxury of being thoughtless about the kind of home to its employees it wants to be.

Fourth, there is the question of what kind of citizen in its environment the organization wants to be—call this the realm of the *Sociopolitical*. Beyond products and services ordered from and delivered to stakeholders, and beyond minimal compliance with the letter of the law, what kind of relationships does the organization want to have with its many different constituencies? How does it want to think of them, and be thought of by them? What is "quality of organizational life" for the organization, and what efforts is the organization prepared to make to achieve it? These are groundbreaking questions for many organizations, yet I suggest that these questions are already being posed to organization managements every day in a host of different ways.

Last is a more philosophical category. Beyond all the things that it is and does, beyond all its policies and practices, what does the organization want to mean at a deeper level to those who work in it and do business with it? I propose the term *Transcendental* for this category. It is perhaps an overly grand term, but it gets at this character of "something more" that so many people are feeling the need for these days. If people are going to try to work "spiritually smarter," as I suggested in Chapter One, they will want a context that is friendly to that quest. If the organization wants loyalty, affection, and sacrifice from its people—and in permanent white water, I think that an organization just about has to receive these things to survive—it has to work out a set of values and priorities that are aimed at making it deserving of such contributions from its people.

Here then are five categories within which some serious evaluating and choice making need to go on: the Economic, the Technological, the Communal, the Sociopolitical, and the Transcendental. The five aren't absolutely distinct from each other, and choices you make in one are going to have effects on the choices you make in others. Ultimately, indeed, the search is for a value *system* (how often we use that phrase without really hearing it) that will provide for needs and interests on the variety of fronts that the modern organization moves toward.

Chapter 4

The Peak Performance Cult

This chapter is about the work that I think is yet to be done on the subject of organizational excellence and peak performance. I'll admit that my title is a little provocative. There are lots of dedicated people working in this field. Furthermore, there is nothing phony or shallow about the subject of doing substantially better at both the personal and organizational level. Nevertheless, there is cultishness, in my view; I think that it derives from four sources and that its net effect is to impede progress in the field. I want to discuss these four sources first, then say why they are impeding progress, and then close this chapter with a discussion of six categories in which I think we still have a lot of work to do on the subject of excellence and peak performance.

Despite the concerns I express in the pages that follow, I want to be clear that this topic is my favorite subject. My own writings about it date from 1972. There is nothing I have worked on over the years that is more important to me either professionally or personally. The comments that follow, therefore, should be understood as the feedback that only best friends will give. In caring a lot, of course, best friends sometimes care too much, and their good intentions become windy fretting. I have decided to take the risk.

Sources of Cultishness

By *cultishness,* I mean strong doctrine articulated by strong and colorful personalities who have succeeded in developing substantial bands of followers around them. The feeling from the outside is that one either buys the approach or one doesn't. It is not presented as a "field of inquiry" where divergent views, debate, and the expectation of further development are the norms. In Chapter Six, I devote some further discussion to the difference between a field of inquiry and a cult, because my own hope is that organizational excellence and peak performance ideas can be primarily a field of ongoing inquiry, for scholars and leader-managers alike. For the moment, let's look into why this cultishness as I have described it is developing in the organizational excellence and peak performance field.

Compatibility with cultural traditions has to be a major element in the cult problem. What the excellence and peak performance experts are saying "sounds right" because their views are so consistent with the traditional American values: commitment to high standards, the importance of teamwork, "practice-practice-practice," the crucial role of inspirational leadership for motivation and loyalty. Furthermore, these characteristics are presented and illustrated with what might be called the "compelling anecdote," a brief portrayal of some member of the excellent organization engaging in some action that perfectly illustrates the point being made, and inviting us to agree that this or that characteristic of excellent organizations and peak performance has now been proved. This is a particularly troubling habit regarding the subject of leadership, because it is so easy to find numerous colorful examples of fascinating leaders doing fascinating things, yet the real cause-effect relationship between how they act and what happens in the organization is never stated and defended directly; it is only implied. It is not surprising that Peters and Austin (1985, p. 292) find they have to deal with the fears of some readers that their personalities aren't brilliant and scintillating enough for them to be like the executives in the book. The authors don't seem to realize that they have *trained* their audience to think that colorful, charismatic leaders cause excellence in organizations; if they did, they would not be surprised when a questioner attaches more importance to brilliant leadership than perhaps is necessary. The truth is that the world is full of colorful, charismatic people. Only a very few of them are associated with sustained organizational excellence.

Urgency and timeliness are a second set of characteristics that create pressures toward cultishness. As I made very clear in my opening chapter, we are indeed in a deep crisis of leadership, management, and organizational effectiveness. Under these conditions, there is a polarizing tendency operating: an idea either is useful for the work of revitalizing an organization or is too vague and fuzzy and "academic." Furthermore, ideas that do look like they have practical value should not be tinkered with. Instead, the impulse is to "get on with it"—to engage in the effort to revitalize the organization without delay.

The commercial value of the ideas is also an important force promoting cultishness, and of course this notion doesn't apply just to the excellence and peak performance movement but has been a characteristic of the management and organization development field for forty years. I do not fault those who want to earn a living by purveying ideas to managers. I do suggest, however, that you can't be changing your mind all the time about your theory if you are going to market it successfully in a competitive, commercial environment. The temptation, therefore, is to freeze one's approach or theory into a persuasive, professional package of "deliverables." The problem then is how much change to permit in them, and at what rate. As everyone knows, the spectrum is wide, with extreme packagers at one end and nonstop tinkerers at the other. In the excellence and peak performance movement, the stakes are high, the fees are substantial, and the competition is becoming intense. I think that at the present time there is an inordinate amount of pressure toward the packager end of the continuum, supported unfortunately by too many managers who are themselves under enormous pressure for efficient and effective packaged solutions to their organization's problems. Not only the organizational clients but the consultants and theoreticians themselves are caught in white water where it is not clear how to manage a body of ideas effectively. This makes the temptation to crystallize some scheme into a cultish dogma all the more tempting but, of course, fruitless.

Finally, there is pressure toward cultishness in the intrinsic character of the subject itself. The data show that in excellent organizations there is a willingness to commit oneself, to believe, to keep the faith no matter what. Members of these systems do not sit around wondering whether they are going to be able to be excellent and stay excellent. Thus, when presenting ideas about excellence and peak performance to a group, you're aware that you are not just reciting facts about excellence but rather that in the here and now of the presentation or the article you are initiating a process of faith and commitment. You behave accordingly, and once again the temptation to let oneself become a cult figure beckons because it seems so markedly to enhance the effectiveness of your message. There is a deep paradox in the situation where a message whose content is about the importance of inspiration and commitment often sounds silly and simplistic unless it is presented in an inspiring and committed way. Every preacher probably struggles with the trade-offs that this paradox poses. My concern is that the excellence and peak performance experts seem unaware of the problem and are thus in danger of erring too far on the side of becoming cult figures and gurus, to the possible detriment of the longer-run vitality of their ideas.

At bottom, my conviction is that in a world of permanent white water, all bodies of knowledge and speculation are themselves in a race to stay just one jump ahead of obsolescence and irrelevance. To the extent that the subject of excellence and peak performance becomes the property of a cultish ingroup of cognoscenti, the subject risks being overtaken and passed by the actual issues real managers and leaders are facing, and then we may begin to hear the managers say ruefully, as they have had to say so many times before about once-promising approaches, "Excellence? Oh yeah, right, we've already tried that."

Some Unsolved Problems of Excellence

In Chapter Three, I argued that every organization is facing a whole range of new priorities and new values, and that leadership and management are really about defining and adhering to a desired mix amid all the turbulence and change. I called this process "purposing." Now I want to talk about a different kind of problem that is also facing every organization. Not only is there a continuing stream of new issues to try to be excellent about, there are problems to be coped with in the very way that we *are* in excellent organizations. These problems aren't getting enough attention, in my view, and they are especially hard to address if we take a dogmatic, cultish view of what excellence looks like in day-to-day relationships among human beings— the "process of excellence," you might call it. Striking, charming, amusing, "outrageous" attitudes and actions have been widely documented in excellent organizations, usually in very admiring terms. In documenting some of the very unusual things that people think, say, and do in excellent organizations, I think those of us who have been doing this research have performed a real service. But I think we also need to question some of this behavior, and I see much less of that going on. What follows are some features of the process of excellence that aren't so pretty and that I think we need to be working on, both theoretically and practically.

Purposes and Objectives. In Chapter Three, I discussed at length the complex process of getting clear and staying clear on basic directions. We still don't understand this very well. Understanding it better is crucial to understanding how excellent organizations can be developed, a subject I deal with below in the section on "Undesignability." There is ample empirical evidence that in excellent organizations there is remarkable clarity, consensus, and commitment about purposes and objectives, but we have to keep asking ourselves how this happens. In the best case, it is an extremely elusive process. In the world of permanent white water, it is further complicated by being continuously altered by all the changes going on in the environment. What motivated the players last year may not motivate the same players this year.

Burnout. In many of my presentations about the nature of "high-performing systems"—my term for excellent organizations—someone almost always raises the question of burnout. I think this is a legitimate concern. It has caused me to think carefully about what it is we mean by "burnout." I don't mean just the symptomology, although that itself is an important subject and is discussed at some length in Chapter Fourteen. If "burnout" is some kind of an inability to function at a high level of excellence, what could cause it?

In the first place, a "burned-out" person is usually someone who formerly was functioning at a high level of excellence. That's why it occurs to my audiences to ask about it in reaction to my recitation of the characteristics of high-performing people. Having once been a high performer means that the person had the deep commitment to the system's goals that is uniformly characteristic of high performers. I think in "burnout" the psychological meaning of these goals changes, however, and the person loses the enthusiasm he or she once had for the task. But this is not the whole story, for we all lose enthusiasm for once-meaningful tasks all the time without going through burnout. Two other things are present that produce the agony of burnout. One is the retention of an abstract commitment to the task, even if concretely one's heart is not in it. And the second is remaining in the system and subject to its culture and expectations. This can be because of "golden handcuffs," commitment to the other members of the system, belief that one will soon be able to shake off the burnout, or other things. I think these three things therefore combine to produce the acute stress we call burnout: (1) loss of commitment to perform the task at an excellent level, (2) continued belief in the importance of the task and of the groups and organizations performing it, and (3) remaining in the system and subject to its culture. This topic is of special importance to excellent organizations because they place such extraordinary demands on their members. We need to know a lot more about what might be called the "psychology of enthusiasm"—what its healthy and unhealthy forms are.

Groupthink. Group norms and expectations are implicated in burnout, but there are other issues as well that make this subject an important one to the future of excellence. The most obvious problem with groupthink is innovation. Once a high-performing system has learned how to perform some activity well and has begun to reap the benefits of its hard-won proficiency, it may be difficult to get it to see that it needs to be concerned with the future and with the possibility that no matter how excellent it is, it should think of itself as a perpetual learner. This is a very sophisticated awareness; it is much easier to rest on one's laurels, fall prey to overconfidence, even arrogance. Folk wisdom knows this one very well: "The bigger they are, the harder they fall"; "What goes up must come down"; and so on. There may indeed be organizations, such as IBM or 3M, that have incorporated innovation right into their concept of what being excellent is. We need to learn all we can from them, and we need to keep developing new approaches.

Second, even after the awareness of the need for continuous learning has been achieved, there is still the problem of the kind of "microlearning" that has to go on in the changed context in order for excellence in new activities to be attained. Just because a school has developed an excellent M.B.A. program is no guarantee that it will be able to develop an excellent executive development seminar. In fact, over and over organizations make the mistake of thinking that because they have proved that they can do one type of activity well, they should have no difficulty with another type of activity. What they forget is the white water: the new task may reside in a very different environment, where the terms of excellence may be radically altered.

A third problem with groupthink is the question of how flexible members are able to be about who qualifies for membership. The fact is that members of high-performing systems develop strong opinions about the type of individuals who qualify. These opinions and standards are primarily task related (although there may be cases where the standards are racist or sexist or otherwise improper). But even if they are task related, there is still the possibility that the group will define the requisites for membership too narrowly, or fail to note that qualified people are emerging in new places, or fail to anticipate the skills that members are going to need in the future.

In true groupthink, members are not able to question the way the group or organization or team is proceeding. Indeed, they are not able to *think* of questions; that is, extract their minds from the flow of group operations and think afresh about it. This can be a deadly affliction in the world of permanent white water, and high-performing organizations are by no means immune. Just how a group stays open to its evolving challenges and opportunities while remaining closed enough to perform excellently is an unsolved dilemma.

Boundaries and Linkages. High-performing systems are very conscious of their boundaries, and so are individuals and groups who are on the "outside." From the inside out, the feeling is that "no one can understand exactly how special we are," and from the outside in, it is frequently a mixture of admiration, envy, and fury. Early in my studies of excellent organizations, I coined the phrase "nonguilty exploitation" to capture the unconcern with which high-performing systems took resources from their environments—information, people, equipment, budget, space, and so on. With extraordinary ease, they could conclude that they needed these resources more than anyone else possibly could, and that whatever actions were necessary to get these resources were all right. This is the organizational form and process that Peters and Waterman (1982, pp. 211–212) referred to as a *skunk works*. There is no question that a skunk works is a powerful organizational form, capable of amazing accomplishments. But it can also be a powerful organizational problem, capable of amazing arrogance.

My point is that we haven't been thinking enough about the linkage problem. If our thinking about organizations is going toward decentralized networks, loosely coupled systems (Weick, 1976b), then we should be thinking more about how we are going to hold these aggregates together, not in a tightly controlled pyramid, certainly, but as some kind of "community of vision and feeling" that will still permit us to call the aggregate an "organization." Companies such as Shell and Digital Equipment already are testing these limits.

"Visionary leadership" is one strategy for fostering a community of vision and feeling. I discuss this at greater length in several succeeding chapters. Another strategy is what one might call "high-performing boundary spanning." The more excellent various component units become, the more important the liaison function becomes. The component units will not give any more attention to the matter than they have to, and the higher performing they become, the harder it becomes for them to see themselves in the broader organizational context and the more resentful they may become about restrictions that are placed on them by the larger organization. We need a concept of high performance for the liaison function, including a lot more ideas than we have at present about how individuals and teams can learn to play this role effectively. Liaison per se is not the main mission, most people would say; the excitement is elsewhere.

For the moment, let me speculate that high-performing boundary spanning is quite different action, qualitatively, from what the peak performance people seem to have in mind. Basically we are talking about literal facilitation of others' energies. The facilitator's energy is a different kind of energy, I think. It can't afford to go "head to head" with the energies of the parties to the situation, for if it does, it simply becomes one more party in need of someone else's facilitation. On the other hand, it is not passivity and wishy-washiness, despite all the jokes about facilitation. It is a kind of leadership, to be sure, because it entails showing the parties ways to work together, but it's less a Western, inspirational leadership than it is a "Taoistic" leadership. What this is I develop at greater length in Chapter Twelve. Let us simply note for now that the facilitator of high-performing components can't be the same kind of a zealot that the parties respectively are. What kind of zealot one *can* be is at the moment an open question.

Short-Term Bursts: Can the Future Be Now? Time is a funny thing in excellent organizations. Not much has been said about it, but my students and executive clients have frequently noted that a lot of the excellence research tends to be about organizations that "zoomed to the top" in a short period of time and/or were project teams that had to perform their mission within a fixed period. What about organizational life, day after day after day, one might ask. What if you're not on an all-out crusade?

More pointedly, one senior executive in a large manufacturing company told me that he thought short-term bursts of excellence were positively bad for his people, that they increased the roller-coaster feeling and the burnout rate among them and created all kinds of loose ends that didn't occur when things proceeded at a calmer, steadier pace. Is this executive opting for mediocrity? Some of the talk from the peak performance people might have you think so. But I am not so sure.

Figure 1 is a picture of the problem. This figure suggests that our aspirations for excellence have to be developed in relation to time. The *exact* relation is not known. It is a balance we are seeking between going too fast (which ensures resistance and disappointment) and not going fast enough; that is, not pushing hard enough (which ensures that not much will change). I don't interpret the executive I referred to above as seeking the region of business as usual shown in Figure 1. He's trying to avoid what the diagram calls the region of instant gratification. The problem is to stay within the envelope of optimal unrealism, as I have called it. Excellence is unrealistic—always has been and always will be. But that doesn't mean that it has to be frantic and maniacal. There's an optimal region there somewhere that we don't understand very well. The slope and width of the envelope obviously are going to vary from system to system, depending mainly on the culture of each. The trick is to find the envelope, and stay within it—year after year. There are organizations that have done it, that have fostered a "culture of excellence." But to endure year after year in the world of permanent white water and absorb all the different kinds of challenges and surprises that entails requires a balancing act such as the one suggested in Chapter Three with the five value categories of Economic, Technological, Communal, Sociopolitical, and Transcendental. This balancing act is anything but a short-term burst type of activity.

Undesignability. If some of the other problems of excellence and peak performance are matters of concern, this one is more than that. It is a real bugaboo. Let me state the issue quite flatly: many within the excellence and peak performance movement

Figure 1. Excellence and Time.

ghest levels of
rformance we
1 now imagine

The region of "instant
success and gratification,"
trying to "do too much and
move too fast," and so on.

The region of realistic
progress and achievements
by organization members;
the envelope of "optimal
unrealism."

The region of "business as
usual," "gradualism," "no big
deal," "wait and see," "things
will take care of themselves."

lay's level of
anizational
formance

Today

5–10 years
into future

Time scale

are leading managers to believe that one can learn exactly how
to bring about excellence in the organization. Yet my own data
and judgment suggest that you can't design the process by which
excellence is going to be achieved.

I know how tempting it is to try, for we see men and
women seeming to foster excellence in their organizations. It
is certainly understandable that we should seek to discover how
they are doing it and then translate that into strategies and
techniques that others can apply in other organizations. Now
I don't want to be too black and white about this. I certainly
agree that there is much that can be learned from excellent organizations and individuals who have a hand in these achievements. Overestimating what can be learned, though, is very
easy, and it is especially tempting when there is such an eager
and affluent market for cookbooks and techniques.

Members of high-performing systems will frequently say
that they can't explain just how the system got so good. They
will fall back on cliches, such as ''getting it all together,'' or

attribute their success to luck or to a divine providence—someone up there who likes them. They will often say that some crisis or disaster in the past is what finally got them—in Ben Franklin's words—to hang together. Members of high-performing systems never say they used someone else's protocol for how to become excellent—something that those of us who write such protocols often forget!

There is something existentially mysterious about how very high levels of performance come about. For any system, of any size and in any field, the process of excellence is an ongoing blending of two things: the dynamic emerging opportunities and constraints of the environment and the evolving feelings of system members about how they are doing and what is possible. These two currents of awareness are far more important than any preset plan about how to proceed. This is not to say that excellent organizations don't make plans, but rather that they almost always find themselves significantly modifying their plan or improvising as they go along, and, therefore, how they *think* about what their plan is and is not is crucial. It is the lower-performing system that either has no plan at all or can't let go of one that it has.

It is also important to remember the argument in Chapter Three when it comes to "designability." If "winning" is what members *mean* by winning, it means that designing a process for achieving excellence requires that members' own evolving standards of excellence be designed in also. But since we cannot know exactly what these evolving standards are going to be until the activity is under way, no complete design can possibly be formulated. In short, what looks like "winning" from the outside is often not felt to be winning. About the best we can do with a plan or protocol or design is choose a target and then try to specify a process for reaching it.

Since we know that the meaning and value of the target will change for members as the activity proceeds, the real question is not "design" so much as it is the evolution of what might be called an "on-line metaguidance system"; that is, a process that can be operated in the real time of the system for thinking about how it is doing, what its accomplishments are meaning to members, and what interventions, if any, are needed to more effectively fulfill both environmental opportunities and member feelings about doing well. These feelings are found in the categories of the Communal and the Transcendental described in Chapter Three. It is a *meta*guidance system because it is above the guidance system that the organization uses to conduct its operations.

"On-line metaguidance system" is an awkward phrase, one that I am sure a hands-on leader with a track record of sustained excellence would snort at, but I am just trying to describe what I think such people do. How they really operate is what I think we have to keep trying to understand.

Closed Value Systems. It will seem strange, after all I have said about the importance of owning a value system, for me now to argue that the unsusceptibility of the system's values and standards to the influence of the outside world can be a real problem. Excellent organizations become very sure of the rightness of their concept. They know how hard they have worked to hammer out an approach that works, that fulfills their values and has proved to be effective in their environment. Still, like any organization, the excellent organization makes decisions and pursues courses of action that various stakeholders in the environment may question. This is where the problem lies: the excellent organization has trouble throwing its value system open to external scrutiny and commentary. It is a matter not of totally open versus totally closed but of finding the right balance. However, the often self-absorbed excellent organization may not be in a good position to seek that balance.

At the end of the previous chapter, we discussed five categories within which values clarification is going to go on, and I forecast that stakeholders associated with each category can be expected to speak up energetically about what they think the priorities should be. These same five categories—Economic, Technical, Communal, Sociopolitical, and Transcendental— are the categories where excellent organizations are going to have to seek the balance I just described. Putting the two sets of comments together, it seems clear that these five categories identify the basic paradox that an excellent organization has to contend with: In order to become excellent, it needs to conduct among its members and stakeholders a creative process of values clarification in all five of these categories, including their inter-relationships; but the more excellent it becomes by its own values, the more it will feel that the need for continued discussion is not necessary, while its stakeholders will feel that the organization's growing potency (excellence) makes the need for such continuing discussion more necessary than ever.

In summary, these are the main issues that together constitute a profound challenge to what I have called the "process of excellence" and, especially in permanent white water, the *future* process of excellence.

Chapter 5

The Grand Paradox
of Management

Comprehension of what is going on in the organization and *control* of what is going on there are the unique things that the manager is supposed to bring to the system. Even though the point is rarely stated quite this flatly, these two key functions run through all degree programs in management and all management development programs: the task is to understand the system better and get it to do what you want it to do (that is, control it) more effectively and efficiently (Barnard, 1938, p. 56). All the content we have been teaching and all the experiences we have been fostering come back to these two objectives: comprehension and control.

There has been more of this rationalistic analysis, design, and control of human systems in the last fifty years in America than possibly anywhere else in possibly all of the rest of human history. So here is a research question for someone to take a crack at: Why in the face of all this do those living in the midst of these systems, including managers, continue to find them mysterious, recalcitrant, intractable, unpredictable, paradoxical, absurd, and—unless it's your own ox getting gored—funny? This is the "grand paradox of management."

Some will complain that I am asking this question at an unfairly high level of abstraction, and that there are countless examples of systems that *do* work and that for the most part don't drive people crazy. Admittedly, at the borders, the objection might continue, the rationalistic model breaks down, and some large-scale errors and disasters can occur. But this does not invalidate the model's basic assumption: More comprehension = more control = more benefit for society.

My response is that it is the objector who is speaking at too high a level of abstraction. It is in concrete organizational experiences that paradox and absurdity are felt. Specific organizational achievements are always only approximations of what was intended. Fudge factors and allowances for overruns abound. Reliability is achieved through backup systems and other redundancies. Financial practices are replete with "creative accounting" that makes possible the kind of financial results that management has *decided* it wants (see Chapter Three). Even though we tend not to recognize it in official policies, organizations are worlds of "more or less" and of "good enough." Simon's (1981, p. 35) "satisficing" names what common sense has known for years and what, in the guise of "Do it/Fix it/Try it," Peters (Peters and Waterman, 1982) declares to be one of the hallmarks of excellence. Lindbloom (1980) called this way of talking the "science of muddling through," as opposed to the theoretically correct approach to organizational action where everything is rationally designed on the front end. He is absolutely correct in his assessment. This chapter is intended as a contribution to "muddling through" in the world of permanent white water.

"Systems thinking" is about the nearest thing we have in the management field to a direct embrace of and confrontation with paradox. Systems thinking does not flinch from complexity and is willing to be surprised by the "counterintuitive" character of many organizational events and processes. Like lots of theories that purport to apply to human events, though, systems thinking has been much easier to enunciate as theory than it has been to absorb into one's everyday way of experiencing, interpreting, and acting on the world. I am satisfied that systems models of organizational events are far superior to simple

"Tinkertoy" models, or linear cause-effect ("domino theory") models as *descriptions*. I am not at all satisfied with systems models as *guides to action in the real time of system events*. Systems models aren't much better defended than any other models against two kinds of chronic and intense potentiality for paradox. One kind is the condition of permanent white water—the theme that keeps recurring through these chapters. Permanent white water defies *all* models, and, indeed, the more comprehensive we attempt to make our organizational models, the more we can detect phenomena outside the model that are influencing the organization. The horizon of what we know accelerates away from us.

The other kind of chronic and intense paradox that may transcend a systems model is the action taker's own presence in the model. The leader or manager is always part of the system being acted upon; this individual is certainly no more fixed an element than any other and, indeed, may be more variable *just because* of possessing action responsibility. Just how the consciousness of this person is going to "dance" with events in the system cannot be known. It cannot be known by an external observer in any very complete way, and it certainly cannot be known by the person him- or herself. This means that "understanding of the system" (comprehension) at any moment and "action in the system" (control) at any moment cannot be known.

As with so many other subjects, common sense is much smarter and more subtle than formal, official theory, even systems theory. Millions of members of modern organizations laugh daily at the latest manifestation of Murphy's Law. Every office you go into has signs about blessing this mess and getting organized . . . next week, and having "earned my nervous breakdown." Organizational life is filled with wry and rueful humor. "Where are we on the FUBAR/EGBAR scale?" ask the people in Wilson Learning Corporation, *FUBAR* meaning "fouled up beyond all recognition" and *EGBAR* meaning "Everything's gonna be all right!" They have even enshrined the scale on company sweat shirts. Managers and employees in the organizations of the developed world have no illusions about just how crazy and absurd things can get.

Words such as *mysterious, recalcitrant, intractable,* and *absurd* are value judgments as well as attempts to describe. *Paradoxical* is a little more neutral, not quite as loaded with feelings of puzzlement, frustration, and disappointment. Paradoxes are conflicts and collisions among apparent truths. Paradoxes refuse to dissolve or be reconciled by such normal methods as getting more facts or being more careful with logic. Paradoxes—if they are really paradoxes and not just accidental oversights or verbal trickery—just sit there to be contemplated. As noted above, it is easy to find the real paradoxes of organizational life captured in sayings, wall hangings, greeting cards, and bumper stickers. There is a more weighty although not always more serious genre of commentary on organizational paradoxes in such books as Stephen Potter's (1971) "gamesmanship" books, Cornford's (1933) *Microcosmographica Academia, The Peter Principle* (Peter and Hull, 1969), and *Parkinson's Law* (Parkinson, 1957). There are more acidic books, such as Whyte's (1956) *The Organization Man* and more recently Scott and Hart's (1979) *Organizational America* and Denhardt's (1981) *In the Shadow of Organization,* all of which bitterly condemn the nature of organization as we know it in America. Authors such as Kafka, Camus, and Joseph Heller further escalate the attack to a level where commentary on organizational paradox becomes a portrait of the human condition in the twentieth century. It is not an exaggeration to call the literature on the paradoxes of organizational life gigantic. One can laugh at organizations or one can rail at them—the energy behind either approach is the same: there is wide agreement that *man* and *organization* combined are a recipe for pain.

Interestingly, "man-in-organization" was the phrase Fritz Roethlisberger always insisted upon as his name for the basic phenomena of the field of organizational behavior (Roethlisberger, 1968, p. x). As coauthor of the "Hawthorne studies," he would be on anyone's list as a founder of the entire field. He realized that his concept was an elusive and arguable synthesis; for example, titling his autobiography *The Elusive Phenomena* (Roethlisberger, 1977). However, he does not seem to see his concept as naming and containing a fundamental paradox.

Argyris's (1957) *Personality and Organization* argued for the basic incompatibility of the healthy personality and the machine-like bureaucracy and as such is one of the foundation books in the field of organizational behavior and development. But, significantly, Argyris did not accept the mismatch between personality and organization as a paradox. Rather, it was a condition to be remedied by the redesign of organizations and the reformation of managerial conduct to make them consistent with the realities of personality. Others were moving in the same direction in the 1950s, notably McGregor, Likert, Herzberg, and Lewin's descendants at the National Training Laboratories (NTL). As a result, our official, professional, "research-based" view of the job of the manager and leader has never been friendly to paradox, tending instead to treat paradoxes as problems to be solved in the service of greater "comprehension" and "control."

If mainstream management and leadership theory had given more consideration to the mentality that is "friendly to paradox," I think management education and training in both universities and training departments and institutes would look very different. There are suggestions throughout this book of what the difference might look like if we took more seriously the paradoxes felt by action takers in the world of permanent white water. A key piece of the difference lies in understanding the enormously important role of values as described in Chapter Three. But, more especially, the difference lies in understanding that *the manager's values, the manager's comprehension, the manager's actions,* and *the nature of the system* are four kinds of interdependent phenomena, all affecting each other, and all evolving together. Any approach that treats one or more of these four as fixed or of no importance almost guarantees that the leader-manager will become trapped in intense paradoxes and absurdities and have to endure the painful feelings that accompany them.

A mentality that is "friendly to paradox"—what sort of a mentality would that be? It would be a mentality that is both good at and comfortable with the "muddling through" that Lindbloom (1980) spoke of. It would be a mentality that is both centered in itself and accepting, indeed loving, of our benighted immersion in paradoxical organizations. It would be a mentality that was not fighting the responsibility it bore. It would accept itself as a "being-in-the-world-with-responsibility" (Vaill, 1984). It would be a mentality that had a different way of thinking about objectives than the problem-solving mentality.

It would be a mentality that lived the *process* of excellence I described in Chapter Four. It would be a mentality that experienced itself not so much as operating *on* the organization from a detached, omniscient perspective as growing from within the organization and influencing it as an expression of that personal growth process. What a stunning reversal of the prevailing ethos of management and leadership: influence and control as an emanation of a growing, dawning comprehension of what is going on and of what is needed. Action taking as learning!

This way of thinking—this mentality—is centered in something. It is centered in a value system or point of view that goes beyond technical learning about what management and leadership are all about. I suppose you could call it a "professional" mentality, but that word has been utterly debased by those for whom "professionalism" is the possession of the body of compreension-and-control techniques that I have been questioning. As I said in Chapter Two, it is a mistake to think that this body of techniques exists apart from managers and leaders as persons. The world of permanent white water has pretty much undercut this kind of professionalism, and those who espouse and possess only this external suit of clothes are finding it inadequate as either a guide to right action or, more significantly, a foundation of personal being in organizations. They are today's hollow men—and women.

The mentality that is willing to let one's action be guided by one's own growth as a responsible person has a center that is deeper and more personal. It is a working credo in the literal meaning of that term—a set of personal beliefs about oneself, the world, and one's role and responsibility in it. I call it a *working* credo because both its content and its meaning develop with experience, just as the rest of the personality does. Change will be relatively slow and even painful, however, for we are talking about hard-won wisdom and awareness. Change will be especially painful if the credo does not contain a provision for its own development as a statement of beliefs; indeed, without such a provision, change may not occur at all.

What is the world of permanent white water saying to us about our credos? This is another way of asking the question I asked in Chapter One about how the manager's job has been changing. The discussion in Chapter Three about values and in this chapter about paradoxes makes it clear, though, that the changing nature of the leader's and manager's job is implying personal change of values and attitudes at a profound personal level. We can't *do* these jobs possessed of (by?) outmoded ideas about comprehension and control, or we will constantly be immersed in paradox.

"There is nothing like a paradox to take the scum off your mind," Justice Holmes said in a letter to Laski (Curtis, 1957, p. 83). For paradox is in the eye of the beholder. That is not a point one hears very often, but a moment's reflection will, I think, demonstrate its truth. Paradoxes do not exist as contradictory bundles of facts utterly external to ourselves as perceivers. We enter situations and live within them holding theories and assumptions about what the situation is and what our role and responsibility in it are. We perceive in situations what we are prepared to perceive. We react to the interaction of our assumptions and experiences with what are called feelings, many of which can be very intense.

The paradoxes that arise around comprehension and control are the fundamental ones, I think, for leaders and managers. We can't do away with them completely, but perhaps we can "outframe" our thinking about comprehension and control in such a way that some of the more common paradoxes diminish in intensity. I do not think that paradoxes can be done away with entirely, for to be playing a game you have never played before is by definition to be continually confronted with anomalies and surprises.

Chapter Fourteen explores credos further in relation to the notion of "vision," and Chapter Twelve also contains many thoughts about how to remain friendly to paradox, couched in a discussion of the relevance of Eastern philosophy. To conclude this present chapter, I want to describe briefly some ideas for our managerial credos that may help us remain friendly to paradox.

Probably the most important thing to say is that the best defense against being thrown utterly off stride is to *know* that one is in a situation that will seem to be filled with paradoxes. This means, though, that we have to resist the seductive idea that the concrete world becomes more rational as we invent more and more rational ideas about it. The concrete world is in truth oblivious to our rational ideas about it.

A second notion is to cultivate our ability to think holistically. Deep in our Western managerial psyche is the compulsion to break wholes down into their component parts. Once we have the parts scattered about, they often don't appear to fit together, particularly if the original whole was an organic whole. "Paradoxes" arise when parts are ripped from their organic settings.

The feeling of paradox will frequently turn on a static view of the world. This is a third notion of considerable importance. If we ask instead how a situation is moving and evolving, we may well find natural forces working to resolve the tensions and contradictions that, in stop action, appear paradoxical. The other virtue of this thought is that it may save us from interventions that actually compound the absurdity in a situation rather than relieve it. "To straighten things out" is such a common turn of phrase that we rarely hear it for what it often is—a fantasy of omnipotence.

Can we release some of our cherished fixities in order that we can navigate more easily in the white water? Can we release the fixity of our facts and knowledge, for one thing, and come to see them instead in all their relativity? Can we release the fixity of our role and see ourselves more as an inventor of our job than a performer of a preexisting list of duties? Can we release our structural fixity, drop the assumption of our prerogatives in a hierarchical position, and instead see ourselves as just another player in what is in fact one big network? The urge we feel to rise in a hierarchy is often an urge to retreat from the complexity, contingency, and craziness (paradox) of the "work level." What an irony that paradoxes don't disappear with more and more authority and eminence. If anything, they just become bigger and more tragic. Better to think of oneself as part of a network (team) no matter how close your name is to the top of the page.

In addition to releasing the fixities of our knowledge, our function, and our position, I think there is something in releasing the fixity of ourselves in career. Weick (1976a) once observed that it is better to think of your career as the predicate of your efforts than to think of it as the subject. He wants us to think of our career as what happens to us through time as a result of our making the most of the opportunities that come to us hour to hour and day to day. Weick was not talking about avoiding paradox, but his observation applies. The more you think that there is someplace in particular to get to (the ''career objective''), the more you may not seem to be getting there at any moment, the more you may seem to be getting somewhere else, and, of course, the more paradoxical your career will feel.

Finally, there are the paradoxes of objectives in general. I said earlier that a mentality that is friendly to paradox has a different way of thinking about objectives than a mentality that experiences the world as a menu of problems to be solved. The neatest expression of the difference that I know of is from a speech Fritz Roethlisberger gave forty years ago to a class at the Harvard Business School (Athos and Gabarro, 1978, pp. 560–566). Roethlisberger was trying to develop for these young tigers of the postwar era a different way of thinking about ''success.'' Among the several things he said was an observation that he admitted sounds paradoxical. Yet the moment I read it, I knew he had uttered a truth that releases the hypnotic hold on our minds of objectives as places out in the future that we are somehow trying to get to. He simply suggested that instead of thinking of the present as the means and the future as the end, we think of the future as the means and the present as the end. He noted—and I am sure with an elfin twinkle—that the present is all that we have, no matter when it occurs, so can't it really be the only true end that there is? And don't thinking and planning ahead then become something that enriches our awareness of the present, rather than something that ignores the present or takes from it in service of some dream that does not now exist?

Between Weick and Roethlisberger, I think the point is that in the world of permanent white water, it is not wise to plan too intently on getting to any particular place at any particular time in any particular way. Not only is it certain that these plans will not be realized; more importantly, we won't be able to enjoy or have much influence on the ride we are actually having.

These are some ideas, then, that may help us remain friendly to paradox. I do not think that, in the turbulent modern world, paradoxes can be done away with. In fact, I am certain that their frequency and intensity will only increase. What I think consciousness can do, however, is *reflect* on paradoxical situations rather than only anguish within them or attempt to stamp them out. The reflection I have in mind is not necessarily high-powered cognitive analysis, though. Reflection, it turns out, is itself a rather paradoxical process—one that the next chapter bravely undertakes.

Chapter 6

Reflection and
the Technoholic

Once upon a time, a physicist, an engineer, and an economist were placed on a desert island and told that each must use his technical skills to figure out how to open a can of beans and thus avoid starvation. In due time, each was asked for the solution. The physicist's approach utilized an artful application of air and water pressures and the sun's heat to create differential pressures, thus popping the can open. The engineer had devised an extraordinary Rube Goldberg system of bits and pieces, which nevertheless appeared as though it might produce enough of the right kind of leverage on the can to get the top off. Taken aback somewhat by the complexity of his two colleagues' approaches, the economist smiled ingenuously and said, "Gee, nobody said different, so I just assumed I had a can opener."

I don't really have it in for economists in this chapter. This story can be turned around so that it insults any profession that we like. I do want to talk at length in this chapter, however, about the qualities of various technical fields and professions that make it possible to tell jokes like this in the first place. I should also note at the outset that one of the key pieces of the whole picture is not discussed at all in this chapter, but instead is reserved for the next chapter. I call it "Satchmo's

Paradox''—the problem of how one who possesses complex, sophisticated knowledge ever does explain to a lay person just what it is that the knowledge consists of and how it works. The archetype is Louis Armstrong's famous reply to the question what is jazz: "If you have to ask what jazz is, you'll never know" (*Bartlett's Familiar Quotations,* 1968, p. 1046).

The main thrust here is to describe what I call a "technoholic" and develop the consequences of this affliction for our thought and action about leadership, management, and organizational effectiveness. *Technoholic* is a rather lurid term and admittedly not one we are likely to apply to ourselves. That is my intent in this chapter, though—to get us to think about the extent to which we *are* technoholics as I will define them, whether we like it or not.

I have already suggested at several places in this book that we are bedeviled with a linear-logical, cause-effect style of thinking, inherited from two or three centuries of thinking about action taking and leadership. But I have been saying that the world of permanent white water keeps upsetting this style of thinking. In particular, this style of thinking requires the assumption of a relatively stable goal or end point of action toward which to orient some prescribed sequence of action steps. If the end point is going to float about, require constant reinterpretation as the world changes and revitalization as organizational members change, then it calls linear-logical thinking and action sequences seriously into question.

What Is a Technoholic?

As noted in Chapter One, the issue is *compulsion,* by which I mean inability to think any other way than to try to specify a step-by-step method for reaching a goal.

> I label "technoholics" those of us who are most seriously addicted to cookbook techniques. Technoholics are found among line managers, staff people, academics, and consultants who mistakenly think precise how-to-do-it prescriptions are their

chief value to managers. We find them among
authors . . . and even among editors. A technoholic
is on a fruitless quest in human affairs: a quest for
liberation from contingency, from messiness, from
politics, from the fundamental back-and-forthness
of all human interaction. A technoholic wants to
front-end a project by imposing a technique or protocol on some stream of organizational events—a
tendency labeled "preactive style" a few years ago
by Russell Ackoff (1974). Technoholics don't like
to feel their way along. . . .

In particular, technoholics need to work on
three things: First, they need to learn to detect
"domino theory thinking" in their approaches to
issues. Second, they need to learn a lot about what
is called "reification." And third, they need to learn
to handle why-to-do-it questions as insistently as
they now handle how-to-do-it questions [Vaill,
1987].

Planning is the specification of a sequence of events or
action steps that will move a system from where it is at present
to some intended new state, usually called the planning objective. So far, so good. But the *logic* of a sequence of events depends
on the surrounding context within which the events are to occur and on the nature of the objective. If the context changes,
the sequence may no longer make sense. Yet too often technoholism leads one to try to hold to the plan of action, even though
the steps may no longer make sense in content or sequence or
both! The plan as a means to pursue an objective, as a *technique,*
has acquired a normative value all its own. It has become an
imperative, no matter what the surrounding context is suggesting. A curious "moral determinism," you might call it,
creeps in, where the hope is that if we cling to the plan, somehow
the steps it contains will *cause* the results that we originally
wanted, no matter how much the *current* context may have in-
validated the earlier planned steps (Barrett, 1978, p. 191). This
is why I call the first characteristic of technoholism "domino-

theory thinking." Of course, enlightened planning theory is aware of this problem, but it is not planning theory I am talking about; it is organizational practice. One of the larger absurdities of organizational life is that millions of managers are expected to hold their systems "on plan," no matter how much contextual pressures and realities diverge from what the original plan assumed.

> "Reification" is making a thing out of what is not a thing. Human organizations and events within them are not *things* but *systems* of perceptions and meanings and communications. An intended flow of action in an organization is not a thing but a very fragile and "iffy" process—dependent on a host of assumptions, future contingencies, and the ability of members to achieve consensus. But when the PERT chart is drawn, when the phase model gets up on the wall, or when the steps-to-completion get frozen on overhead transparencies, the process loses its fragility in people's minds and becomes the "thing-method," the "thing-approach," the "thing-strategy." When events occur which are not allowed for in our reified "action plan," what do we do? We ignore them, or we reinterpret them to fit our reified plan, or we throw our protocol out in a fit of cynicism. That is, technoholics do these things. Reification imprisons the technoholic in his or her thinking.
>
> Why-to-do-it co-exists with how-to-do-it in every project. Yet in the high pressure of the modern organization, the can-do attitude is far more often focussed on finding a means to a *given* end than it is on considering and choosing ends in the first place, or in being willing to re-think and re-negotiate ends along the way. You might say that retaining the capacity to examine and re-examine *why* we are proceeding as we are is our principal

defense against technoholism. It consists of recon-
sidering objectives, re-examining assumptions, and
constantly checking the degree of consensus in a
group or organization about the value of the activity to prevent it from descending into empty
ritual (Harvey, 1974). Possession of methods and
techniques does not free us from the need to keep
asking what those methods and techniques are—
and are not—for [Vaill, 1987].

Objectives, the technical method being followed, the degree
of consensus and understanding among participants, and the
validity of assumptions about surrounding context constitute
four categories in which it is vital that a leader-manager be able
to reflect—and not just as an individual, but as a member of
a management team. What I have been calling "technoholism"
is the interruption of this reflective ability by a fascination with
technical method and a belief that it is powerful and valid enough
to somehow override disturbances coming from the other three
categories. Cultishness of the sort described in Chapter Four
is another force that can interrupt reflection. Cultishness is fundamentally a disturbance of the flexibility of thinking. Thinking is thus forced to have a dual referent: the merits of the question and the fit of the ideas one is having with the norms and
values of the cult. This dual referent always exists to some extent, for no reflective process can be conducted in a social vac-
uum. But the amount of social pressure one feels and the degree
of narrowness of the norms can make all the difference as to
whether a new idea gets considered.

I have already said a lot about how the meaning and value
of objectives can change as a project proceeds, and I have called
the process of trying to keep objectives relevant and meaningful
"purposing." A tremendous amount has been written about
the problem of gaining and maintaining consensus in groups,
and in Chapter Eleven I say more about it myself. I devote the
rest of this chapter to the subject of identifying surrounding contextual assumptions.

Assumptions and Contexts

For several generations, management students have been exhorted by their teachers and trainers to "define your assumptions!" The phrase has become such a shibboleth that it is hard to hear it with fresh ears. For all the exhortation about assumptions, not one instructor in a hundred can say very much about how to identify assumptions. And even when one accepts and understands the injunction and endeavors to practice it, there is still the need to consider what it means under conditions of permanent white water. Within a rapidly changing context, assumptions are as fluid elements of the situation as anything else. They can no longer function as "givens."

Let us define a "technology" as a standardized method of any sort for producing some intended output or consequence from some set of inputs. A hammer is a technology. So is a violin, and so is a sermon. A spontaneous dance in a disco at midnight probably isn't, but the disco itself is (an entertainment technology), and certainly the music is (a dance-inducing technology). Standardized method is in my view the hallmark of a "technology." Despite the common connotation, it need not be machinery. The question for any designer or developer of a technology is "What needs to hold true in the surrounding world in order for this technology to work as intended?" To answer the question, the designer or developer is going to have to reflect on and critique the technology. This is what techno-holics have such a hard time doing.

Below are twelve considerations about the kinds of assumptions that will be found surrounding any given technology. When technologies fail, it is very often the case that forces and factors within these categories have turned out differently from what was assumed; or worse, it was not realized that the assumption was even being made, so unanticipated forces began to undercut the effectiveness of the technology right from the start. This latter condition is very common in implementation of public policy.

1. Every technology contains a claim about validity (that it does what it says it will do) and reliability (that it does it

consistently). What is the *ceteris paribus* that goes with all such claims?

2. All technologies require input resources in certain amounts and at certain levels of quality, delivered on certain schedules at certain costs. What assumptions are made regarding input resources? This might be called the "batteries not included" factor.

3. What assumptions are made about the fit of the technology with known biological and psychological laws governing the human beings who will operate the technology and be affected by its outputs? This might be called the "three easy lessons" or the "simple instruction book included" factor.

4. What assumptions are made about the fit between the intended output of the technology and the needs in the environment that these outputs are supposed to meet? This is the "up to spec" factor. Another way to phrase this issue is: What assumptions are made about how close to spec is close enough?

5. What assumptions are made about side effects—their nature, their extent, their seriousness, their cost in relation to the value of the main intended output? This is the "break some eggs to get an omelet" factor.

6. What assumptions are made about the nature and extent of side effects of the main side effects? This exploration of second- and third order consequences should in principle be thought of as extending indefinitely.

7. What assumptions are made about costs—to buy, operate, maintain, and upgrade a technology?

8. What assumptions are made about the start-up phase of the technology? This is the "shakedown, debugging, and break-in" factor.

9. Given that human beings will almost always introduce spontaneous change into every technology as they learn to operate it and use its outputs, what assumptions are made about the likelihood and nature of such changes and about the consequences of such changes for the technology as designed? This is the "high-tech/high-touch" factor.

10. What assumptions are made about the fit of the technology

with existing norms, mores, and taboos in the culture in which the technology will exist? This is the "we've never done it this way before" factor.

11. What assumptions are made about the commitments to future action implied by the existence of the technology? If people are kept alive longer, for instance, what responsibilities does this create that would not arise if it were not possible to prolong life?

12. The "factors and forces" that surround any given technology are themselves usually technologies. Which assumptions on this list need to be carefully considered for the operation of these "support technologies"?

I will be the first to agree that many of these kinds of assumptions are routinely studied, often by very sophisticated methods for some technologies. And I will agree that there are many technologists for whom such careful examination of all aspects of a technology is business as usual. Despite this, however, my opinion is that this style of thinking is not as generalized in our society as it needs to be, and I think that the many critiques of the impact of technology on society bear out my perception that we are not systematically examining technology with anything like the thoroughness these categories imply. There are many "technologies" by my definition that don't receive this kind of analysis at all, as a matter of fact. A university degree program is a technology, for instance, but there aren't very many university degree programs that receive the kind of multidimensional consideration the twelve categories entail. Many toys ("play technologies") are sadly, even tragically, lacking in this kind of consideration. The whole history of the automobile and of television in America is a history of unexpected costs, of unrealized capabilities, of multiple unanticipated downstream consequences. Applications of computer technology are constantly running afoul of unanticipated sticking points resulting in missed deadlines, cost overruns, and, worst of all, shattered hopes for presumed benefits. The list is a long one. Our capacity to make things, fashion technologies, has run way ahead of our capacity to evaluate the implications of a technology for the wider socioeconomic framework in which it exists. I am suggesting that this history has bred and continues to reinforce a style of thinking about technology that I have been calling "technoholism."

The twelve categories of assumptions above will go a long way toward helping with the identification of assumptions that weave through the operations of a technology. However, still unaddressed is the question that I said not one professor out of a hundred knows how to answer—the question of how to identify assumptions, the question of how to proceed when you don't have a list of twelve categories to start you thinking. What, in other words, triggers our realization that we are making assumptions? I am not aware that this question has been addressed as such by psychologists or other investigators. Furthermore, we shouldn't try to answer the question by specifying a clear-cut protocol, for our protocol (a technology) would itself be subject to all the invisible assumptions that I have said pervade all technologies! We would find ourselves in an infinite regression.

Chapter Four made passing reference to the difference between a cult and a field of inquiry. Technoholics are cultish about their favorite techniques. They have trouble being flexible and playful with their technologies, contemplating defects, treating the technology as a matter of continuing learning and discovery. As noted above, they don't like to feel their way along. Is it hopelessly idealistic to suggest that any operating technology should continue to be thought of as a field of inquiry, regardless of how standardized and routinized it has become? At first glance it may seem so, but wait: consider how high performers talk about the technologies they employ. Whether musicians, athletes, craftspeople, or just plain workers doing whatever they do with high degrees of excellence, the behavior is the same: They talk lovingly about their tools and equipment. They anthropomorphize them, give them personalities and biographies. They may speak with delight or with irritation about how their equipment is working, but they always speak with intensity and a kind of humbleness about the complexity of the process of achieving excellence with their equipment. Here is astronaut Michael Collins, for instance, talking about the space capsule's basic power source: "Those fuel cells . . . are funny things. It's not that they either work or don't work. They are like human beings; they have their little ups and downs. Some of them have bad days and then they sort of cure themselves. Others are hypochondriacs, they put out lots of electricity, but they do it only bitterly with much complaining and groaning, and you have to worry about them and sort of pat them and talk to them sweetly'' (Mailer, 1971, pp. 239–240). It is no exaggeration to say that for a high performer, the possibilities and the limits of technology are definitely matters of ongoing, creative inquiry.

The last chapter counseled friendliness to paradox, and this is one of the moments for it. The identification of critical assumptions that affect the success of a technology is always going to be something of a bootstrap operation in which there will be heavy reliance on three things: (1) the knowledge that there is an issue here that needs to be thought about; (2) creative use of one's general knowledge of the physical, economic, and social context of the technology and one's experience with past technologies under similar circumstances; and (3) discussions with others in order to get feedback and commentary about the assumptions that one has been able to identify. This last category declares that the process is a social enterprise as much as it is an individualistic, analytical enterprise. We have discovered yet another case of the need in modern organizations to learn to work ''collectively smarter,'' yet another case where our inattention to the need to improve our ability to work with others is having serious consequences. High performers know that inquiry into the possibilities of their tools and equipment is a social enterprise. This is why they can sit around for hours talking shop. They never get tired of discussing the infinite subtlety and mosaic of fine points that exist between the human being and any technology.

The way of thinking about technology sketched in this chapter is intended as an antidote to technoholism. Although the tone has been very sober—for, indeed, the stakes are very high—the truth is that human beings find technology fascinating, and it is far more often invented and operated in exuberance than viewed with alarm. People's adventures with technology can also be very funny, as we shall see in the next chapter. I

will close this chapter by quoting a little fantasy I made up several
years ago to suggest to my own professional colleagues that while
we may disdain the common person's search for an all-purpose
cookbook, we are hardly immune from the compulsion ourselves:

> We've all heard managers and students ask
> for a cookbook (and among ourselves we speak con-
> descendingly and even disdainfully of such needs).
> But what would the cookbook look like as written
> by the contemporary OB [organizational behavior]
> professor? Well, it would probably take a systems
> view and discuss at great length the interactions of
> cook, ingredients, utensils, sink, stove, and diner.
> Reading it, one would not be able to tell if the book
> was addressed to the spoon, the salt shaker, the
> cook, or the dough. If well done, the book would
> of course be hailed as a breakthrough. Its writer
> would be featured at the Academy of Management.
> Its contents would be regurgitated in bluebooks
> (I choose not to pause to explore the image of re-
> gurgitating the contents of a cookbook). Worst of
> all, cooks would read the book dutifully, seeking
> insight into cook*ing*.
>
> As the field of cookbook theory matured, sub-
> specialists would emerge. Two-factor [Herzbergian]
> theories of the cook's motivation would be offered
> (borrowed in the best cross-disciplinary tradition
> from the field of Organizational Behavior). As time
> went on, articles would doubtless appear with titles
> like "Some Neglected Variables in the Kitchen,"
> "Test-Retest Reliability of Vaill's Diner Satisfac-
> tion Inventory," "The Emerging Culinary Para-
> digm," and so forth. Ultimately, the heavy-hitters
> in cookbook theory would be sitting in endowed
> chairs, satraps in a game which, long since, had
> relegated the *cooks* to the sidelines.
>
> Am I communicating? [Vaill, 1979, p. 2].

Chapter 7

Satchmo's Paradox

In one way or another, all of these chapters are about "unlearning." That word is one we have all heard countless times, but rarely if ever is it defined. It's just a noise we make when we want to suggest that somehow a person has to reorganize his or her way of looking at the world. That is what this chapter is about: unlearning. I call it "Satchmo's Paradox" because Louis Armstrong declared the paradoxical quality of unlearning with powerful simplicity when he said "If you have to ask what jazz is, you'll never know." (*Bartlett's Familiar Quotations*, 1968, p. 1046). Ironically, this comment is usually quoted when the intent is to declare the mystery and ineffability of some phenomenon. Armstrong's comment has virtually become a rhetorical device for closing off discussion of some complex subject. It amounts to a put-down, as if the questioner were some kind of a lunkhead for thinking that anything so special as the thing in question could ever be easily explained. In all likelihood, the good-hearted Armstrong did not originally mean the statement as a put-down but rather as a simple statement of the fullness of his own awareness as well as a feeling of helplessness about ever conveying what it really meant to him.

The following quotation from Chester Barnard expresses quite succinctly why Satchmo's Paradox is important to this book:

> The executive functions, which have been distinguished for purposes of exposition and which are the basis of functional specialization in organizations, have no separate concrete existence. They are parts or aspects of a process of organization as a whole. This process in the more complex organizations, and usually even in simple unit organizations, is made the specialized responsibility of executives or leaders. The means utilized are to a considerable extent concrete acts logically determined; but the essential aspect of the process is the sensing of the organization as a whole and the total situation relevant to it. It transcends the capacity of merely intellectual methods, and the techniques of discriminating the factors of the situation. The terms pertinent to it are "feeling," "judgment," "sense," "proportion," "balance," "appropriateness." It is a matter of art rather than science, and is aesthetic rather than logical. For this reason it is recognized rather than described and is known by its effects rather than by analysis [Barnard, 1938, p. 235].

I have found this remarkable statement to be worthy of continual rereading and reflection. Sadly, it is inconsistent with the way Barnard is remembered in the management field. We think of him as the rationalist supreme, the person who did more to put management on "solid theoretical ground" than anyone else. It is as if we remember him only for the first part of the key sentence in the above quotation. Barnard did indeed contribute a great deal to the discovery of the "concrete acts, logically determined." Yet he himself did not stop with that, declaring very clearly that there is something else that is much more important: "sensing of the organization as a whole and the total situation relevant to it.'' The theory of how to develop and transmit "feeling," "judgment," "sense," "proportion," "balance," "appropriateness" is far less developed, if it exists at all, than is the theory of "intellectual methods and the techniques of discriminating the factors of the situation." In the fifty years since Barnard wrote these lines, not a great deal has happened to alter the judgment of the last sentence: we know it when we see it, but we can't define it very well.

It is not an exaggeration to say that there is no statement in the entire leadership and management literature that more neatly captures what I am interested in. I am fascinated by the challenge of finding better ways of talking about this "specialized responsibility," and I am fascinated by the many and various ways that this responsibility is discharged by real people in real situations. The two things intertwine, too: the more adequately we can talk about it, the more clearly we can see it for what it is; and the more we can see, the better our conceptual understanding and our capacity to educate others become.

Both of these dimensions—talking about it and doing it— are dogged by Satchmo's Paradox. Barnard as much as says so himself at the end of his statement. Both the theorist of the process and the practitioner of it have awarenesses—feelings, judgments, senses—that are very difficult to articulate. In the phrase of Norman Mailer's (1971, p. 124), they keep "running off the edge of the word system." The theorist would like clearly to explicate what this "aesthetic" aspect is. Even more importantly, practitioners would like to be able to make their visions and strategies clear and meaningful to other members of the organization. Barnard does not address this communication aspect of the problem at all.

This chapter discusses Satchmo's Paradox as it affects the practitioner. In the next chapter, I explore the metaphor of leadership and management as a *performing art* and make some further comments about the general problem of developing better images and concepts and the significance of Satchmo's Paradox to that process. The question that guides us in this chapter is how does a leader or manager make the organization and its purposes meaningful to members and key constituents, especially in a world of permanent white water, where meaning is constantly buffeted by new issues and events and a pervasive confusion about what is going to happen next? In Chapter Three, I used the term *purposing* for this process and said that the objective is to develop clarity, consensus, and commitment. In this chapter, purposing is shown to depend on transcending Satchmo's Paradox.

The Many Forms of Satchmo's Paradox

Let us start with a little fuller discussion of what Satchmo's Paradox is. Here are some everyday examples:

1. Children give hilariously incomprehensible accounts of things as simple as their day at school owing to their inability to "hear their story in the ears of the other." Children are not unique in this, however.

2. A very common example of the paradox occurs where someone is giving us directions in a strange city, and we gradually realize that the direction giver can't imagine how lost and disoriented we actually are and hence makes many unwarranted assumptions about our understanding of the area.

3. Another very common experience is trying to follow the action in a game that one does not understand very well. Without a gestalt on the game as a whole, you can't understand specific actions. The fans around you are cheering or groaning, and you don't exactly know why. Attempts by them to explain what is happening are usually quite inadequate.

4. Doctors, lawyers, automobile mechanics, and instruction booklets are famous for giving us instructions and explanations that we can't follow.

5. Although public signs by and large do anticipate the sign readers' needs pretty well, each of us has had plenty of experiences with signs on roads or in airports that are maddeningly ambiguous as to what they are telling us to do.

6. Cross-cultural communications are plagued by Satchmo's Paradox. Even if we understand the dangers of taking too much for granted in our own culture, we will tend to underestimate just how much unspoken knowledge about the surrounding culture even the simplest statements rest on—until we are the giver or, worse yet, the receiver of information across a cultural boundary.

7. Organizational life is full of examples. The phrase "user friendly," in fact, has come into vogue just because so many experts in organizations keep writing policies and prescribing methods that managers and other employees can't understand. "What is this memo really *saying*?" is commonly heard. People walk out of meetings all the time scratching their heads about what the boss actually wants.

These are enough examples to make the point and doubtless to set the reader thinking of other personal examples of this phenomenon. In all cases, the intention is to communicate, not to obfuscate. In all cases, (1) someone with expert knowledge or direct experience tries to convey it to someone else (2) but fails, or succeeds only after many false starts, puzzled looks, and mutual frustration, (3) because the expert communicator is unable to experience what the world is like for someone who does not have the expertise and/or the gestalt that the communicator has, and (4) the person who lacks the gestalt has trouble framing a question that will cue the expert to the confusion that is developing between them. The expert cannot "unlearn." The expert doesn't even realize that there is a need to unlearn, because the expert does not understand the nature of knowledge in the first place. "Meaning is context" is an old slogan from the field of semantics. Without context, statements that are apparently simple and obvious can be utterly perplexing.

Faced myself with the need to make Satchmo's Paradox meaningful to management groups, I wrote the following poem (Vaill, 1985b) to try to capture the essence:

The Layman's Lament

You understand something and I don't.
You understand that I don't understand, but
You don't understand what it is that I don't understand.
I understand that I don't understand, but
I don't understand what it is I don't understand.
Not only do you not understand what it is I don't understand,
You don't understand how you came to understand
What it is that you understand.
You understand that your understanding is more advanced than
  mine,
But you don't understand exactly how it is more advanced,
Nor do you understand how to make yourself simple again like
  me.
I understand that your understanding is more advanced than mine,
  but
My understanding doesn't feel simple, rather,
It feels chaotic and confused.
I can't begin to explain simply to you
What it is I don't understand
So that you can help me understand it.
You and I have a problem
If I am to come to understand what you understand and
If you are to come to understand what I don't understand.

Satchmo's Paradox derives from two interconnected aspects of knowledge: first, facts and ideas exist in and have meaning within larger gestalts; and second, those who possess these
gestalts don't know exactly how they acquired them, don't know
how to look at the world afresh without them, and don't know
how efficiently to transmit their gestalt—their "big picture"—to
others.

Top Management's Distinctive Competence

"The big picture"—for how many years have we been
saying that possession of the big picture is the hallmark of the

top-level executive? In the last decade, the more fashionable term has become *paradigm,* and we have been talking about how organization members, especially leaders, have to learn to drop their old paradigms and adopt new ones. The whole implication of Chapter One is just that, and my discussion there can be understood as an attempt to use the permanent white water metaphor to contribute to a new paradigm. I hope that I have demonstrated here, though, that we don't just put on and take off these gestalts, these big pictures, these paradigms, casually. Not only do they become deeply embedded in and completely interwoven with the rest of mental functioning; they are powerfully supported from the outside by social mores and pressures. It is a major achievement to get outside one's gestalt and experience the world as those with other gestalts are experiencing it. Making the big picture real for oneself and others is top management's distinctive competence and distinctive responsibility.

The question that is guiding us in this chapter is how leaders engage in purposing so that clarity, consensus, and commitment survive in the white water. What emerges from this discussion of Satchmo's Paradox, though, is the idea that communication at the level of gestalts, big pictures, and paradigms is a very special sort of communication. It is not one that the leadership literature has taken as seriously as it should. The literature seems to assume that members of an organization are "informed about the mission" or "inspired with the vision" in pretty much the same way that everyday communications occur. The mission or vision or grand strategy is the gounding for everything else. It is broader, "softer," longer range, probably more metaphorical than workaday instructions. It is probably more a passionate personal expression of top management values than it is a set of technical instructions. At least these are the things that everyone is *saying* about organization missions. The point I am making in this chapter is that too little thought has gone into the very tricky business of communicating a fundamental gestalt, for Satchmo's Paradox does make it a very tricky business.

Chapter Fourteen discusses the content of visions, missions, gestalts, and paradigms; in this chapter, I am concerned with process. What can we say about how it happens that gestalts do get transmitted? For, despite calling it Satchmo's *Paradox* and despite my poem and all my illustrations, we know that human beings do muddle through to mutual understanding of each other's views of the world.

Probably the most common method we use, and one that higher-level people are particularly prone to, is force. We just simply keep insisting on our way of looking at things until the person or group we have targeted just gives in and accedes to our version of truth. As we all know, sometimes this process is conducted at top volume with much sound and fury. Sometimes it is accompanied by threats—the mailed fist in the velvet glove. Bribes figure in here, as do manipulative attempts to restrict any other world views from getting through, a device well developed in totalitarian societies but by no means unknown in American organizations. Various grounds may be invoked to buttress the appeal, and indeed all the different values listed in Chapter Three may appear as part of the gestalt that is being advocated.

Nonstop forceful promulgation of a party line, of a philosophy to undergird and give meaning to daily activity—it works, or seems to. Should we be concerned about finding other methods? I think the answer is yes. I think we have to bend over backward to keep coercion out of the process as much as possible. We wouldn't want it done to us, and this obligates us not to advocate doing it to others, no matter how tempting. Human beings become strange when they are coerced, and they become especially strange when they are coerced at an ideological level. If the process works, or seems to, leaders are then faced with a group or organization that is strongly committed to a vision or mission that, for certain, will become obsolete in the white water. This necessitates a new process of unlearning and relearning—coercively, remember—in order to keep the vision or mission relevant. The problem is that missions in the world of permanent white water require creativity, initiative, and embellishment by those who are to implement them. We *can* create blind, unthinking loyalty to the current doctrine, but do we really want to? If coercive promotion of the mission fails, on the other hand, we now have an organization that lacks focus and direction, that may be torn with dissension, that in the best case is a centrifuge of ill-coordinated busyness and in the worst case is in an ugly, rebellious mood. No, when you think it through, imposing one's big picture coercively, while superficially efficient, is a poor strategy.

Some Noncoercive Alternatives

What are the alternatives? I spoke at length in Chapter Five about what it might mean to be "friendly to paradox." Those qualities certainly are relevant to this problem of unlearning old gestalts and effectively communicating new ones. As noted there, paradoxes exist within a given frame, a frame we are often hardly aware of. Part of the process of understanding the paradox is to understand the frame that contains it. The question is what kind of mental bootstrapping is involved in understanding the underlying pattern or organizing principle of one's knowledge. By definition, the frame is normally taken for granted. In giving meaning to the ideas it contains, it cannot itself be problematic, or at least not problematic in quite the same way. But indeed this is precisely the effect of the world of permanent, unpredictable white water: our frames *are* problematic; in fact, they are in many cases hopelessly fractured and cannot be put back together again in their former coherence. This is what I think is meant by Emery and Trist's metaphor of "the ground itself is moving" (Emery, 1969, p. 249): our underlying frames, gestalts, paradigms, big pictures are everywhere in doubt. The task is to understand how we acquire frames, how we communicate them, and how we change them in ourselves and others.

Satchmo's Paradox functions as a kind of null hypothesis for this effort: maybe it can't be done. Maybe we are wiser to keep silent. I don't really believe that, and certainly leaders and managers don't have that luxury in any event. But I am also pretty sure that we can't communicate our gestalts in ordinary unreflective ways, using whatever mixture of forcefulness, presumed logic, and charm that occurs to us at the moment. We have to be more reflective about the process, I think, because the moving ground affects the process of communicating a new big picture, even as it affects the content of it.

In a sense, all the principles of "good communication" are relevant to the process of discussing underlying frames. It is definitely a values clarification process, but values clarification at quite a profound level. It is the exploration of a value *system,* not just an examination of unitary values.

The process of discussion needs to go on in felicitous circumstances. This is easy to say until it is realized how thoroughly the North American managerial mentality is geared for crisp, technical communication, occurring in the context of a structured agenda, with someone clearly in charge of the discussion to "keep it on track," with "action steps" coming out of the discussion, followed by a taking up of the next item on the agenda. The military briefing is paradigmatic, and of course even the military is finding that a great deal of its business can no longer be transacted in that frame. It would make an interesting research project to try to discover how much actual chafing is going on in American organizations over the very restrictive structures for communication we have evolved. Certainly millions of managers walk out of meetings daily rolling their eyes over the superficiality of the discussion, appalled by what they see as chronic skirting of "the real issues." The real issues are the ones that it is hard to talk about—they go to the level of what business we are really in, of what is happening in the world around us, of whether this organization has much chance of becoming the kind of place we want it to be.

What is called "strategic management" tries to deal with questions such as these. Even conscious discussions at this level, however, easily drift back into very structured modes of discussion. Questioning the foundations of one's world is anxiety generating. We can learn to do it, and I think we have to, but it hurts. To some extent, it probably always will (see Vaill, forthcoming).

Going away from the office to an off-site meeting in the woods has become standard procedure in thousands of organizations (though there are still many for whom it is a mysterious, questionable act). The woods can be a more felicitous place for discussing basic frames and gestalts, provided that organization members remember to leave their office clothes and office formalities at the office, and provided that they are willing to let their discussions have a more conversational and open-ended quality than they ordinarily demand, and provided that they do not demand of themselves that the meeting yield concrete, deliverable "next steps." This, in fact, is a crucial barometer of whether a group has really taken advantage of the freedom that an off-site meeting provides: if the intent was to dig deeply into each other's basic points of view about things, the event has failed to the extent that people feel a compulsion to be taking something specific back with them. Since I conduct many such meetings myself, I am aware of the sad reality that participants often do feel compelled to take home ideas that they can implement immediately. Some, indeed, have to report in detail when they get back to the office and distribute materials that were generated at the retreat. All this, of course, distracts a person from the kind of meditative conversation and reflection that entertaining a new big picture entails.

Under more relaxed circumstances, whether in the office or away, we can adopt different points of view if we want to. We don't have to be pushing our own. I am talking about trying to view the organization from other perspectives than one's own. How does the organization look to its various key stakeholders? In their eyes, it may be easier to see what the new game is and what is involved in playing it. Taking the stakeholders' point of view can be a matter of research, or it can involve some imaginative role playing, or both. There is no reason why stakeholders can't be part of the process, for they too are careening in their own white water.

In Chapter Four, I spoke of "high-performing boundary spanning" as a key function in the complex networks of contemporary organizations. In the present context, I am talking about the need to learn to live on the boundaries of *ideas* and to compare and contrast and integrate across the boundaries. Our traditional paradigms tend to be closed systems of ideas. The most open system of ideas that we know is empirical science, and even that has its dominant organizing principles that change fitfully and with much groaning (Kuhn, 1962). Our ideas about people and organizations are less consciously open and it takes more effort to imagine that there might be very different ways of organizing, of leading, of defining responsibility, and of treating people than the notions we have evolved in growing up. This is why the myths of management I cited in Chapter One are so important: most of us can't say exactly where we got those ideas; they have just always been with us. Yet those myths are the very notions that the white water has worn away.

"Practice, practice, practice" was the punch line of a beer commercial in which very high-quality action was displayed. I find many organizations forgetting this precept when it comes to discussion of basic missions, underlying frames, visions, and so forth. There is not a concept of practice in the first place— that is, that this is a type of discussion that has to be viewed as a learning process. And certainly there is not a concept of *repeated* practice. Yet we are talking about a kind of activity most of us have not done very much, whose essence is to muse about highly anxiety-producing matters. Put this way, it is almost funny how clumsy some of our attempts are and how silly we are to hold ourselves responsible for highly efficient behaviors that smoothly move us to a new understanding of the big picture for the future. If Ralph Siu (1980), inventor of Chinese baseball, is right, the very nature of the game requires continued discussion of what it is fundamentally about, making an acceptance of ourselves as perpetual learners all the more important. It has to be okay to be clumsy at this game, for otherwise it will not be played at all.

Another thing we can do when we are able to enter a more relaxed, more meditative state with each other about what the big picture is all about is to make fuller use of all the media we have available to us. We can look at videotapes and films, play music, make collages on walls, and get up to our elbows in fingerpaints. We can build physical models of what we think is going on, and we can write poems about it. We can spend time alone honestly meditating or reading things we never get a chance to read when we're immersed in our current in basket. We can keep stranger hours than we normally do—watch sunrises and take afternoon naps. In short, we can more fully explore the truly incredible range of channels through which we can communicate and dance with the people and things around us. I call this ability with a wide range of channels *mediaease*. We have the abilities and the resources for genuine multimediaease. It is a tragedy of major proportions that our culture classes a lot of the work we do through these channels as "fun and games" and "touchy-feely." If we have ever had any of the good experiences that arise in these modes, we shouldn't let go by unchallenged some of the casual and cynical dismissals we hear. We are talking about fledgling ideas and methods through which people are trying to hold their world together and keep their sanity.

Under the right conditions, we can get a wholly new frame or point of view about some broad situation or problem. We can have the well-known "aha" experience. These experiences are our chief evidence for the idea that Satchmo's Paradox does not close our sharing of our gestalts. When we have this "aha," I think something like empathy is going on. We are finally standing in a different pair of shoes. Vistas open out that we could not see from our former viewpoint. What used to be interesting now may look ordinary or humdrum, and what used to be mysterious, scary, or outright invisible now looks . . . interesting. Curiously enough, I am not aware that very much is known about the psychology of empathy. It is a crucial bridging process among human beings, but it is rather ineffable itself. For purposes of empathic understanding of each other's organizational visions, though, I think something I'll call a process of "flagrant unrealism" is going on, and this will be this chapter's final thought about how to transcend Satchmo's Paradox.

"Flagrant unrealism" is the capacity to drop the idea that there is an external standard of truth somewhere against which to measure all our gestalts, frames, and broad visions. I call it "unrealism" because it stands somewhat in contradiction to philosophical realism, the school of thought that declares that there is objective reality, independent of human awareness and perception. Actually, the technical arguments for realism are strong ones, and I am certainly no advocate of conscious irrationality. As a practical matter, though, each other's perspectives are all we have. We have no external standard of truth, only a multiplicity of opinions to choose from. Flagrant unrealism declares that all reality is a "social construction" (Berger and Luckmann, 1967) and that the real operative problem among human beings as they communicate with each other in real time is the creation of a community of vision and feeling, as I called it in Chapter Four. You can't empathize very successfully if you are at the same time saying to yourself, "Of course, he might be wrong," or "I wonder if she has her facts straight," or "They're famous for playing fast and loose with their data, of course," and other such mental reservations that impede understanding and acceptance of where another person or group is coming from. These mental reservations postulate that since there is external truth somewhere, we had better be careful about swallowing whole any particular person's view.

By calling it a *community* of vision and feeling, I am saying that a multiplicity of points of view need to be considered together as fully and flexibly and, indeed, gently as we can. "Feeling," "judgment," "sense," "proportion," "balance," "appropriateness," said Chester Barnard (1938), and I think it is some of these actions I have discussed that can implement those qualities. We are developing new big pictures out of the white water world of the present, trying to peer together into value systems and world views that are unfamiliar, themselves evolving, and in many cases completely untried. I do not know what these big pictures are or will be, although I am right in there speculating with everyone else. But I am sure that we won't get very far unless we face up to Satchmo and his paradox.

Chapter 8

Managing as a Performing Art

In Chapter One, I said that three themes would keep recurring throughout the book: (1) how the jobs of leaders and managers are changing, (2) how these jobs are going to be learned, and (3) at a more fundamental level, what these processes are suggesting as new ways to think about what life and effective action in organizations really are. All of this could well be going on without the other theme that has run through all the chapters so far—the notion of "permanent white water." Under conditions of permanent turbulence and unpredictability, we can't be merely adjusting and fine tuning our understanding of the management job and of the process of learning it. I think we are dealing with a different kind of world than traditional ideas about learning and about performance presume. A paradigm shift is under way, and as we reach for better ideas about what action in organizations is, we have to let this transformation occur, I think, even if it takes us into some very unusual places and invites us to consider some rather offbeat ways of talking about management and leadership.

Chapter One lists some of the major myths about management that influence and restrict our capacity to think afresh about what managers are up to in organizations. Chapter Two is an argument that "management" and "leadership" cannot be understood as freestanding functions apart from the consciousness and style of the people in the positions. In Chapter Three I argued that the leader or manager has to take charge of the definition of success, that it cannot be a presumably "objective" thing apart from the value systems of those involved in the process. Chapters Four through Seven explore various challenges to thinking posed by leading and managing in the modern organization.

Treating what the leader or manager does as a list of functions is one of the most fundamental problems in the whole question of what action is and can be in the modern organization. It is this question that the present chapter addresses, using the metaphor of "management as a performing art" as a point of departure (Vaill, 1974).

The List-of-Functions Approach

The list-of-functions approach to action is overwhelmingly the dominant model of action in organizations. By the list-of-functions approach, I mean focusing on the effect that the leader or manager has or is supposed to have on the organization, and then letting this desired effect stand for the actual action—in the sense of concrete behavior—the person supposedly takes. Thus, if the organization needs a plan, we "gerundize" this desired effect into some kind of behavior called "planning"; if the organization needs goals, the corresponding action becomes "goal setting"; and so forth. There are lots of different functional theories of the management job; for example, Koontz and O'Donnell's (1972) famous *planning, organizing, staffing, directing,* and *controlling* or the many modifications of it. What I am criticizing here is no particular functional framework but the style of thinking itself. Chester Barnard, who earlier was quoted with admiration, had as much as anyone to do with getting the study of management off on this foot. Barnard, indeed, specifically makes the "essential executive functions" depend directly on the "elements of organization" he has defined (Barnard, 1938, p. 217).

Here, though, is the problem: it is much easier to say what a *plan* is than it is to say what *planning* is, and so on with any of the other desired functions. It is much easier to point to new recruits and to say why they are needed than it is to say how to go about the action called "recruiting." The desired effect can be described as an objective entity. It can be defined independently of differences among individual action takers. It can be held steady in time if that is desirable so that it doesn't change as a desired effect with changes in the personnel of the organization or with conditions in the environment, even though the action needed to achieve the effect may change radically through time as personnel and surrounding conditions change.

In short, the list-of-functions approach results in a normative model of how the organization is supposed to be, and then reasons that the role of leaders and managers is to fulfill this normative model in actuality. Managerial action is "performing the function." Notice, however, that it is impossible to "perform a function." That is just sloppy use of the language with enormously confusing consequences. A function is an abstract statement referring to an effect. The *function* is not the concrete *performance* of the action. More than the name for the function is needed to talk about the nature of the actual performance. Note that I am not criticizing the specification of needed functions. That has been a fruitful approach. It defines the territory that managers and leaders are concerned with and names the effects we want them to have. It is what the list-of-functions approach forgets that I am criticizing.

The list-of-functions approach forgets that action taking is a concrete process before it is anything else. Furthermore, it is a concrete process performed by a whole person in relation to a whole environment populated by other whole persons (that is, not other lists of functions). This whole process is embedded in time and is subject in the real time of its operation to all the turbulence and change that surround it, that indeed suffuse it, because the turbulence and change are within action takers as much as they surround them. Simply to name the function to be performed as though it were the action ignores all of this richness of the actual action-taking process and, worst of all, ultimately masks the richness and leads to an empty model of what the action-taking *process* is. This is why generations of students have had such a hard time figuring out what leading and managing are from the statement of functions. Treating action as a thing rather than a process is a particularly thorough and harmful case of the "reification" I attributed to the techno-holic mentality in Chapter Six. If it did not cause so much confusion and misunderstanding, it would be hilarious.

Let us consider further this model of a "whole person in a whole environment in relation to other whole persons, embedded in time, with all actions viewed as concrete processes, and the entire process thoroughly suffused with turbulence and change." This is a rather mind-boggling phenomenon to try to theorize about, and it is not surprising that the list-of-functions approach has been substituted. It is so much easier to talk about, to use in performance appraisals, in research and teaching; so much easier to write about. But it is very misleading, especially in an environment of permanent white water.

There are probably lots of different names we could give the "whole person in a whole environment . . . " model for convenience's sake. "Holistic process model" comes to mind, for example. However, I find the phrase "management as a performing art" a good deal more suggestive and down to earth. It has the advantage of suggesting analogies from other fields, which an entirely new name does not. It builds on the intuition many observers have had over the years—that there truly is an art to leading and managing. The performing aspect picks up the dynamic, fluid quality that the list-of-functions approach has such a hard time with. And I, at least, find the phrase intriguing because, frankly, it offers a kind of romance and creative verve to the four-square business of management.

Lessons from the Performing Arts

The remainder of this chapter is a meditation on what the performing arts might have to teach us and remind us about leading and managing. For my purposes, the "performing arts" are the familiar ones of theater, dance, and musical performance and variations on these. Radio and television have also spawned many forms of performance, which may not be quite as "artistic" as the classical modes but which we should consider. There may also be spectator sports that have something to teach. It is not necessary to be overly precise or technical about it. The search is for forms of dynamic, goal-directed action occurring under pressure and responsibility that may have something to teach us about workaday organizational management and leadership. I should also say before proceeding that I will be using a somewhat idealized version of what the performing arts are. Close up, any given theatrical troupe, dance company, symphony orchestra, or movie company will be seen struggling with the same white waters and problems of leadership and management as beset everyone else. The use I will make of the performing arts metaphor in this chapter depends more on how the performing arts *intend* to be and on how they differ from work organizations that historically have intended something else. Thus, I will be arguing that what the performing arts have traditionally intended may be relevant to managers of work organizations in the difficult new conditions. By implication, I might add that arts organizations might have something to learn themselves from their traditions.

Since I have just spent considerable time indicting the list-of-functions approach to managing and leading, this issue is a good one to begin with. What do the performing arts suggest that might prevent us from falling into the list-of-functions trap? I think the answer is fairly obvious: if you think of action taking as a performing art, there is no danger that you will confuse proficiency in a component with proficiency in the rounded performance as a whole. Furthermore, you will be pushed to consider what the "rounded performance as a whole" in fact is; that is, what the overall process of your managing and leading activity is intended to be. A staff meeting, for example, might be understood more easily as a whole than as a series of discrete agenda items. We know that some leaders intuitively do this anyway and think about what mood they want the group to be in at various points and in connection with various items. Matters are positioned on the agenda with their overall fit in mind.

Interestingly enough, thinking of action as a performing art does encourage consideration of critical functions or components; both the whole and the parts are considered in relation to each other. The list-of-functions approach I have criticized assumes that there is only one basic set of functions that apply in all situations. Looking at action as concrete performances reveals that for one occasion or another, a particular function will be of more or less importance; indeed, it may be the key to the whole activity, or may be absent entirely. The performing arts metaphor disabuses us of any doctrinaire ideas about what the key functions are.

There are two further implications. First, "functions" are specific to a given performance and are not general categories at all. "Set design" as a function, for example, would be considered as much in relation to the role it was to play in a given theatrical production as in relation to abstract "principles of good set design," and indeed, if it ever came to a trade-off between conforming to abstract principles versus fitting into the specific need of a given production, there would be no question that the latter should take precedence over the former. This puts a very different meaning on the idea of standard management or leadership functions. A second implication is that once a key function is identified for a given performance, then great attention is paid to getting the function correctly defined, getting adequate resources for it, and rehearsing it until it is "right." Ironically, in the management and leadership field, if a lot of time is spent on getting a function right, people often become impatient. They may complain about getting bogged down in minutiae. They may get bored with rehearsals or have pangs of conscience about the lengths to which the organization is going to achieve a certain effect. Thus, it is clear that reflection on the list-of-functions approach to management using a performing arts metaphor reveals subtleties about it that we might not identify otherwise.

Hovering on the edge of awareness in any consideration of the performing arts is a notion of what a "quality" performance is. There can be nothing automatic or formulaic about it, no canned definition of quality that can be taken off the shelf.

As argued in Chapter Three, "quality" remains in the eye of the beholder: it is up to those conducting the performance to decide what they are going to mean by quality. Yet we cannot quite leave it at that, for there are "artistic standards" that transcend the values and perceptions of any particular set of performers. What they actually have to do is a complex act of integration between what they want and feel that they can achieve in their particular situation with what they perceive to be more timeless standards of quality and of taste. Furthermore, this will often be a *passionate* integration, not just a mechanical one, not just a "nod" to the standards of the wider artistic community. Performers often have very intense feelings about how the quality of what they are doing relates to standards of the wider artistic community. They may feel that their work is in the grandest tradition; they may feel that it takes traditional standards to new levels; they may consciously be out to revolutionize standards for a particular work. The main point is that they are unlikely to be indifferent and unaware.

How different this is from the often one-dimensional discussions in work organizations of whether or not the "job got done." If management is a performing art, the consciousness of the manager is transformed, I think. One becomes much more interested in the quality of the process and much more aware of how a given course of action does or does not resemble other things that one has done or that others have done. One is *thinking* quality throughout. Isn't it interesting that this is precisely what the excellence literature is trying to get managers to do?

The notion of a quality *process* deserves further thought, too. The typical American management mentality is that we will do whatever it takes to reach the objective. The performing arts would tend not to look at it this way, but instead would hold themselves to staying within certain forms in pursuit of the intended result. Indeed, the forms *are* the art; if the forms are violated, the result is not of the same value. Forms do change, of course. We play Bach on synthesizers now as well as on traditional instruments. The point is, though, that in the performing arts the form *matters*. There is a balanced relation between form and function that is of great importance, and in the course of the activity, this balance is kept clearly in mind and highly valued. Contrast this with the debate in management about whether the end justifies the means and the frequent sacrifice in modern pressured conditions of means to ends. Perhaps leadership and management cannot be as conscious of form as the arts are, but awareness of the role of form would help many a leader to anticipate the impact of various actions on the system, for whether the leader is form conscious or not, the members of the system certainly are.

Attaching importance to form also makes it possible to take pleasure in the quality of the process that one is conducting or participating in. In management, you don't hear much about the pleasures to be derived from the operations of the organization, except in one type—namely, high-performing systems. Where members have learned how to operate at high levels of quality, they take pleasure in the sheer conduct of the process and attach great importance to proper execution. The performing arts show that this pleasure in the process can occur even though "world-class quality" is not being achieved. Sousa marches are fun to play at any level of expertise. Themes of play and of personal enjoyment run all through the performing arts. And the arts prove unequivocally that these themes do not detract from getting the job done. Quite the reverse: play and enjoyment are integral to getting the job done. What an intriguing priority for a manager to consider in any type of organization: making sure that members derive some pleasure in the process. "Job satisfaction" and, more recently, "quality of work life" are the terms we use for the idea of taking pleasure in the process. In my opinion, consideration of these ideas is greatly enriched by thinking of the meaning of pleasure in the process as it is found in the performing arts. It might help us to resolve the old debate about how important job satisfaction is and to understand it in process terms rather than as a reified, measurable "thing" that a worker either has or doesn't have.

There is a connectedness here, too, in the performing arts—a connectedness between the importance of the form and the ability of participants to take pleasure in it. If the form is regarded as unimportant or is constantly being upset and tinkered with, members may have trouble discovering the pleasures that are available in any particular form. This is yet another manifestation of the permanent white water problem, for it upsets organizational forms constantly. Still, there may be more that managers can do to defend forms against external turbulence, but it will require that they attach more importance to form in the first place. This whole discussion should cause managers to think very carefully before they perpetrate yet another reorganization on their people.

There are three further qualities in any organized activity that the performing arts demonstrate unmistakably, yet that are often overlooked in discussions of management and leadership. These qualities are particularity, variety, and contextuality.

By *particularity*, I mean the utter uniqueness and concreteness of every event. It is impossible to conduct a "generalized performance." You can only conduct *this* performance, and it is what it is for better or worse. I am sure it is possible to become "jaded" in the performing arts; that is, to lose the ability to treat each performance freshly. But that is a perversion of what is considered desirable. How different this is from everyday life in organizations, where there is often a kind of dumb acceptance of "routine" and little in the traditions of effective management and leadership to suggest that a manager should strive to prevent a feeling of "routine" from creeping through the organization. In fact, bureaucratic theory suggests that "routinization" is something desirable! Even with all that has been written about inspirational leadership, participative management, and the like, I have seen virtually no emphasis on the idea that organization members should be encouraged to discover uniqueness and specialness in daily activities. Just because the performing arts seek magic in each performance does not, of course, mean that managers of work organizations should, but the lack of emphasis on discovering the "essence of the particular" is certainly worth pondering.

Ignoring the particularities of a system supports and encourages the fiction that a science can be made out of management. A science dares not assume that there is anything decisively unique about any system, for if there were, the science's general laws would not apply. No one is foolish enough to think that the performing arts can become applied sciences. Why do we make that assumption about the management of organizations?

With the notion of *variety*, I am referring to the basic heterogeneity of all human systems. The performing arts are very conscious of "fit" and "blend" and "meshing," of "harmonizing" the various elements of the system. This is one of the reasons so much attention is given to rehearsal. It is why "prima donnaism," while as common in the arts as anywhere else, is regarded as undesirable. All this preoccupation with blend and fit is due to the fact that every purposeful organization is a mixture of "apples and oranges." The various elements of the system conform to different laws; they react to external influences differently; they often do no occur together in nature, and so there is no natural organic unity. To the extent that organic unity occurs, it is achieved through the investment of substantial time and energy. The performing arts bring enormously varied parts together in productions. They demonstrate the problem, and they demonstrate strategies for dealing with it. The performing arts prove that even though there is not an organic unity of *things* in a system, an organic unity of *feeling* can be developed and that this unity can bring a coherence and flow to what would otherwise be only a loosely related collection of parts. The key lesson is in the time the arts take to develop this feeling in any production. It is the main thing you strive for—not some peripheral nicety.

Once again, this characteristic of variety shows how ridiculous it is for us to talk about a management science. No given manager can choose what elements and their interrelations shall be present in a situation being managed. Science selects phenomena to study scientifically and seeks to standardize and regularize these phenomena; that is, control their variability. The manager or leader, on the other hand, is always confronted with mixes of phenomena that probably will not have been studied scientifically. The system is existentially a melange. The manager cannot choose to banish from the system elements for which there is no adequate science, or if such an attempt is made, the banished elements may merely lie dormant until the efforts to keep them out of the situation cease; then they flow back in. Thus, the manager's situation is much more like the problem faced by a movie producer, an orchestral conductor, or a director of a play than that faced by a scientist. Like these counterparts in the arts, the manager can seek to discover and develop an organic feeling among participants for what the business is basically about. "Every employee must understand the essence of the business," said James Treybig of Tandem Computer (Magnet, 1982). This is the principle the performing arts demonstrate so vividly.

Contextuality is the idea that the elements of a system are not atoms standing in mechanical relationships to each other, and further that they exist together in time. The slang word is *chemistry,* and hard as it is to define, its reality is unquestioned in any system where effectiveness depends on close coordination among the parts. What the performing arts make so clear is that contextuality is really a matter of the culture of the system and that this culture is something that develops over time and exists throughout a given field of endeavor rather than singly in one system. Because of contextuality, the performance of any single element depends heavily on its degree of fit with its context. It means that individual people can perform way above or below what appears to be their individual potential, depending on the degree and kind of support they get from the surrounding system. It means that individual performers will be intensely conscious of the kind and degree of surrounding support. It means that parts cannot be exchanged like chess pieces; transfers in and out of people, replacements of equipment, and so on are felt intensely. One reason that "the show must go on" is such a powerful norm in show business is precisely because of how sensitive the performing system is to the context, and how many different reasons there might be for the show *not* to go on. If the system were intrinsically resilient, the powerful norm would hardly be needed.

In managing work organizations, we don't like to think about how sensitive the system is to changes, especially changes of the white water kind. It is more convenient to believe that various elements can be interchanged and moved around pretty much on management's whim. The performing arts constitute a powerful reminder, if one is needed, of how unrealistic this belief is.

Not only are human beings contextually interconnected at the physical level, they can also think about it, form opinions about it, make judgments about what they like and don't like about it, and make modifications in it on the basis of these perceptions. I will have more to say in the next chapter about awareness of context. How often managers wish their people would not ask questions, would not think *about* the organiza tion but instead just do its work. In asking that, a manager is asking a person to become unconscious! Put this flatly, it is clearly a ridiculous impulse, yet managers feel it all the time, even managers who should know better. What it means to manage a system of contextually interconnected actors who are also contextually interconnected consciousnesses is one of the most complicated issues in the whole field of leadership and management. It means that people are interconnected in their perceptions as well as their behavior. Person *A* and person *B* can be making beautiful music together in the view of person *C*, but *A* and *B* are also listening to the same music and forming opinions about it, opinions that may or may agree with those of *C* or of each other. The music then is contingent on the factual actions each person is taking as well as on each person's perception of those actions. If *C* is the boss in this case, it is little wonder that he or she might wish that *A* and *B* would just go ahead and make the music and leave the evaluation of it to *C*. In wishing for this, of course, *C* wishes for too much. In most cases, *A* and *B* can't be kept in the dark. Human beings can't turn off consciousness even if they want to. The performing arts demonstrate that what can be done is that *A* and *B* can learn to integrate their consciousnesses as well as their actions. They can come to share a common vision and common standards. In fact, most performances are not possible without integration at this level, which is why the culture of the performing arts supports learning of each other's tastes and preferences as well as just practicing physical actions. The sheer mechanical integration of actions without integration of consciousness produces a stilted and tentative performance that lacks rhythm and flow. It seems to me that there are direct translations of these ideas to the question of what it takes to lead and manage a work system effectively and of the kind of help system members need in order to perform effectively together.

I said earlier that the expressiveness of the artist is more important than mere technical competence with the tools, actions, and traditions of the art and that a mentality that is friendly to paradox will practice influence and control as an emanation of a growing, dawning comprehension of what is going on and of what is needed. Both of these observations have to do with creativity, a subject that is very important to leadership and management. What do the performing arts have to contribute to our understanding of creativity? The main thing, I think, is the obvious idea that it is assumed that creativity will occur, that various participants in the artistic activity will be continually seeking the dimension of personal expressiveness in everything they do in the performance. But there is an additional bit of wisdom here, I think, for if all the arts wanted were spontaneity and individuality, what you might get would be a centrifuge of expressiveness with everyone going off in their own direction. So the creativity has to occur within some framework and has to be subject to some discipline. Somehow, a curious union of opposites has to occur where performers have to find creative freedom in the closely interconnected workings of the system. To be sure, there is a provision for "soliloquies" and "arias" where an individual performer is highlighted and showcased and everyone else is in supportive roles. But I am suggesting that creativity and personal expressiveness have to operate during the "ensemble" parts also, when everyone is playing or performing together.

One mistake the arts would never make is to presume that a part or role can be exactly specified independent of the performer, yet this is an idea that has dominated work organizations for most of the twentieth century. The part or the role in the arts defines and frames a context within which the performer is expected to operate artistically. What a different idea with what interesting implications for management of work. There have been various intuitions of the power of this idea for the past fifty years in management, but it has still not caught on as a basic operating principle as it exists in the arts. It is still

considered a kind of luxury that a leader or manager can practice under special conditions. We think, for example, that emphasis on creativity is more "appropriate" for certain tasks than
for others. We talk about "enriching" jobs, as though some
jobs have no creative dimension in them and have to be hyped
somehow. The arts make no such assumption. The spear car-
riers are expected to give as much thought to their roles as the
star. What is at issue here is the question of whether the human
being is naturally creative and expressive versus the notion that
the human being has to be engineered into circumstances that
call for creativity. The arts make the former assumption; the
world of work tends to make the latter. My own opinion is that
the arts have a far healthier and more valid view.

There is one more thing to be said about what the arts
can teach us about creativity. The arts stand open to the possibility that the individual person is capable of spontaneously generating astonishing new material, material that goes far beyond
what anyone imagined was possible. It might not be an exaggeration to say that the expectation of such periodic breakthroughs
is the most powerful thing about the arts and what gives them
their most profound human meaning. They demonstrate thrilling things about human nature. In this age of permanent white
water, where the basic viability and effectiveness of organizations are everywhere in doubt, we are in acute need of similar
creative breakthroughs in all sectors of society. We need new
products and new services and new ways of working together
and new approaches to the chronic problems of society. The
corporate excellence literature is demonstrating that occasionally
it is possible to get a company set up in such a way that unusual
levels of creativity, quality, and quantity of production emerge.
I think the performing arts demonstrate the same thing, but they
show additionally how an ethos of quality and creativity can
pervade and undergird an entire field or discipline, transcending time and space and welding thousands of people together
in a shared adventure. A "universality" is regularly attained.
This is the next level we should be working toward in the leading
and managing of work organizations. The performing arts and
the human organizations in which they find their expression consistently demonstrate that it can be done.

Chapter 9

It's All People

All management is people management, and all leadership is people leadership. The reason for this is that there is nothing that a manager or a leader can do that does not depend for its effectiveness on the meaning that other people attach to it. How and why people attach meanings to things, how and why these meanings change, and how and why people's meanings and people's actions are interconnected are the subjects that managers and leaders should be concerned with. But they aren't, at least not as often or as thoroughly as they could be. This chapter is about this problem and its consequences and about some ideas for trying to recover the truth that "it's all people."

I suppose that it must be granted at the outset that it may be trite to say "it's all people." What else could it be, any reasonably thoughtful person might ask, particularly one who has been concerned with making organizations work better. The fundamental importance of "the people factor" is regularly affirmed among managers. I am sure that many of my colleagues have had the same experience I have had of hearing alumni say that they wish they had taken more courses in human behavior when they had the chance. The strategic planner I quoted in Chapter One speaking about the importance of people is expressing an increasingly common thought. Peters and Austin (1985) devote more than sixty pages directly to "People, People, People," and indirectly their entire book is a celebration of the people factor. The popularity of Peters's books, as well as those by authors such as Weisbord (1987), Kanter (1983), Bennis and Nanus (1985), Bradford and Cohen (1984), and many others, certainly establishes the existence of demand for new ideas about people and, by implication, an understanding of the importance of the subject. One of the best public demonstrations of the notion that "it's all people" is the continuing example of organized competitive sports, especially at the professional level. All the other factors that might explain wide differences in performance are relatively constant: the amount of funding a team receives, the quality of its equipment, the rules it plays by, the wider regulatory environment it exists in, the background training and experience of its players and coaches— these factors are all virtually equivalent. Even frequency of injuries tends to balance out across teams. The big thing that is left is the kind of leadership a team receives and how the members play together as persons; in other words, the people factor. Competitive sports demonstrate conclusively the futility of hoping that high levels of effectiveness are going to come by any easier or more efficient means than through people. The priority of people in the conduct of the organization has never been put better than Gardner put it in the original "excellence" book, a work that remains as persuasive and inspiring as anything currently on the market: "What we are suggesting is that every institution in our society should contribute to the fulfillment of the individual. Every institution must, of course, have its own purposes and preoccupations, but over and above everything else that it does, it should be prepared to answer this question posed by society: 'What is the institution doing to foster the development of the individuals within it?'" (Gardner, 1961, p. 142).

So what is the problem? We appear to be more aware than ever of the central importance of the human being to organizational effectiveness. It hardly seems necessary to argue this point for its own sake, but that is what this chapter does.

At several points in these chapters, I have indicated my dissatisfaction with the way we are talking about people in our management and leadership disciplines these days. I want to bring those concerns together in this chapter and give the whole issue more focus. Chapter Two, for instance, closed with a somewhat cryptic remark about the "impoverished ideas about the nature of the human spirit" I find in the managerial competency movement, and this comment deserves elaboration. In Chapter Three, I suggested that values clarification is a five-dimensional matter. At least two of the dimensions, the Communal and the Transcendental, are directly about human feeling and should be kept in mind as the discussion proceeds. I described at some length in Chapter Four my concerns with the peak performance movement, and much of my concern rests on the view of the human being that I find this movement taking—basically an instrumental view of the human being as something to be motivated, programmed, and inspired. This is totalitarianism—there is no other word—for, despite its benign intent, it treats the human being as an object to be lifted out of itself for its own good as well as the organization's (see Scott and Hart, 1979).

I also said in passing in Chapter Four that a body of ideas is as hard to manage in the world of permanent white water as an organization is, and I think this is a quite important point. It implies that our judgments about ideas are not immune from turbulence—our judgments about the quality of ideas, about the adequacy of their grounds, about how they hang together, about where one goes with them, about their fundamental validity. We live in an age of shrill brilliance where the well-known marketplace of ideas is a cacophonous place and the scramble for advantage is ferocious. In this context, we need to keep thinking about how our "image of man in organization" is developing. We need to keep asking ourselves whether we are remaining true to human nature as fully as we know it, or whether we are instead settling for images that play better, have more leverage and appeal. None of us is immune from the technoholism described in Chapter Six, and it can be a particularly pernicious affliction when we let it influence, nay determine, who we think the human being is. Given that the greatest minds

of human history have been unable finally to determine who
the human being is, we do well not to adopt too closed an attitude ourselves, no matter how much some OD project or "total
systems design" or "organizational transformation" seems to
require a fixed view, and no matter how inspired that view is!

The behavioral sciences as they have been employed to
understand organizational behavior, manage it, lead it, and
change it have evolved various basic views of who the human
being is. There have been "Economic Man," "Social Man,"
"Self-Actualizing Man," "Team and Group Man," "Socio-
technical Man," "Complex Man," "Peak Performer Man,"
"Postindustrial Man," "Neural Net Man," and so forth. Despite the seriousness of these efforts, I sometimes wonder whether
we haven't tended to settle for a rather superficial view of who
the human being is—"Superficial Man," if you will.

Superficial Man

Who is Superficial Man? Well, until very recently, we
have settled for letting him be a middle-class North American
white male adult, assuming that whatever is found out about
this demographic archetype probably applies to everyone else
as well (Theory X and Theory Y, for example). Superficial Man
"behaves," and his behavior is observable and classifiable. He
does not do anything utterly novel—that is, unprecedented—
so his behavior is therefore predictable, or at least the *tendencies*
of his behavior are. The meaning of Superficial Man's behavior
can be decided irrespective of what he thinks the meaning of
his behavior is; in fact, his own opinion of the meaning of his
behavior is *never* taken to be of primary significance. Rather,
those who study Superficial Man always understand more about
him than he understands about himself. It is possible, by the
way, for one's study of Superficial Man to be affected by some
of Superficial Man's own characteristics—although usually not
the ones being studied. You can "get too close to your subject,"
as the experts in objectivity are fond of saying. This poses a
sometimes difficult but, it is assumed, never insuperable challenge to research methodology.

Superficial Man's understanding of the world outside his skin, including his relations to other Superficial Men, exists as atomic ideas, discrete units of consciousness, so to speak. Superficial Man can report validly and reliably on these units in what is called his verbal behavior. He does manifest nonverbal behavior, but it exists as curiosities, anomalies, anecdotes, and punctuations of his verbal behavior and has no independent, systemic existence of its own. Furthermore, verbal and nonverbal behaviors taken together cover all the significant modes through which he might try to express himself. Superficial Man does not have a childhood, or an unconscious. In principle, everything about Superficial Man is nameable and explicable. Furthermore, it is assumed that the concepts and category names that psychology invents for characteristics of Superficial Man mirror his concrete characteristics completely for all intents and purposes. While abstraction entails simplification and separation of characteristics, the assumption is that by itself abstraction is not distortion. The only real sense in which there are mysteries about Superficial Man is that the behavioral sciences have not yet got around to investigating everything there is to investigate about him.

From time to time, Superficial Man has experiences that seem relatively rare among Superficial Men at large. Owing to the metapsychology just described, however, any individuals having such experiences are treated as suspect outliers to whom rigorous evidentiary tests must be applied. Examples of such experiences include unaccountable bursts of creativity, idiot savancy on sophisticated subjects, fire walking, amazing feats of strength or memory, talking with God, levitation, extrasensory perception of various kinds, spontaneous healing of incurable diseases, mental manipulations of huge masses of data, and out-of-body experiences. The null hypothesis is that Superficial Man sui generis does not have such experiences. This null hypothesis depends for its plausibility on the other assumed characteristics of Superficial Man. It is perfectly understandable that Superficial Man *thinks* he has these experiences, but, as noted above, what Superficial Man thinks about his own experience or what he naively thinks about the experience of others is always subordinate to external, more objective tests.

Except under special circumstances, Superficial Man seems not to mind being regarded as I have described him. This is an empirical statement. Just why Superficial Man is able to live in relative indifference to the theories that are held of him has not itself been a matter of curiosity to behavioral scientists. Superficial Man does become questioning of the theories when their application directly affects his interests as he feels them to be and articulates them to himself. Usually, his behavior on these occasions is explained by behavioral scientists as "resistance to change," showing a "lack of tolerance for ambiguity," or revealing a "threat to the self-concept." There is little or nothing that a specific person can do to alter the Superficial Man model that is held of him. In groups and organizations, Superficial Man is connected to his fellows in something called "structure," a phenomenon that can be adequately modeled by drawing squares and circles and connecting them with lines. The idea of any bonding to his fellows that may run deeper than prescribed structural relationships, while sometimes casually considered, is basically seen as a romantic notion, and in any event these deeper bonds are assumed to be modifiable by inspired leadership that will get Superficial Man to change his "culture." As one final salvo: The theory of Superficial Man just sketched does not apply to those who study Superficial Man, or to anyone one knows well or loves.

The question, I suppose, is just how possibly overdrawn and irresponsible this sketch is. I will quickly agree that various psychologists and others are quite aware of the absurdity of one or more of the statements above and that much creative work has been done and continues to be done to develop better ways of thinking and talking about human nature. Some will find some truth in some of these statements about Superficial Man. I don't know how many will find it on the whole a satisfactory account of how the applied behavioral sciences think of members of organizations. My own opinion, nevertheless, is that this is the dominant image of the human being in the field of organization development, in the organizational behavior and management departments of our nation's management schools, in our textbooks, and in the values and priorities we communicate to our students, including our most advanced students. It is a distressing image. The sentences I have written above reflect, deliberately, a host of mistaken assumptions, misunderstandings about science and about the philosophy of science, value-laden agendas masquerading as objective principles, and outright mis-statements of fact. It is a consciously outrageous portrayal. But I wonder whether, if I had written it a little more evenhandedly, some of us, myself included, might not have found ourselves approving of one or more of the propositions for investigating and managing Superficial Man.

The Study of Superficial Man

The list-of-functions approach to management so roundly criticized in the last chapter is an example of how we have described a managerial job as held by Superficial Man. No live human being carries a list of functions like this around in his or her head, parceling out little packets of action to one func-tion or another. Anyone who talks about personality charac-teristics as things ("needs," "feelings," "perceptions") is super-ficializing the real complexity of consciousness. The simple block diagrams of how organizations are hooked together in chains of command make sense only if we assume additionally that it is dumb, dependable Superficial Man who inhabits such an organization. No one who knows anything about how organi-zations operate thinks that a chart on a piece of paper describes anything of any significance. Only Superficial Man responds with automatic joy to an "enriched" job and doesn't insist on being consulted. Only Superficial Man is "reinforced" by a "reward" that a moment's reflection would tell him is worth little or nothing. Only Superficial Man is easy to "slot" into the need hierarchy. Only Superficial Man has a Myers-Briggs type (Myers, 1980) that tells us about all we could want to know about his perceiving, his judging, and the orientation of his consciousness.

I am trying to get us to root around in our favorite theories and techniques of management, leadership, and change for the self-serving assumptions we may be making about ourselves, the people we work with, and the people whom we are trying to influence. It is not possible to relate to as complex an entity as another human being without holding a theory or theories about it. I am asking about the adequacy of those theories and about what I perceive to be our relative complacence with those theories—indeed, our actual pride in them. My position is that, relative to our hunches, intuitions, and dreams about the human being, our theories are rickety, flimsy affairs, in need of constant tending, criticism, and the most creative development we are capable of. I am suggesting this as a norm of the intellect— that we should never let our images of the human being rest, for the phenomenon they attempt to model is inexhaustible.

The Shortcomings of Utility

The problem is not so much that our theories of human nature are wrong as it is that we create them and evaluate them primarily with criteria of utility. Every graduate student has heard the old saying that the test of a good theory is that it works. Secondarily, most of us have been taught to value economy and elegance, but never over utility. Occam's Razor usually gets mentioned along in here, too, with its counsel to choose that theory that rests on the fewest and/or the most well-founded assumptions. But I daresay few if any readers have ever been counseled to choose theories with an eye as much to matters of stewardship as to matters of utility and of verbal elegance. By *stewardship* I mean an ethical criterion, a criterion that asks whether this is the way we *want* to think of the human being, whether this is a *good* way to think about the person, whether this theory *values* as well as describes the individual. The supposedly tough-minded response to this is to say that the theory that is *truest* is in the long run the theory that is the best steward of our faith in the human prospect. This statement may seem right on its own terms, but the definition of *truest* turns out to be very tricky. If one adheres to a narrow, empirical, objectivist standard of truth—basically a physical science standard— one ends up throwing out most of the theories of human nature we are currently using *and* throwing out whatever humanistic values still survive in our philosophies of inquiry. One is driven back to mechanistic models that deal with the human being as a neurophysiological entity and/or an operantly conditioned "organism."

I think we need an enormous strengthening of the stewardship role played by our theories of human nature. The killing technological powers of the twentieth century broke upon us before we had developed sufficiently persuasive theories of the value of human nature to prevent the loss of hundreds of millions of human lives. Now as we approach our own *fin de siècle,* the problem of the value of human life is no nearer solution. Meanwhile, we have confronted ourselves with two or three more global challenges to human *being:* We have a pharmacological revolution and a worldwide drug epidemic that everywhere calls into question the value of human consciousness and the locus of self-control. Just behind that in the queue of assaults on being is the artificial intelligence revolution, promising to transform whatever it is that we mean by mind. Clamoring for the floor in the increasingly fretful discussions of what to do are the behavioral engineers, promising solutions to problems through the development of criterion-referenced, behaviorally anchored task specifications with satisfactory performance guaranteed through the creation of finely tuned reinforcement schedules, the whole thing designed and administered by someone to whom this white rat theory of personality does not apply (Skinner, 1976, p. 258).

I don't see how anyone can say that our understanding of human nature is secure, when such sophisticated technologies and such ambitious political and social programs are being brought to bear on it. Every one of them has its own image of humanity built in, an image of humanity that functions not in stewardship but rather to justify the objectives and techniques of the particular program or course of action. Where then *will* an image of humanity centered in stewardship come from? How will it be brought into the discussion of a given program's value? Whose job is it? The problems I am talking about are right on the doorstep of every leader and manager. They are not vague, far-off "social trends" that are somehow going to osmose into the social body without any stress and strain or disturbance of our own everyday organizational practices. I am hardly alone in expressing these concerns. Critiques of "technological" or "mass" or "organizational" society abound. The one contribution this discussion might make is to bring home the seriousness of the problem to people who are developing and practicing theories of leadership and management for application to specific human beings—that is, employees, associates, and stakeholders.

Toward a Robust Stewardship

What does our conviction that "it's all people" need to make it more valid and more strategic for the future? I think the answer is fairly straightforward, although it is relatively revolutionary in the sense that to implement it will require some fairly extensive changes in our thinking and our procedures. I am speaking now particularly of and to those who would say that they have been doing the best that they can to keep a humanistic view of the human being alive in the midst of all the mechanistic systems and bottom-line obsessions that pervade modern organizations. I am one of this group. I am not too satisfied with the way I find things, as this chapter shows, but in another sense, I can certainly say for myself that I have been trying in my way to keep an enlightened concept of human nature in front of my colleagues, my students, my readers, and the managers I talk to.

The straightforward but uncomfortable approach to the assaults on our image of humanity is to quit cooperating with those who are interested in a theory of human nature only for exploitative, manipulative, and dominative purposes. This is one form that a true and robust "stewardship" can take. I am not exactly sure, by the way, who "they" are—the exploiters, manipulators, and dominators. There are millions of men and women in jobs that seem to require them to exploit, manipulate, and dominate who yearn for an alternative; who want to feel better about themselves in their jobs and in relation to the people around them. They feel trapped into this kind of behavior because they haven't been able to develop an alternative themselves, they're not aware that anyone else has developed one, and they don't feel that they can take too many risks on their own because they feel that they are surrounded by people who they are afraid will take advantage of them—people who are in fact hurting just as much. As on so many other matters, Pogo was right. There by and large is no "they." It's us. There may be some who are irredeemable, to be sure (Kelly, 1988), but even toward these a different strategy from the one we have been practicing is warranted. Toward the close of this chapter, I include a quotation that says what that strategy might be.

To say that we must quit colluding in the image of Superficial Man is one thing; to develop a more positive approach is another. Fortunately, I think the ingredients of a positive approach are already there—an image of the human being that is both responsible stewardship and sound management and leadership theory. The rapid development of the field, the permanent white water conditions, the proliferation of specific organizational problems, the general explosion of interest in approaches to the human problems of organizations have all combined to diffuse the positive images of humanity and distract workers in the field from doing the development work that needed to be done. We have tended to rely on the humanistic philosophies of the pioneers in the applied behavioral sciences, often without understanding these philosophies very well, without understanding their roots in the broader and deeper history of ideas, and in particular without understanding the scholarship and concern that went into the development of those ideas. We don't know much about what people such as Mayo, Maslow, Lewin, Jung, Rogers, Bion, Piaget, and others went through to lay down their fundamental notions. And we haven't been curious enough. The students of the students of these individuals are the mainstream of the field now, and the next generation is just a few years from ascendancy. It has been too long already since very much new material has penetrated the core of the management and leadership field.

The Many Forms of Stewardship

What if we tried to develop the questions to be asked of any new theory of the human being so that we could see what kind of stewardship the theory contained? What would those questions be, those concerns we might have about the quality of life that a given theory presumed and sought to foster? What interests do we have in the best theories, using a definition of *best* that goes beyond mere practical utility? (By the way, the debate with the tough-minded objectivists with their ideas about rigor *is* a debate about what *best* means; in other words, a debate about values and therefore not decidable by the kinds of criteria the rigorists are most comfortable with.)

In the remainder of this chapter, I propose a few tests of a good theory of human nature. My thoughts about these tests are tentative, and my broader intent is to start some discussion of this question rather than to settle things. In the considerations I discuss below, there are many familiar echoes, and this is as it should be. The applied behavioral sciences as they have evolved in the management and leadership field *have* tried to be humanistic, and, as noted above, there have been some extraordinary contributions made to our thinking about the nature of the human being. I want to keep that process going. I don't know how else to raise these considerations except as a listing. In practice, they will function more as a rounded awareness of what some theory is really saying.

To what extent does the theory realize that it is a theory? This first question may seem a little odd, but in many ways it is the most important one on the list, for the problem is dogma, the belief that the theory is not just "theory" but truth. Take any five of today's best-selling management books and consider them according to criteria of tentativeness, humbleness, openness to being falsified (Popper, 1985), or explicit awareness of their own limitations. My perception is that they don't do too well. Responsible stewardship requires both bold creative thinking and complete willingness to be proved wrong, both "conjectures and refutations," as Popper (1965) has aptly titled one of his books.

To what extent does the theory take a "process view" of human beings? The view of the human being as a "being who is continuously becoming" has been part of the applied behavioral sciences from their beginnings (Allport, 1955; Vaill, 1984). The pressure in the last few years, however, has been toward more

static views, partly because of the explosion that has occurred
in higher education and in the so-called stand-up training field.
I don't want to sound too cynical, but we have needed pictures
to draw for rooms full of students and trainees. Pictures inev-
itably become static lists and diagrams, and while we may say
that our model actually is "dynamic," what gets copied down
and remembered is the stop-action list or the neat block diagram.
How to powerfully convey a process view and consciousness to
students and executives is an unsolved problem in education.
The field of so-called experiential education is aware of the problem but has not made much of a dent in it.

Another way that a theory can fail to take a process view
is by "pigeonholing" people into categories and then treating
them as possessing the presumed characteristics of the category.
Does a theory, say, of the motivation of coal miners permit one
to talk to a real, live coal miner in such a way that the person
is not just being forced to demonstrate the attitudes and values
prophesied in the theory? Behind this question is the proposition that the nature of a person is not determined by the aggregate nature of a category a person may belong to, no matter
how good the theory and research on the members of that category may be. This is the "hard edge" of the philosophy of becoming: the actual, live person transcends all categories.

*To what extent is the theory one that the theorist believes applies
to him- or herself?* One of the oldest jokes in the field is that management experts don't know how to manage and that consultants
have all the same problems they are billing the client for. There
is some deep wisdom in this perception, I believe, perhaps so
deep that all we can do is laugh about it— nervously. It would
be interesting to know how many teachers and consultants are
honestly attempting regularly to apply to themselves their favorite theories, their favorite ideas about how one should act to
be effective, about how one's own behavior can contribute to
a problem, about the causes of motivation and the ingredients
in effective communication. I think it is a fair question to ask,
but if we did ask it, I am afraid we would find that a lot of very
popular and influential notions are not taken all that seriously
by the very people who have invented them.

These three characteristics—the theory's honesty about itself, its openness to change in the phenomena it refers to, and its advocates' own willingness to take the theory's medicine— are the three key qualities that will produce a responsible stewardship in theories and theorists. There are a few additional characteristics that add to our picture and one final one that I am going to take the risk of stating flatly.

To what extent will the theory, if communicated to those it refers to, be accepted as a reasonably valid set of questions about their world? My own definition of *manipulation* is that an act is manipulative when the true motives behind it cannot be shared with those toward whom the act is directed, for they will disapprove of these motives (and presumably then resist the act) if they learn them. Current theories and research methods are full of tendencies that are manipulative by this definition. Even such simple things as questionnaires have theories behind them that often cannot stand the respondents' scrutiny. But what then becomes of our search for truth about humanity, it might be asked, if we are going to have to check our motives with the subject at every step of the inquiry? Is knowledge about humanity going to be dependent on knowledge that research subjects approve of? To some extent, yes, for this question is intended to reduce irresponsible meddling in people's lives, virtually spying on them for no good reason. But more profoundly, this question does not close off any research project that can withstand the scrutiny of its ethics by such groups as peer review panels and by groups, such as unions, that can act on potential respondents' behalf. Too much industrial research on workers has been authorized by management. This authorization may have disinterested motives, but more often it doesn't. In the consulting field, one of the key questions is "Who is the client?" I think this question needs to be changed to "Who is the client, and to what extent is my expertise in service of the client's needs at the expense of the client's subordinate's needs?"

Subjecting a theory's content to the opinions of those it applies to is *intended* to foster more theories that don't just describe people in the world but *help* those people in the world, help them better understand themselves in their environment. We have

been dominated by an ethos that says, "Get the facts first; helping people comes later." In OD it is called "diagnosis." That
separation of facts and values may work in the physical sciences.
In the social sciences, it has turned human beings into objects
for manipulation. Too often, the help never comes, or it comes
to people other than the human objects on whom the data were
collected.

   To what extent does the theory avoid "scientism," defined as
substantial modification of the theory's content in order to conform to
presumed methodological standards of clarity and reliability? This did
not used to be such a problem in the applied behavioral sciences.
From the 1930s through the mid-1960s, the emphasis was more
on developing interesting new concepts of management and
leadership and new ideas about the people that managers and
leaders are working with in organizations. But for the past twenty
years or so, we have been getting more and more preoccupied
with methodological considerations, and it has been having a
stifling effect on conceptual thinking. As Maslow notes in his
little-known critique of "means-centering" in science, emphasis
on methods drives out creativity in content (Maslow, 1954, chap.
2). A recent exciting reopening of the debate about the depress-
ing effect of scientism on our study of human nature is Wilbur's
(1983) *Eye to Eye.*

   To what extent does the theory recognize the tension between con-
formity and freedom? This question is especially acute in an applied field where there is great interest in change and, as noted
in Chapter Five, in comprehension and control. The phrase
"training and development" is a very common one in the management and leadership fields. Lots of organizations have departments with that name. There is a national professional society
with the name. The phrase appears frequently in article and
book titles. But with all this usage, I have never seen it pointed
out that the two ideas of "training" and "development" are
basically antithetical. Training has to do with conformity and
control. Development has to do with increased realization of
personal potential. Our lack of sensitivity to this antithesis is
mirrored more broadly in management and leadership. We have
a lot of theories these days that purport to show leaders and

managers how to get employees to do various things and refrain from various other things. Of course, in Skinnerian operant conditioning theory, we have a whole school of thought devoted to the subject of control of behavior. Strange that this school has developed no doctrine of "behavioral emancipation" to go along with its control-obsessed "behavioral modification." How to free a person from a reinforcement schedule—what an intriguing idea! The main point is that we should question a theory of human nature on its relative interest in control versus freedom. Since control is such a strong interest of managers, and utility is such a popular criterion for evaluating theory, we have to be careful of the subtle equation developing: A good theory equals one that creates controls on behavior effectively and efficiently. But sadly, the train may already have left the station, for I think that there are thousands of professionals who already accept that equation. In accepting it, they are implicitly rejecting the role of theory in freeing human nature.

These questions are intended as methods we can use to be responsible stewards to an ethical and enlightened image of who human beings are and theory of their nature. Theories that cannot answer these questions adequately, or that may in fact reveal indifference or contempt for the question itself, should not be sponsored or used by the men and women who lead and manage our modern organizations.

Before I offer my final question for a responsible stewardship, I want to quote something from a book of meditations I have always liked: "The real corrupters of society may be, not the corrupt, but those who have held back the righteous leaven, the salt that has lost its savor, the innocent who have not even the moral courage to show what they think of the effrontery of impurity,—the serious, who yet timidly succumb before some loud-voiced scoffer,—the heart trembling all over with religious sensibilities that yet suffers itself through false shame to be beaten down into outward and practical acquiescence by some rude and worldly nature" (Tilestone, [1884] 1934, p. 221).

Finally, *to what extent does a theory of human nature make it easier for me to respect, to appreciate, indeed to love those I am applying it to?* I have deliberately phrased this last question in the first person, because I do not see how you can make such a personal assessment for anyone but yourself. I cannot tell you that a particular theory prevents *you* from respecting, appreciating, and loving other people. I think that each of us does have to make this assessment for ourselves, though, and following the quotation above, I think we have to be as tough as we can about the many theories that fail the test of this question or that are indifferent to the question.

Actually, this may not be quite as idealistic a question as it first appears to be. The fields of organizational behavior and organization development have been accused from their beginnings of being "soft" on people, and they have managed to withstand these attacks. The thrust of my argument, buttressed by the above quotations, is that we have to keep on withstanding those accusations, that indeed we must be much more assertive than we have been about what the field of management and leadership and organizational effectiveness is all about. More than twenty years ago, one of the founding practitioners of the field of OD answered my question about his philosophy of change by saying, "Love the people and hate the system." This is what it is all about. Offhand and slangy as the phrase may be, "it *is* all people."

Chapter 10

The End of Culture and the Dialexic Society

It is fitting that this chapter should follow one that argues as urgently as Chapter Nine does that we have to pay more attention to the ethical quality of our theories about human nature. One of the areas where the stewardship urged in Chapter Nine is most needed is the way we talk about human cultures. This chapter makes some interpretations of what is going on in the field of culture applied to management and organizations. The basic position I will take is that we have been misusing the idea of culture and promoting misunderstanding of actual cultures. There is a challenge in this world of permanent white water, and the concept of culture is involved in understanding it. I want to show in this chapter how the idea of culture helps us to understand this challenge, but only if we use the concept differently from the way we have been.

The challenge I refer to is how coordinated streams of action among people are possible when everything is *changing*. That is the theme that has been with us from the beginning, but in this chapter it is faced a little more directly. I have been saying that it is hard to survive in permanent white water, hard to play Chinese baseball, hard to continually play a game at which one is a beginner. Most of what I have said so far about actually doing these things has dealt with our individual consciousness, with our ability to think about what is going on, test assumptions, not get trapped in technoholic thinking or succumb to facile promises. The ability of each individual to perceive clearly what is going on is indeed crucial, but the fact is that we face these conditions *together* in groups and organizations. I have made a few references to networking and working collectively smarter and becoming better team players; now all this needs to be discussed in more detail. In this chapter, the focus is on the idea of culture. In the next chapter, the same problem is discussed in terms of the ability of executive teams to function effectively together.

This Juicy Notion of Culture

I am sure readers of this book are fully aware of how popular the idea of culture has become in the past few years. Several good books and articles have come out, and there have been numerous conferences. As editor of *Organizational Dynamics,* I can personally testify that organizational culture has been the most common topic among articles submitted in the past three years. "Changing the company culture" is on everyone's lips. I want to question quite sharply this easy and hopeful way of talking about organizational culture. But before I get to my own critique and why I think it is important, I want to speculate a bit further on why there has been this explosion of interest in the idea of culture.

For the past few years—and less visibly for the past fifty years—the subject of culture, and especially the culture of large organizations, has attracted more and more theorists and researchers. In fact, we are at a point now where thousands of people know how to characterize a cultural milieu and are doing so regularly. What makes the natural history of organizational life so interesting? I can see four things going on as the members of some organizational culture hear the natural history of it described, and these help explain why the subject of culture is so popular and why managers and others interested in change think that the concept is so promising.

First, the details of a culture we know well and feel strongly about are so *juicy*. That perhaps is an insufficiently technical term, but I am trying to capture the colorful, palpable quality of stories and observations about cultures we know well. We experience the shock of recognition. Deep memories are stirred. We *see* ourselves in the scenes and surrounded by the people. I think stories of cultures we know well and feel strongly about make us feel more real. We can enjoy the texture of our experiences, and we unabashedly let ourselves be drawn into exchanging anecdotes and telling ingroup jokes. There is an interesting feeling of security that arises as we let our consciousness fill with the nature of some culture that has meaning for us. It isn't that the cultural information is news to us; in fact, its essence is that it *isn't* news. Without putting the information in story form, however, all our knowledge and experience will tend to remain ill structured and latent. In sum, members of a culture love to reexperience the nature of the culture through words and pictures as told by someone who can make it all come alive.

Second, even though this information is vivid and powerful and can be very moving, it is typically not psychologically threatening. This may not be true for someone who has been scarred deeply by some culture. For most of us, though, I think it is more likely that the feelings evoked by the cultural material will not be too painful to deal with. This characteristic means that you can tell a group of executives things about their company culture that have extremely personal meaning for them, things that are very serious and sobering, that may even be dangerous or illegal. As long as the focus is kept on the culture and the finger is not pointed at particular people or actions, my experience is that a sustained discussion of the nature of the culture is quite easy and in fact very enjoyable because of the energy generated by the juiciness of the data. I think that cultural material fosters a realization that in some ways no one is responsible for the culture. It just is what it is.

The concept of culture provides an excellent vehicle for talking about the attitudes, values, and actions of the people in the culture. As the last chapter showed, there has been a rapid increase in interest in the "human factor" among managers. Discussion of culture lets a manager or management team feel that they are really focusing on what the people in their organization are like, that they are really paying attention to people. This is a third thing that is going on as an organization's culture is considered.

But then an odd kind of reversal can occur, and this is a fourth thing going on when culture is being discussed. It seems to become clearer and clearer that all the cultural patterns are highly determinative of what is happening in the organization, highly determinative in particular of all the different measures of performance the management might be interested in. The "odd reversal" is to move gradually from talking *about* the culture to beginning to think about what can be done *to* the culture so that its energies pull more in the direction that management wants for purposes of organizational effectiveness. Hardly before it realizes it, a management—aided and abetted by in-house staff, external consultants, books and stories from other organizations, and an acute sense of urgency—is thinking of organizational culture as a management tool and is beginning to listen seriously to plans for how to change the culture to something presumably more desirable.

The subject of organizational culture is one of the most plausible new forms of leverage on the organization to come along in years. I think it is also very oversold and unreliable. Given a serious definition of culture, which I will offer in a minute, I think it is more likely that you can't change organizational culture, and efforts to do so only empower the existing culture and result in resistance. Far from advocating methods for changing culture, this chapter suggests that the real problem is that more and more organizations lack a culture of any power and that this creates a different kind of issue for leaders and managers than what has been presumed by those who have been focusing on "how to change organizational culture." The first step into this argument is to get clear on what this thing called a "culture" really is.

Yet Another Definition of Culture

There are literally dozens of definitions of *culture*. It is one of those concepts, such as "personality" or "communication," that we intuitively know are getting at something very important, but this "something" is so diffuse that there is practically no limit to the number of possible turns one can give the kaleidoscope. And turns beget turns; the more definitions there are, the freer any given writer feels to create his or her own. So here is mine: A culture is a *system* of attitudes, actions, and artifacts that *endures over time* and that operates to produce among its members a relatively *unique common psychology*.

I have italicized the key phrases in this definition, the things we must not forget, in my view, if we are really talking about a culture as distinct from some other kind of aggregate that isn't just a random mass, but that is still not crystallized to the extent that we assume that cultures are. Especially the "unique common psychology" (UCP) is important, I think. It is the UCP that attaches meaning to the various attitudes, actions, and artifacts of a culture, and different UCPs can result in objectively identical attitudes, actions, and artifacts with dramatically different meanings. The UCP is how we know people from the same culture—what we can see that they have in common even if they can't see it themselves. Without "uniqueness," there would be no identity or boundary to the culture. "Commonness" is probably more obvious, for it is the subtle likeness among members of the same culture that makes it possible for us to tell that they are members of the same culture. Finally, I would make "psychology" an essential element. We are not talking just about quirks and superficial traits; we are talking about fundamental similarities of thinking and feeling, perceiving and valuing. Culture runs deep into the psyche, or else we are not talking about culture. Furthermore, the common psychology is what makes it possible for members of a culture to feel so much closer to each other than they do to others who are not members.

Making Sense as Culture

The more we are able to make sense of the idea of culture, the more we can see that the role of culture is to help us make sense to ourselves and to each other. More exactly, it isn't the abstract category of culture that aids the sense making but all the concrete "attitudes, actions, and artifacts" that constitute a culture. These familiar things are grouped, combined, embellished, and played off endlessly as we live and function in our cultures. The most ordinary, taken-for-granted, everyday actions exist within a cultural framework, a framework we pay no attention to until it buckles on us—as it does to one degree or another when we travel to other countries or interact with groups within our own nation whose UCP is different from our own. These groups within a society—professional groups, hobbyist groups, political and religious groups, certainly inhabitants of particular geographical regions (such as Minnesota)—can be just as sharply bounded from each other as national cultures traditionally have been. As noted several times, organizations can be cultures, too, provided that the definition I have given applies. In all of these situations, it is possible to feel the sharp differences between one's own cultural perspective and that of some group that has a different UCP.

When a management group talks about its own organizational culture, this kind of talk is governed by its own UCP and by the norms for such activity within that organizational culture, although in some organizations it pushes the limit of what is permissible for discussion. Such talk is supported by the norms of the broader managerial culture cutting across organizations and advocating anything that increases managers' comprehension and control of the organization (see Chapter Five). Such talk is further supported by the norms of the broader culture of educated people that supports the idea of rational analysis of the situations we find ourselves in, provides vocabulary and standards for thinking and talking about things, and certifies the value of the activity. Such talk is supported by the norms of the even broader national culture, which says that we have a responsibility to lead and manage our organizations as effectively as we can, especially in the current period of global competition. There are doubtless other influences from one sort of culture or another that help to make sense of the idea that discussing the organization's culture is a rational and proper thing to do.

It is very important to remember that managers' ideas about organizational effectiveness are themselves made credible and valuable by cultural norms and influences. The values clarification I described in Chapter Three is possible only to the extent that there is enough shared culture to make a discussion of various values possible. What a management group is going to be able to talk about doing to or with its organizational culture is powerfully influenced by the culture itself. This is the point we keep overlooking when we talk facilely about changing the organizational culture. It is not possible to just sit down with a clean slate and describe the kind of culture an organization ought to have. Even those who are not involved members of a particular culture have on their own cultural ''glasses'' that influence what they are able to see in a given organization and what changes they are able to imagine. Furthermore, to talk about changing an organization's culture involves talking about changing everyone's behavior and UCP. It is true that management groups usually include themselves when spelling out needed changes, but usually the changes they decide on for themselves tend to be unitary things such as ''more delegation of authority,'' ''more emphasis on innovation,'' and so on. These changes are not conceived as systemic changes and are certainly not understood by managements as interventions into their own UCPs. There are sometimes external consultants and other observers who realize that true change in the UCP is called for in a given management, but realizing it is one thing; making the point as an effective consulting intervention is quite another. There are few consultants today who have the competence and the courage to do the latter. He or she who undertakes to change the ''unique common psychology'' of an American top management team is carving out a formidable task. More will be said of it in Chapter Eleven.

True culture change is systemic change at a deep psychological level involving attitudes, actions, and artifacts that have developed over substantial periods of time. The changes that most organizations actually are undertaking these days exist at a much more superficial level than real change in the culture. There is nothing wrong with this per se. But calling it "culture change" sets up the expectation that the UCP of organization members will change as a result of the interventions and in the direction intended by the interventions. In fact, the UCP will not do anything of the sort. Instead, it will continue to operate as it always has, only now with the organizational changes that have been made to deal with. The UCP will ignore most of these changes, will accommodate casually to those that are not too bothersome, and will resist everything that actually seems to involve a direct confrontation with the UCP itself.

The belief that the UCP can be manipulated, conditioned, coopted, or cajoled into cooperating in its own transformation is one of the more worrisome ideas floating around in the management field these days. If a management group thinks that it is intervening in the UCP of the organization when it isn't, it is setting itself up for disappointment and disillusionment. Even more seriously, it is setting itself up for renewed attempts to confront the existing UCP, for it is true that American organizations are filled with UCPs that are ill suited to permanent white water and that are inhibiting the organization's capacity to adapt to the changing environment. These renewed attempts are likely to become increasingly Byzantine and manipulative or, alternatively, increasingly punitive and coercive. Either way, a management that has become convinced that a UCP has got to change is going to evolve into an increasingly totalitarian frame of mind. A given management group's *own* UCP is partly the organization's, but it is also heavily influenced by the UCP of the American management culture, and this latter not only authorizes, it *encourages* the kind of extreme steps I am talking about.

The "Dialexic" Society
and Real Change in the UCP

The UCP of all cultures and subcultures is changing, but by a process of cultural tectonics that goes well beyond anyone's direction or control. Permanent white water conditions have combined with technologies and values of the so-called information age to create an amazing new condition, and it is this that constitutes the real challenge I spoke of at the beginning of this chapter.

My main thesis is that culture—as implicit and taken-for-granted attitudes, actions, and artifacts that create and sustain a unique common psychology—is dying and that we are becoming a society devoted to commenting on everything we do and think. This compulsion to comment I have dubbed *dialexic,* because its essence is to speak "on the other hand"—that is, dialectically—and its reflex is to assume that things are not what they seem. I am also stealing a little connotative energy from the term *dyslexic,* for what I am talking about may be every bit as much a cultural pathology as the impairment of the ability to read that *dyslexia* refers to.

One of our cultural heroes since World War II is the "commentator." In a world where nothing is what it seems and there is a compulsion to "commentate" on everything, it is more and more difficult for what occurs to become part of culture. The atmosphere is brutally irreverent and soul-searching, so inexorably *conscious* and self-analytical that the attitudes, actions, and artifacts of culture as I define it never achieve any formal meaning. Anything that starts to become influential is immediately undercut, first by analysis by legions of experts, actual and self-styled, who exist for every subject; then by parody, including all the attempts that go on to simplify, standardize, and often commercialize an idea or practice or event; and finally by ennui, the loss of ability to take various attitudes, actions, and artifacts of a culture seriously. The best index of ennui is the American ability to watch television hour by hour without remembering either the content of programs or the message of advertisements. The throwaway images of TV have no past— only a future. "What's on next?" has become the grand organizing question of the American evening.

We generate theories, interpretations, and commentary on phenomena in the dialexic society even as the phenomena themselves arise. One might say that dialexia is a new culture, which is producing its own attitudes, actions, and artifacts and beginning to evolve its own psychology. This is the way the information age, the postindustrial society, the "New Age," and so on have been discussed. But who is doing the discussing? These new "ages" are not just subjects, they are objects, and the more thoroughly they are made into objects, the less likely they will be to become woven into the existing UCP of society and gradually contribute to change in the UCP itself. Dialexic thinking is being applied to these macroconcepts even as they are being invented. Dialexic thinking itself is only minutes old in the reader's mind, and already I, and probably the reader, too, are "commentating" on it and bending its evolution away from any process of subsidence into the existing UCP of society. No, the dialexic society is not really a new culture in the sense of my definition. It is really an anticulture—not deliberately, of course, but its effect is to prevent an attitude, action, or artifact from achieving cultural significance and enriching the UCP of any existing culture. The dialexic society is a new social phenomenon where nothing can be out of awareness and taken for granted for long.

Furthermore, the attitudes, actions, and artifacts of the past that *have* been out of awareness and thus have shaped each one of us are being relentlessly brought to the surface by the dialexic society and analyzed, parodized, and gutted of meaning. Freud's opening up of unconsciousness to consciousness is, of course, the landmark event, and the subsequent proliferation of ways to get at what is out of awareness has completed what he began. All he needed to do was demonstrate that there was something *there*—that what is out of awareness can profoundly influence what happens—and the rest is really the psychic history of the twentieth century. Nowadays we have a massive "knowledge industry" devoted to pressing the work forward in all cultures and subcultures, at all levels, from the most deeply personal to the most macro trends affecting the planet as a whole.

Dialexia and Integrated, Habitual Flows of Action

The function of culture is to provide and sustain frameworks within which the following kinds of cycles can occur: (1)

actions suggest themselves to us; (2) we can choose from these (3) and then act in the confidence that what we are doing will be understandable to others (4) and that the same culture will then suggest things to others (5) that they can respond to us with (6) that will be understandable to us (7) and that the same culture will then suggest new actions to us . . . and so on. Cycles like this operate within a culture for anything—from ordering lunch in a restaurant to proposing marriage; from hailing a cab to writing a book. The essence of what culture does is to make it possible for us to execute probably hundreds of these cycles a day without having to think about it. But in environments of rapid change such as modern organizations, there are more and more "courses of action," as we still call them, that cannot have the steady, direct, repeatable quality that the phrase "course of action" suggests. In the world of permanent white water, this kind of stable, taken-for-granted process is becoming more and more fragmented. The more fragmented it becomes, the less we can know what action will fit the world we are in and the people we are trying to relate to. We are thrown into studying the increasingly problematic situations of the world of white water, activating the dialexic modes where situations can be one thing, "but on the other hand," they can be something else, and so on. Our study involves the theory and research literature—all the tons of concepts and frameworks that are available. Our study involves us with all kinds of experts and leads us to hire consultants to help us think about all this. In the best case, this study is called "planning" and "reflection." In the worst case, it is called "obsession." There is a very fine line between "planning" and "obsession," a line that the harassed, pressured modern manager may be more prone to cross than is realized. The main difference between the two is that planning occurs in relation to missions and objectives that are understood and deeply valued, while obsession is the triumph of the form of analysis over its function. Obsession is going "round and round." Along with obsession, of course, goes its companion "compulsion." The former deals with thinking, the latter with action. Compulsiveness is the continual returning to an action whose primary objective is not the accomplishment of work in the external world, but rather the calming of the churning world within. "Workaholism" is probably the most common form of compulsiveness in the organizational world. Dialexia in action is the behavior we call "fire fighting." In all organizations there will be some crisis management. But where we find a management handling the same kinds of issues over and over in a crisis mode, it is a management in which compulsiveness rules and planning and decision making have been driven out.

Dialexia is obsessive-compulsiveness of the mind, body, and spirit where the normal, culturally grounded linking of thought and action is constantly interrupted, negated, thrown off stride, brought up short, taken "off line." In sum, modes and cycles of behavior that an effective culture permits us to take for granted increasingly cannot be taken for granted because of all the changes that are occurring in the world. The main resource we have for coping with the situation is a type of intellectual analysis that may merely get us going "round and round." It is interesting that "situational management" could in this sense be understood as an invitation to a manager who's not sure what to do to go "round and round" for a while dialexically! All kinds of action takers in the social and organizational worlds have already experienced the terrors of obsessive thinking, the going round and round in one's mind about how to handle some situation, the anxiety, the self-disgust as you realize what you're doing to yourself—"mind games" we call it in the dialexic society.

Dialexia and Commitment

The change that has gradually invaded the "unique common psychologies" of the cultures and subcultures of the developed world is that they have become brutally self-critical and questioning of everything—the condition I am calling "dialexia"—where "on the other hand" is never out of order. To compound the situation, the world of permanent white water creates a situation where each person is coping dialexically with the white water he or she experiences, but less and less can any two people be sure that they are in anything like the same white water! It is a world of infinite variety in the content of things that one can get involved in and continues to expand and complexify at a geometric rate. Thus it is that we have the common feeling of "everybody going different directions." In the dialexic society, it is a very easy matter to study one's problems and to talk with others about them, but it is very difficult to find people who are willing to join one in action; that is, accept joint responsibility for some project or activity. (Another variation is that verbal commitments and promises of cooperation will be given, but then there is often no follow-through.) It is easy to find people who will talk, hard to find people who will commit. Thus, in the modern organization, we spend millions of hours listening to each other brief the group on the status of this or that project. The person whose project it is asks for ideas and feedback but knows that asking for help in action is not appropriate.

Some managers feel that they spend all their time going to meetings. The dialexic talk of the meeting is the dominant mode of action they engage in, and millions of us are very good at it and even find it for the most part enjoyable, especially if the groups we meet with are congenial. But dialexic talk doesn't go anywhere. Mission-oriented talk goes somewhere. Mission-oriented talk wants to get out of the meeting and get things rolling. The problem is how to convert dialexic talk into mission-oriented talk. Dialexic talk, remember, is engaged in obsessively-compulsively by people who feel that they are already working hard on very important problems and who don't really see or feel any real bonds with others apart from common employment in the organization or membership in the project. Dialexia is anticultural, as noted above: it gives reasons for *not* committing, for *not* getting any more involved and entangled than one feels one already is. Dialexia is very motives conscious and speculates endlessly about what some other person is really up to. Dialexia is very form conscious, and the effect of this form consciousness is that now and here are never the right time and place. Dialexia modulates feelings very carefully to make sure that there is no uncontrolled gushing or bleeding. Cordiality is the closest that dialexia can get to love; silence is the worst thing that one can do to another: it can mean boredom, anger, or hatred. "That's interesting" is the highest compliment dialexia can pay.

At the present time, there is a tremendous amount of talk about how to gain commitment in the organization, make the mission live, communicate the vision, get people to "sign on" and become project champions. This talk itself does not yet seem to have fallen into dialexia, but if I am right about the pervasiveness of the dialexic mode, we will soon be talking "on the other hand" about how to get a group of people excited by a new mission. Whether talk about mission and vision becomes dialexic or not, it is misdirected if it assumes it can just implant commitment to mission or vision where it does not exist in a group. Dialexia has changed that culture, that UCP. Dialexia now permits the members of that culture to ask such questions as:

> "Why should I?"
> "Run that by me again."
> "Is this the way the Japanese do it?"
> "Is this what that consultant told you to do?"
> "Didn't we try this once before?"
> "How does this fit in with our charter?"
> "Where are the data to justify this?"
> "It's not in the budget, is it?"
> "Don't we all already understand the mission?"
> "Let's kick it around awhile and see how it plays out."
> "Haven't we got an awful lot on our plate already?"
> "I was just reading something about this."
> "Every year about this time we start talking this way."
> "Is there something we can read about this?"
> "This really ought to be on the agenda for our next off-site meeting."

We have all heard remarks like these. We have all *made* remarks like these! They are the ordinary conversational noises of the dialexic society. Their effect is to move further into a verbal morass of subpoints, exceptions, and subtle distinctions. In a dialexic culture, we seek distinction by making distinctions.

Universities are the only organizations whose mission is to seek distinction by making distinctions. Most other organizations make their distinctions for the purpose of gaining greater clarity about who is going to do what toward what objective. As Harlan Cleveland remarked, ''The management of large organization systems will require a great deal of talking and listening, in an effort to take every interest into account and yet emerge with relevant policy decisions and executive action. The world's work will not be tackled by identifying our differences, but by sitting down, preferably at a round table, working hard at the politics of consensus, bringing people together rather than splitting them apart'' (Cleveland, 1972, p. 84).

This statement was intended as an invitation to action, indeed a call to arms, but I am afraid it has become a slogan for a dialexic managerial culture where a discussion of mission and vision in such phrases as those listed above takes the place of the active pursuit and fulfillment of the mission and vision. When a group is discussing mission and vision, they are discussing the family jewels, as it were. Dialexic undercutting of such discussions is fatal to the coalescence of feeling and energy and shared understanding that everyone agrees you have to have to get coordinated action among human beings. Dialexia has discredited most of the forms and values we have inherited from the past, and dialexia prevents new forms and values from becoming the kind of routine, taken-for-granted, jointly understood and believed-in principles on which coordinated action can be founded. Dialexia reads the Cleveland quotation above and remarks, ''Interesting. Let's put on a workshop built around that idea,'' or, ''Let's get him as a speaker at our next executive update seminar.''

Dialexia is a deep condition, part of today's UCP. It may already have occurred to the reader that in a sense dialexia is a luxury. It is ineffective and inefficient behavior, but up to about the mid-seventies, it was possible for managements to engage in it without too much obvious damage. The luxury derives in American society from two sources, one outside in the competitive environment and one deep within the individual spirit. The ''organization'' is a field or a frame, as it were, where the real energy of its human members meets and copes with opportunities and threats from the external environment.

Many commentators have noted that the organizations of the industrialized West have had it relatively easy since World

War II, enjoying expanding markets, cheap raw materials, enormous infusions of public capital in defense spending and other things, and relative political and economic calm. This has all blown away in the past twenty years, of course, even though there are still lots of managers who don't realize it.

What fewer commentators have noted is that the other half of the organizational equation—the authentic real energy of the individual member—has also been eroding over the past quarter century. "Loss of will," "spiritual malaise," "me generation," "culture of narcissism" (Lasch, 1979), "pursuit of loneliness" (Slater, 1970), "the age of anxiety" (Auden, 1947)—these are the kinds of phrases we have been hearing; but less often have these concerns been brought concretely to a focus in the individual person's capacity to participate in organizational life, and in particular to cope with permanent white water. One of the major reasons why observations about the plight of the individual in society have not been applied to organizational members is that these people have worked very hard to keep themselves together on the job. The stresses and strains of life at work are now acutely and poignantly evident and are being regularly documented, but they were there for many decades before anyone took them seriously.

We are living in a period of simultaneous buildup of pressure—the global social-economic-political-ecological crisis from without, and the spiritual crisis from within. These two meet in the organization's conduct of its affairs. Yet this very organization, at what is truly a crisis of its institutional life, has a fragmented, discredited culture that has long since lost its capacity to provide the effective bonding that people need to think and act together. And it has a set of communication and problem-solving processes that are highly technoholic and dialexic. The crunch that organizations are feeling, furthermore, is causing them to become *more* technoholic and *more* dialexic, for these are now major elements in the UCP of the managerial world. Expert systems, artificial intelligence, and computer networks are the latest toys for the technoholic. Off-site visioning seminars and spirituality workshops are the latest arenas for dialexia. It doesn't have to be this way; or, more pointedly, if technoholism and dialexia do take over, with serious efforts such as these to relieve and renew organizations and people, the absurdity will only continue to compound and the malaise grow deeper.

The reader may have noted that technoholism and dialexia feed on and reinforce each other. Technoholic solutions produce unanticipated negative consequences, causing embarrassing inquiries, more and more cautious analysis, delays and interruptions, and other dialexic actions, all of which creates more impatience and a tendency to embrace new, quick, and dirty technoholic "solutions." The remaining four chapters are devoted to what managers can do to avoid these two inadequate and ineffective modes of action. For the moment, I hope that this chapter has succeeded in demonstrating that those who would "change the organizational culture" have a different and more difficult job than some of them seem to realize.

Chapter 11

What Should the Top Team Be Talking About?

On assuming command of the Continental Army on July 4, 1775, George Washington immediately issued the following general order: "The Continental Congress, having now taken all the troops of the several Colonies which have been raised, or which may hereafter be raised for the support and defence of the Liberties of America; into their pay and service, they are now the troops of the United Provinces of North America; and it is hoped that all distinctions of Colonies will be laid aside; so that one and the same spirit may animate the whole, and the only contest shall be who shall render on this great and trying occasion the most essential service to the great and common cause in which we are all engaged" (from a commemorative plaque on Cambridge Common, Cambridge, Massachusetts). Here is a literal call to arms, an example of the clarity of vision and purpose that everyone is saying is so badly needed from today's top executives. In the case of this call to arms, things have turned out rather well, so far.

There is agreement that the governance and guidance of modern organizations need to be of higher quality. Somehow, we need better answers to the question that forms the topic of this chapter: "What should the top team be talking about?" I have observed this question being asked in many corporations, government agencies, and health systems. It is sometimes asked explicitly by executives. Just as often, however, it is asked implicitly; that is, it is evident that an executive group either isn't sure exactly what it should be talking about or isn't sure how to go about it even if there is some degree of clarity on what the subjects ought to be. In light of the many comments in this volume about permanent white water, there is clearly a greater need than ever for creative talk and action at top levels—everyone agrees about that. If the arguments of Chapters Nine and Ten are accepted, additionally, it means that the talk has to be as much about the organization as a human system as it needs to be about the "business aspects." Top teams are much more comfortable discussing business issues. Permanent white water conditions have put matters on their agendas, though, that may seem far removed from business. Yet in the intensely interconnected systems of the modern environment, everything counts. Top teams have to be prepared to talk about virtually anything and make appropriate judgments on the organization's behalf.

There are two broad categories of issues involved in the question of what the top team should be talking about. One category is the subject of strategic management; that is, the *what* of the top team's discussions. There is still a lot of confusion about what strategic management is and what the top team's role in it is. I want to say a few basic things about the subject as I see it, although my comments will be only a sketch at best. There is so much material already available on strategic management that, aside from my few clarifications, it isn't necessary in this chapter to try to interpret the subject in depth. The second category is the dynamics of the top team itself. There is less material available on this subject. Again, I am sketching out the territory for the moment. I have given book-length treatment elsewhere (Vaill, forthcoming) to what I call strategic management process consulting. This chapter is confined to establishing that there is a need for this new kind of consulting.

The Problem of Strategy

Contrary to much of the strategic planning and strategic management literature, which treats these subjects as matters of great intellectual complexity, my experience is that it is actually very easy to say what you are doing when you are engaging in strategic management, very easy at least to name the categories within which discussion needs to occur. What is hard is *doing* the "strategizing." The block diagram models and the lists of steps and functions are by no means decisive as to how the discussion should go and how it should be brought to periodic conclusion in actions called strategic decisions. I will briefly state a few basics about what I think this strategizing is as executive activity, but I devote the bulk of this chapter to the process of doing it, to what I call "strategic management as organizational behavior." Here are the basics:

1. I like to reserve the word *strategy* for talking about the conduct of some whole unit in relation to its environment. This is a matter of taste more than anything else, for the word *strategy* could also be used for matters that were strictly internal to some group or organization. The "whole unit" can be anything— an entire company, a division or "strategic business unit," a department, a project team, a geographically defined unit, and so on. Saying what the whole unit is then forces a specification of what its environment is, and this is crucial, for the unit will be doing whatever it does in relation to this environment. If the unit is part of a larger organization, I treat the larger system as part of the unit's environment—a very significant part, but not the sole part of the unit's world.

2. Having said what unit we're talking about, the next thing to do is say what that unit is trying to do and to be. This is the question of mission. Most readers know that this question is a conceptual and semantic swamp. One of the reasons the top team has trouble with what it should be talking about is that it often does not have a useful way of thinking about what the mission of the organization is. After a fair amount of experience and soul-searching on this question, I have reached the conclusion that it is not useful to equate the mission with

the content of the business, whatever it is. It is not useful to define a university's mission just in terms of education, a hospital's mission just in terms of treating disease and providing care, an army's mission just in terms of fighting wars; and it is definitely not useful to equate a business's mission with making a particular product, providing a particular service, or making money. The primary content of what the organization does, the primary areas of its distinctive competence, are only part of its mission. The point I am making holds for units that are smaller than total organizations, too. The mission of accounts payable is more than paying bills. The mission of the mail room is more than collecting and distributing mail.

The mission of any kind of organization or unit thereof is to establish and maintain itself as an organization that makes and sells the product or service or otherwise performs the function assigned to it. The mission is to be an organization of a certain sort. It is not to do a certain sort of thing through being an organization. That is a perpetuation of what I called in Chapter One the "myth of the organization as pure instrument." "What business are we in?" is the sine qua non question in strategic management. It wouldn't be such a hard question if managements didn't get hypnotized by their product or service and end up not being able to detach their thinking about the organization from that product or service.

"To go into business" is to acquire a multidimensional mission that is only partly about products, services, and profits. The reason this is hard to understand is because economists have owned the definition of "the firm" for 200 years, and everyone else has had to scramble for conceptual scraps under the table. But all one has to do is pay attention for a while to what top teams are actually facing for the multidimensional character of the mission to be quite obvious. In Chapter Three I suggested that "effectiveness" is a five-pronged affair: the Economic, the Technological, the Communal, the Sociopolitical, and the Transcendental. "Purposing," I said, is the process of gaining clarity, consensus, and commitment on the mission. It follows that purposing is the development of clarity, consensus, and commitment to a concept of the organization, present and future, that integrates strengths, opportunities, and responsibilities of economic, technological, communal, sociopolitical, and transcendental kinds, and *that* is what the top team ought to be talking about. The only way in the world of permanent white water to "establish and maintain oneself as an organization" is to be prepared to give attention to issues in all five of these categories and to be developing skill in integrating them, and that too is what the top team ought to be talking about.

3. Strategies are initiatives; they are acts of leadership. They are acts of leadership even though they might be strategies that have been followed many times before or that other organizations have used. When playing a game that has never been played before, all strategies are very risky. They represent very complex determinations of what should be done, and as such they are acts of leadership. They are declarations of intent to make certain choices in the future when various particular choice points are reached. The opposite of strategy is expediency, just following one's nose, unless a decision has been made to proceed that way, in which case expediency is a strategy.

4. Along with being initiatives, strategies are consciously thought-out choices, determined after considerable analysis and discussion. As such, strategies are value judgments, no matter how persuasive the supporting data may be. The discussion of various possible strategies and how to choose among them, what criteria to use, is a prime area for talk in the top team. In general, top teams are much more comfortable discussing alternative *business* strategies—that is, choices concerning the development and use of the organization's economic and technical competence—than they are with the many other subjects that the five categories named above present.

5. Not mentioned as often about strategy is the fact that strategy is an organizational change process. Too often the imagery employed about strategy has a very linear quality: strategy as following a pathway, strategy as a trajectory, strategy as a course of action, strategy as a broken-field runner, and so on. If these kinds of images were ever appropriate, they are now obsolete in permanent white water. How a strategy is actually going to be conducted is one of the most important things for

the top team to be talking about, since we don't presently have good imagery for the very complex process of changing a system's character through time. The statement of the strategy is a statement of intent to change the organization in some way for some reason. How this intent will play out in the organization is another matter entirely. Sometimes it is called "implementation" of strategy.

The question of how to think about the process of practicing (or implementing) the strategy is one of those subjects where it might be possible to develop some very rich and complex models. Such models would be beside the point if they did not emanate from a particular top team and focus on a particular set of organizational circumstances. What is wrong with the field of strategic management is that we have thought we could model it apart from the energy, enthusiasm, and commitment of a particular management team. A strategic planning/management model is meaningless without convictions of its rightness built right in. It is like modeling churchgoing without including anything about the kind and degree of devotion felt by the attendees. The problem is not to build a complex model of the process apart from a management team. The problem is how the team can evolve a way of thinking about the process that it believes in, is committed to bringing about, and enjoys in the process. (What a quaint notion—the idea that the implementation of strategy should be enjoyable!) Evolving this way of thinking is what the top team should be talking about.

6. The comments above about ownership and commitment, about the environment, and about a change process through time lead me to a very simple model of what the strategic management process is, a model that is so simple that a picture does not even have to be drawn of it. For all the issues that have to do with executives' and other members' values, feelings, energies, and commitments, I employ the word *inward*. For all the questions about the environment of the strategic unit, I use the word *outward*. And for the question of movement through time into the future, not surprisingly I use the word *forward*. The inward-outward-forward (IOF) scheme permits us to add something significant to the definition of *purposing* given above.

In that statement, there is reference to a "concept of the organization." The IOF model tells us where to look for that concept. The five categories of economic, technological, communal, sociopolitical, and transcendental tell us what the concept is going to be about.

As soon as we say that the *what* is these five categories, the *where* is inward, outward, and forward, and the *why* is the fulfillment of the mission—that is, purposing—the question of "How?" naturally poses itself. That most fundamentally is exactly what the top team should be talking about.

Organizational Behavior in the Top Team

The main reason for the question of what the top team should be talking about is the wide agreement that the modern organization can't count on enlightened, creative, effective one-man or one-woman leadership. People such as Lee Iacocca, Rene McPherson, and H. Ross Perot are regularly cited as examples of the kind of strategic leadership we need more of. But, sad to say, we don't know how, as a society, to do much more than we have been doing to provide for the emergence of such individuals. There is a tremendous amount going on among today's executive development professionals trying to see how organizations and other institutions can do a better job of fostering strategic leadership; I think that there are some important breakthroughs coming.

Unfortunately, it is not a question that most American graduate schools of management and administration are capable of taking too seriously, because they have become so heavily "tenured in" with quantitatively oriented technical specialists. Although this chapter is not primarily about long-range educational strategies for developing strategic leaders, I have devoted space at the end to outlining what I think an eighteen- to twenty-four-month educational experience for strategic leadership might look like. The door is standing open for educational institutions to implement such programs if they have or can create the flexibility these programs require.

Strategic management *is* organizational behavior, whether you are one of the towering charismatic leaders with global influence and repute or "just another vice-president" who sits down a couple of times a month in the "executive committee" to talk about how your company is doing and wonders from time to time whether the group is making as good use of its time as it might. The various kinds of "working smarter" described in Chapter One are all relevant to the question of what the top team should be talking about and how. The tendency may be to opt for the familiar modes—the ones that are already about as fully utilized as they can be: working harder, working technically smarter, and working politically smarter. It is perhaps time for top teams to look carefully at the other three modes mentioned in Chapter One: working collectively smarter, working reflectively smarter, and working spiritually smarter.

My perception, however, is that there are severe difficulties facing many top teams—difficulties that have the curious, almost diabolical quality of masquerading as strengths. Consider the kinds of attitudes and skills many executives have developed in order to get into a position to be on the top team in the first place. They have developed a *strong action orientation,* which may be ill suited for the increased complexity of strategic issues. They have had to be *competitive* and have learned how to gain the advantage in meetings and other settings. In American culture, competitive advantage often goes to those with clear concepts and lots of accurate, well-arrayed facts. Strategic issues typically don't fit within clear concepts, nor are they famous for being surrounded with a high quantity and quality of facts. These executives' business sense is often their strongest suit, but now at the strategic level, with its future orientation, knowledge of the present business may not be an asset, may even be a liability, and in any case, the subjects discussed range far beyond the limits of the business in economic and technical terms.

Top team members have developed an *astute sense of the political realities* and know in particular how to defer to the real power at the head of the table. But meanwhile, more and more men and women who are in the position of "the real power" are looking to their top teams for ideas, for feedback, for willingness to work together more effectively. More and more CEOs are realizing that coping with the permanent white water simply has to be a team effort, but when they look at their colleagues, they think they see a group that evidently wants to go on with the typical waltzing around each other they have always done. Meanwhile, team members look at the boss and wonder whether he or she will ever wake up to the perilous shape the organization is in. It is a tragic two-ships-in-the-night problem.

A final quality that deserves special mention is that top team members who have come up through the ranks in American organizations have learned how to control their feelings very well. Control of feelings is one of the strongest aspects of the "unique common psychology" of the American managerial culture. There are strong beliefs that go with it, and there are various well-developed techniques for exerting control. To a remarkable degree, it works; that is, senior executives in American organizations know how to keep control of themselves in the midst of the most extraordinary situations where the stakes are very high, the pressure intense, the uncertainty and ambiguity of the situation enveloping everything.

The problem with a high degree of control of feelings in a top team is that they can't know what is really going on with each other. People can misread each other's commitment. They can possess key pieces of information that they don't feel comfortable sharing. One or more can be deeply concerned, even intensely fearful about how some business problem will be dealt with, but in not revealing their degree of genuine concern, they may be detracting from the amount of effort the team puts into the issue. Where feelings are masked, a norm of "I'll take care of my shop and you take care of yours" frequently develops, and this undercuts any possible collaborations and sharing of resources that might have been possible. Where intense riskiness is felt but not expressed, a norm of "you-first-ism" often develops. No one is willing to put the performance of his or her own unit in jeopardy, so while supporting innovation and new approaches, managers never volunteer their own units as the place where some new experiment will be tried. Controlled feelings often get projected onto the boss, and he or she is blamed for the suffocating atmosphere of the meetings. "After all," as a top team member said to me recently, the boss "is going to do what he pleases anyway, so why speak up? He doesn't really mean it when he says he wants input. If I really need something or have something important to tell him, I'll see him privately." Perhaps most tragically of all, the norm of controlling feelings keeps a person who may be having a personal life crisis from expressing very much of the problem to team colleagues. The existence of the crisis may not be revealed at all. There is a great deal of private anguish in residence around the typical top team conference table. An incredibly powerful belief supports this conspiracy of discretion, the belief that if the team members reveal their humanness to each other, it will somehow hurt the organization. Top teams ought to find ways of testing the validity of this belief. That is definitely something to talk about.

A climate of controlled feelings is very vulnerable to the dialexia I described in the last chapter. Dialexia is ritualistic discussion, the appearance of substance, the appearance of interest. Dialexia fills up meeting time, and since it is about the affairs of the organization, it doesn't appear to be a waste of time. But it doesn't go anywhere. Meanwhile, each member of the top team is sitting there thinking that the meeting is something to be tolerated, a necessary interruption to what is really important—namely, running one's own piece of the business.

In all of this, of course, the strategic agenda of the organization languishes. Each member may be able to give a personal account of what it is; in various interviews with top team members, I have heard elegant, incisive summaries of the organization's situation, present and future. The trouble is that only rarely does such insight get expressed in top team meetings and used in the formulation of the organization's strategies.

Time, Feeling, and Focus in the Top Team

In an earlier essay (Vaill, 1982), I said that leaders of high-performing systems manifest high degrees of what I called time, feeling, and focus. *Time* refers to the consistently long hours leaders devote to their systems. They are usually not compulsive workaholics, but they are working all the time. Also, they typically stay in their jobs longer than counterparts who are not in charge of high-performing systems. *Feeling* refers to the clarity with which they express their respect for and devotion to both the work of the system and the people in it. No one is mixed up about where the boss stands on things. They are the very opposite of the consciously controlled managers I was describing a minute ago. Not that leaders are necessarily emotional, demonstrative men and women. Each has a personal way, though, of coming through as an authentic human being. *Focus* means simply that they know the activity thoroughly. They have an almost incredible ability to put their finger on the two or three things pending at any moment that most need attention for high performance. The things they focus on bear a material relation to the mission; they are matters that pervade system operations; they are matters that are relevant to the system's future; and they are matters that other members can also see need to be attended to.

Members of high-performing systems typically find working with their bosses thrilling. Such people's understanding of what needs to be done is astonishing (focus), their availability and willingness to stay on something until it's done is refreshing (time), and through it all they are interesting and memorable people to be around (feeling). The best purposing is done by leaders who possess these qualities of time, feeling, and focus. They are so effective at making their vision and sense of mission real to others that one can almost reach the conclusion that purposing is in fact quite easy. Of course, it isn't, but the fact that plenty of men and women, as leaders of high-performing systems, do it with ease, do it with hardly a thought about it, means that it is not mysterious, exotic behavior. It is right there in front of us if we can understand it.

It is right there in the top team, too. The biggest problem with top teams is the distorting of feeling that I described earlier. Typically, top teams already possess the willingness to commit time, and typically they possess or can acquire the technical knowledge about strategy for the focus category. But they may feel somewhat blocked about feeling. That's the main sensation—feeling blocked.

How to unblock? What realistically can a top team do, a team that may be beset by competitiveness and suspicion masking as cordiality? There is not a good, single, reliable answer to this. The field of OD has a well-developed strategy called "team development" that might be used, but the problem is that it hasn't been used very often on top teams, and there aren't many consultant-facilitators available who can work effectively with top teams. Explicit team development is a leading edge that has promise, but it is still in its infancy.

The Top Team and Organizational Health

There are two other strategies whereby the top team might improve its own capacity to talk within itself while at the same time benefiting the organization. One is a strategy of immediate intervention. The other is to go back to school together.

Even though a top team might have trouble addressing its own blocked feelings head on, what it can do is initiate a process of working on the whole organization's manifestation of the same problem. Throughout this volume, I have been pointing out what a powerful effect the stresses of permanent white water are having on the members of the organization. Particularly the last two chapters make it quite clear that the modern organization is a place where everyone is just barely holding on. I think that it is time for the top team to start talking about how to relieve some of the pressure on people in the organization. This is a complex issue, of course, and not one that executives should just start jabbing at randomly. But the resources for thinking through strategies for improving organizational climate are available and in many cases are already on the payroll. There is already a large body of case history, for many organizations have already taken steps, in some cases very dramatic ones.

My expectation is that sustained consideration of how to improve the climate of the organization will improve the climate in the top team. The climate of the organization is something they have in common and value in common despite differences in the pieces of the business they are responsible for. It may be a little manipulative to hope that the top team will start talking about feelings within itself by focusing first on the feelings of others, but I don't think so. The dilemmas the top team will face if it takes the question of climate seriously can't help but raise questions of personal values and commitments within the top team. All the dilemmas and trade-offs of my five dimensions of effectiveness suddenly become important to talk about. It becomes important to look inward, outward, and forward to understand what is affecting the climate of the organization.

Going back to school together—the second strategy—capitalizes on three things: (1) that the education in strategic management is needed anyway and that it is best framed as group education, since it will be a group conducting the strategy; (2) that top teams benefit in their work together by getting away from the pressures of the job and into situations where they still must work together, but on matters that are one step removed from operating the business; and (3) that we know that groups are regularly able to have high-quality experiences together in educational settings. These three factors create a powerful synergy for a top team. Any group that together went through what I am about to describe would have no trouble answering the question posed by this chapter.

Ideally, top teams from four or five organizations would go through the program together. It might make a group of somewhere between thirty and fifty people. All would presumably be experienced managers and already familiar, to some extent at least, with the strategic issues facing their organizations. For the most part, even those with M.B.A. degrees would have had little if any opportunity to read, write, and talk about problems of the governance and guidance of large systems. Thus, much of the material would be quite new as academic material, although it would all exist in practical form in the participants' organizations.

The program might consist of four broad themes, each one receiving about four to six months of emphasis. (Obviously, participants would be "in class" one or two days a week, at most, but because of the complexity of the subject matter, several months on each topic is appropriate.) These themes are as follows:

1. *Strategic Leadership*—the whole question of what we think we know about leadership of large systems; theories and data from all organizational sectors; the psychology of large system leadership, the nature of "strategic consciousness"; opportunity for self-assessment of leadership attitudes and abilities; presentations by successful strategic leaders; application of material to each top team's own organization.

2. *Organizations and environments*—building on 1., a detailed examination of how organizations are interconnected with their environments; major emphasis on stakeholders, mutual influence between organizations and stakeholders; considerations of public/private sector relationships, tensions, dilemmas; implications of what this book has called "permanent white water" and of other theories about the same phenomena.

3. *Anticipating the future*—the state of the art on anticipating the future in complex systems; discussion of major social, political, economic, technological trends; how to think about futures in general, rather than just "what's the future going to be like?"; putting themes 1. and 2. into motion, that is, viewing them as processes in time; trying to learn to think in terms of organizational evolution; exercises to lengthen each team's time perspective.

4. *Personal assessment and development*—readings, exercises, and discussions dealing with team members as persons, issues of stress and other medical matters; personal values, adult development, family relationships; career issues; opportunities for deepening relations among participants, strengthening of deep feeling, commitment to each other.

This is only a sketch, but it covers the kinds of subjects and experiences that I think top teams need. As I have said, they particularly need to develop feeling as a group to go with their more developed capacity to focus on the right issues and their well-developed, maybe overdeveloped willingness to put in time. To be high in time and focus without feeling is to be "competent" but not very deep or very real. To be high in focus and feeling without time is to be "wise" but not very energetic.

To be high in feeling and time without focus is to possess what we call "spirit" but perhaps to lack content to go with that inner light. What we want in the top team, and what I think it should basically be talking about, is how it is going to go about developing itself as a group of competent, wise, and spirited persons.

One More Message from George

George Washington doubtless possessed the qualities of time, feeling, and focus when he issued the order quoted at the beginning of this chapter. But a year later he became exercised by something of possibly less strategic significance than that call to arms. He wrote from his New York headquarters: "The General is sorry to be informed that the foolish and wicked practice of profane cursing and swearing, a device heretofore little known in an American Army, is growing into fashion. He hopes the officers will, by example as well as influence, endeavor to check it, and that both they and the men will reflect, that we can have little hope of the blessing of heaven on our arms if we insult it by our impiety and folly. Added to this, it is a vice so mean and low, without any temptation, that every man of sense and character detests and despises it" (from a wall hanging in Washington Hall, U.S. Army War College, Carlisle, Pennsylvania).

Maybe we should give George the benefit of the doubt here and chalk up this directive as a not very graceful attempt at spiritual leadership. But there's a little too much haughty annoyance in it for that. I think that George was having a tantrum. Somehow, it is rather comforting to know that even George Washington occasionally erred in what he should be talking about.

Chapter 12

Taoist Management: "Composedly They Went and Came"

The thirtieth chapter of the *Tao Te Ching* (Lao Tzu, 1972) reads as follows:

Whenever you advise a ruler in the way of Tao,
Counsel him not to use force to conquer the universe.
For this would only cause resistance.
Thorn bushes spring up wherever the army has passed.
Lean years follow in the wake of a great war.
Just do what needs to be done.
Never take advantage of power.

Achieve results,
But never glory in them.
Achieve results,
But never boast.
Achieve results,
But never be proud.
Achieve results,
Because this is the natural way.
Achieve results,
But not through violence.

Force is followed by loss of strength.
This is not the way of Tao.
That which goes against the Tao
   comes to an early end.

This wonderful summary of the ingredients of effective leadership was my first introduction to Taoist thinking. The comments in this chaper are the tentative reflections of one who is both puzzled and fascinated by one of the central concepts of Taoism as developed in the eighty-one chapters of the *Tao Te Ching*—the notion of "wu-wei," or "nonaction." Taoism certainly is not a subject like the plane geometry of the American high school sophomore in which finally, exactly, either one gets the right answer or one doesn't. Taoist thinking is much more elliptical and elusive, to me, anyway. It is a rather meaningless comparison, I suppose, but Lao Tzu, presumed author of the *Tao Te Ching,* precedes Euclid by something over two hundred years. Let us see what we can make of his thinking.

The Question

Supposedly, translation makes a difference when studying the *Tao Te Ching.* Therefore, I have included excerpts from chapters 2 and 3 of the book as rendered by three different translators.

Chang Translation

Thus, the wise deals with things through non-interference
   and teaches through no-words [Chang, 1975, p. 6].
When action is through non-action,
   no one is uncultivated [p. 10].

Waley Translation

Therefore, the Sage relies on actionless activity,
Carries on wordless teaching [Waley, 1958, p. 143].
Yet through his actionless activity
   all things are duly regulated [p. 145].

Feng and English Translation

Therefore the sage goes about doing nothing,
  teaching no-talking [Lao Tzu, 1972, p. 2].
If nothing is done, then all will be well [p. 5].

"In the context of Taoist writings," says Alan Watts
(1975), *wei* "quite clearly means forcing, meddling, and arti-
fice—in other words, trying to act against the grain of *li*. Thus
wu-wei as 'not forcing' is what we mean by going with the grain,
rolling with the punch, swimming with the current, trimming
sails to the wind, taking the tide at its flood, and stooping to
conquer" (p. 76). (*Li* is defined on p. 46 as "organic order as
distinct from mechanical or legal order.")
    In the remainder of this chapter, I want to explore the
relation of wu-wei to the Western managerial idea of "taking
action." To anticipate a bit, I think it is possible that wu-wei
is a more powerful idea about taking action in conditions of permanent white water than anything, at least of a systematic kind,
that we have produced in the West. The Watts remark just
quoted is quite clear, but the application of it to Western organizational situations is quite another matter, calling for considerable reflection.

The Nature of Wu-wei

    So much Taoist writing is in the style of polarity, of com-
ing and going, forth and back. The subtitle of this chapter is
from Chuang-tzu, a successor of Lao Tzu's. "Returning is the
motion of the Tao," says the fortieth chapter of *Tao Te Ching*
(Lao Tzu, 1972). It is a style of thinking that, though not absent from Western consciousness, must contend constantly in
the West with another mode, the idea of "Forward!", with
little recognition of the opposite tendency being simultaneously
present. The wu-wei of nonaction is especially foreign. The
Western mind expects that if vigorous action is not taken, things
that are not wanted will take over. "The future belongs to those
who prepare for it" captures this expectation, with the implication that if you don't prepare, you will get a future you don't

want. "When the going gets tough, the tough get going" again implies that only vigorous action will overcome difficulty. "Overcoming," indeed, is all through our thinking about action. Overcoming tremendous odds is a frequent theme in our mythology of leadership. We love underdogs who triumph. Notice that *what* is overcome is usually left vague and indefinite. It is not a technical statement we are making when we speak of overcoming tremendous odds but a romantic statement. We are describing the *feel* of action rather than the actual field of action. When one looks closely at the true field of action, it is often apparent that conditions were actually quite ready for the action, and the "overcoming" image is not really a good description of what happened. It is our "unique common psychology" that makes us feel we are struggling and overcoming, when another UCP could feel it quite differently.

Perhaps at some level below conscious thought, Western managers and other action takers might be better at "going with the flow" and "moving with the available energy" than we like to think. Montagu (1952) argued that in nature, cooperation is much more common than contention, and that using the Darwinian idea of "struggle" to justify competition, exploitation, and violence is really a vast anthropomorphizing of what actually happens in nature (and, says Montagu, is not an interpretation that Darwin agreed with). If Montagu is right, it helps us understand the frequent appearance of men and women who have a "feel" for what can be accomplished in a situation, who have a "nice touch." Maybe we can recognize in others what our UCP makes it hard to see in ourselves.

Insight into our ideas about action can also be found in sports and in the performing arts, where some physical action has to be performed at a very high level of excellence but where there is also an important mental component. Hitting a golf ball, playing a rapid violin passage, executing a dive or a gymnastic move—these are good examples. It is well known that one can think too much about these actions, one can "press" and break up the routine, habitual flow of motion that is the key to excellent performance. Even the most accomplished performers are not immune to this problem. *Concentration* is the word we usc to talk about some kind of right frame of mind to be in, but this does not begin to capture what is actually going on in the performer's mind, nor does it hint at what the phenomenon "loss of concentration" is.

It is possible that the Taoist's wu-wei is the Westerner's "peak performance" in the best sense of the phrase—the integration and complete attunement of mental and physical and probably spiritual energies and awarenesses. A major difference, though, is that the Taoist drops both notions of "peak" and "performance," I think, and instead seeks to extend that consciousness to all of life. In the West, we have the idea of this type of action sequestered, as it were, in stylized performance. We have a kind of "enclavitis"; that is, we think that really quality action is possible only under very special conditions. A diver, for example, who can give a magically Taoist-like account of the state of mind-body-spirit as she poses for a dive gets no support from our culture to achieve the same state in preparing for the postcompetition press conference. If she does get into a special attuned state for the press conference, it is seen as a personal trait and not a a clue to anything larger or deeper. The press refer to her as "gracious," and the matter is left at that. Our Western UCP is interested in her ability to dive; the Taoist is interested in her ability to extend her diving-being to her life in general.

Language is part of this whole issue. So much Western imagery has to do with overcoming and with triumph, as I have said. Maybe we should just let our tough, exploitative language alone and get on with the quest for Taoist forms of consciousness and action even though we have to talk about them in hard-edged, mechanistic phrases. Management isn't really a martial art, but we talk about it as if it were. Virtually every part of the body has associated with it a phrase that is routinely used to describe what we do to each other in organizations, from little things, such as having one's nose tweaked or knuckles rapped, to fairly major things, such as getting cut off at the knees or drawn and quartered (Vaill, 1984–85).

I don't think that trying to ignore language is a very satisfactory arrangement, though. It is only through thinking and through language that we can get to whatever truth the Taoist has for us. After all, it is in language that Lao Tzu (Waley, 1958, p. 143) says across the centuries, "the Sage relies on . . . wordless teaching." Perhaps wu-wei in its quest for Tao works in words as much as in physical action, especially for our Western minds, which are so soaked in verbosity and dialexia (Chapter Ten). Perhaps in words, wu-wei is most operative not when I am choosing my words but when there is a kind of no-action operating in them—when the ideas are just flowing out, expressing experience and feeling and cognition, without somehow being mediated through some choosing process in which words are crafted "for the occasion" or "for effect." We have all had the experience of seeing how the lecture, the briefing, the testimony starts to get interesting only when the speaker departs from the script and starts coming "from the heart." Spontaneity—once again something that we know well at the level of experience but that we routinely violate in our formal conduct of organizations.

A wu-wei of conversation, of problem solving, of strategic planning—my sense is that we in the West have not tended to think of the promise of Taoist philosophy and practices in terms of the use of words. It has been identified with dramatic changes in life-style, typically in the direction of various ascetic practices, and with the martial arts. A wu-wei on the telephone, a wu-wei of the job interview, a wu-wei of the annual report: these are the kinds of communicative occasions when our Western "forcing" mentality is most evident. A wu-wei of the traffic jam. Later in this chapter, I will try to refocus our view a bit. I will take various highly verbal modes of managerial action and discuss how they might change if we approached them more in a posture of wu-wei than we presently do.

Wu-wei is reaching for a sense of action as the spontaneous expression of being and is calling attention to all the ways that this spontaneity can be distorted, blocked, and otherwise confused by—by what? By thought? But "thought" is part of this spontaneous being. Wu-wei is interested in the integration of our incredible thinking capacity with our action. Thought is not action, and the two can get dramatically split. Thought by itself creates no effects, makes no one angry, moves no mountains, instigates nothing. Maybe wu-wei is a meditation on this: thought is so powerful in its suggestive capacity, but so impotent in its implementive capacity, that it must somehow cast itself in terms that set the rest of the organism in motion. Thought must live in the imperative, for how else can it get us up and doing? Wu-wei is possibly calling attention to this quality of thought in the hope that we will see that in reality thought is only conjectural and cannot compel action. If some need for action is looked at for its own sake, unvarnished by the imperatives, elaborations, and obsessions of thought, one might find that much less action and much gentler action is called for than Western can-do values might suggest, that there is more energy already in motion than thought has noticed, and that there already is implicit a likely outcome of the situation that exists irrespective of what imperative thought wants.

Wu-wei suggests that unless we can see this about ourselves in situations, imperative thought will lead us to try things that are unrealistic, inappropriate, uncalled for, and that our action may then become one more of the complicating elements of the situation rather than having the relieving, resolving effect we intended. Wu-wei seeks actions that fit and that harmonize with situations, with one's own understanding treated as *part* of the situation. By contrast, the Western philosophy of the role of mind and thought would have it independent of the situation, would have it objective, rational, and able to exert itself as a force from outside. This is what is behind the doctrine of comprehension and control that was so sharply questioned in Chapter Five. It is worth pausing once more, though, to note just how profoundly American managers are encouraged to view themselves as detached from the organizations they manage and able in relative freedom to analyze these organizations and plan interventions into them. *Interventions*—the very word implies that one is standing outside. Contrast this with the approach that was suggested in Chapter Five—" . . . a mentality that experienced itself . . . as growing from within the organization and influencing it as an expression of that personal growth process." There may be no more important distinction discussed in this book than this one.

These ideas about imperative thought are also relevant

to the question of what in ourselves we need to confront to move into more of a wu-wei state. The West does have an alternative to single-minded, goal-directed, can-do thought. It is called "critical thinking" or "reflection" or more exotic things, such as "reflexivity" and "self-referencing." Argyris has popularized the notion of "double-loop learning" and makes it the essence of maturity (Argyris and Schön, 1974). But there is such intensity in the way that we are counseled to practice critical thinking, these chapters not excepted. Wu-wei might view such energetic rationalism as possibly a step backward. Just across a relatively invisible line from critical thinking, remember, is the obsessive wheel spinning I dubbed "dialexia."

What might be the problem with critical thought? It always is displaced from the moment—that is its essence, when the Taoist might like us to be more *in* the moment, free of habits and reasons for stepping out of the moment. We step back when we reflect, forward when we plan. We step in some sideways fashion when we "compare and contrast." We step up when we generalize ("The guiding principle here is . . . ") and down when we particularize ("This is nothing but a case of . . . "), and so on. We are all around the moment, but there has not been much emphasis in our culture on just being effective in the moment. About the only thing that one can be in the moment is wu-wei—a kind of nonprincipled, nonjustified, nonthought-out, noncalculated action. It is not a passivity, or not in its essence a passivity, though on some occasions wu-wei might be quiescent, but it might just as easily be terribly concentrated, explosive. It may go on at the top of the lungs. But these adjectives are all beside the point, for as long as they are in the moment, they have the wu-wei quality. "Beside the point," by the way, as an expression that banishes an idea from consideration, perhaps reveals the Western mind's half-conscious realization of how much thinking and action is not really relevant to what is going on here and now.

It is consciousness in relation to the world outside it that I think we are talking about. Wu-wei is conscious of all the ways consciousness can "get it wrong." The Western mind likes problems where only a few things can go wrong, and that are structured enough that you can find your mistake and correct it. Real life is not like this, of course. It is not a problem that somebody made up for you but is instead a continuously unfolding and infinitely chambered set of possibilities. Consciousness has a terrible time figuring out where it went wrong in "real life"; that is, in figuring out why it evidently failed to understand a situation and accidentally produced consequences it did not intend. In the twentieth century, we have put consciousness on the couch, drugged it, operantly conditioned and behavior modified it, preached at it, tried to suppress it with genocide, tried to get it to be born again, tried to lead it and manage it, tried to supersede it with artificial intelligence—it is not an exaggeration to say that the transformation of consciousness has been the twentieth century's chief preoccupation. Wu-wei would see much of all this as relatively fruitless, I think—that is, if the objective is somehow to get *control* of consciousness and to help consciousness understand itself in its circumstances a little better.

"Itself in its circumstances"—that really is the problem. The Western mind wants consciousness to understand its circumstances but not itself *as an ongoing part* of those circumstances. That is what we have such a hard time with as managers and leaders. Too much of our theory depends on the manager being a relatively free agent who will operate on the system from the outside.

The Western mind assumes that with more careful analysis of these "circumstances," it will be able to operate efficiently from the outside. It cites its incredible success in the physical and biological sciences as evidence. This ethos has carried over into our thinking about leading and managing human beings in organizations, even though the transfer is full of very questionable assumptions, as several of the chapters in this book have tried to show.

The Western mind is also very skeptical of the alternative—that is, of *not* attempting to influence events and circumstances from the outside using science or whatever other leverage is available. To put it in positive terms, the Western mind might argue that humanity's special genius is precisely the capacity to make conscious value judgments from the "outside" of situations about what is useful and not useful, valuable and not valuable, good and bad, right and wrong. Humanity's ability to formulate projects, so to speak, and tenaciously pursue them in the face of adversity is the thing that is special about it. People are the creators and achievers of values that would not be created and achieved were people's rational consciousness not operating on the situation. Aren't people fundamentally "countersituational" in that they never accept things as they are? This I believe summarizes the kind of objection that might be made to all this talk about "nonaction" and immersion in the here and now.

I think that this set of objections is a misunderstanding of wu-wei, though—and, indeed, a very Western way of misunderstanding in its insistence on the significance of human achievement. I don't think that there is any project or course of action that is ruled out by Taoist philosophy and the attitude toward action called wu-wei. It is not what is indicated or not indicated by this way of thinking; rather, it is the frame of mind one is in with respect to any action. The stanza with which I began this chapter, after all, puts no limit on the *kind* of results to be achieved but is very concerned about what the meaning of those results is taken to be.

The wu-wei consciousness is looking for synergy in any project. It includes itself as part of the mix but also pays a lot of attention to all the other elements it can identify. It is a perfect consciousness, I think, for action in complex systems. It is sensitive to the problems of peak performance discussed in Chapter Four. It seems quite capable of remaining friendly to the paradoxes reviewed in Chapter Five. I think that it would be free of the technoholism described in Chapter Six and the dialexia of Chapter Ten.

As to whether wu-wei is "ambitious" enough, whether it would set demanding standards, whether it would really strive for *excellence* as discussed in Chapter Three, I think the answer is that "synergic excellence" is a quite different kind of excellence than the sort we are more familiar with in Western culture. Integrating the five dimensions of value discussed in Chapters Three and Eleven quite clearly must be a search for synergy, for in

a very real sense, those five categories are "apples and oranges."
The Economic, Technological, Communal, Sociopolitical, and
Transcendental live by quite different laws and principles, are
concerned with different data, have different terms of success,
as it were. To say that they must *all* be balanced and integrated
is a severe test. A Taoist mentality, by the way, would want
us to be very careful with these five categories to make sure that
we did not drift into treating them as structural properties of
situations within which to accumulate research findings and then
seek to take actions that "optimize" across the categories.

What aerobics is in bodily activity makes a nice analogy
for "synergic excellence" in wu-wei terms. Aerobic exercise is
sustained activity that stays within the body's limits to take in
oxygen and eliminate the wastes that accumulate in the muscles
and blood from the exercise. One seeks not the *limit* but the
balance. "Effectiveness" is maintaining the balance, and over
a longer period of time, through what is called "conditioning,"
the level at which the balance can be maintained rises. But one
does not make the mistake of thinking that it is possible to take
a shortcut to the higher level just by injecting imperatives into
the system that insist that it perform at a higher level. It is not
the imperatives that contribute to the rise, but the conditioning.

There are plenty of Western managers and leaders who
understand their roles this way, who think "aerobically," so
to speak. It is just that they are not getting much support from
the managerial culture at large or from the local reward systems
of their organizations for thinking this way. The wu-wei philosophy contains such support.

On Taking Nonaction

Earlier in this chapter, I said that I would give some examples of what the style of wu-wei as I understand it might look
like in the conduct of leading and managing as we think of it
in Western terms. Clearly, the wu-wei wants to keep our world
from getting carved up into little categories, for no sooner do
we create categories than we begin to evolve structures and forces
to maintain the categories, and after a while the structures and

forces that were created to maintain the categories become objects of maintenance themselves, and so on, and so on. This is the ''segmentalism'' that Kanter (1983) has criticized so tellingly. There are three kinds of fragmentation that especially dog us in management, and wu-wei is very clear about all three. We split off the *present from the future* and become much more interested in the latter. We split off *thought from action* and spend our time building elaborate mental castles in the air, which we find have to be compromised in all directions in order to be implemented. And we split off *manager from system managed* and then spin elaborate prescriptions about what the system needs and what the manager ought to do about it.

To maintain the unity of time, the unity of thought and action, and the unity of self and environment—this is what wu-wei attempts. It sounds tremendously ambitious when phrased in such sweeping terms, but I think that there has actually been much evidence in American management over the past twenty-five years of an urge to reunify these fragmentations. For example, in Chapter One, I discussed seven myths about the manager in the organization. A wu-wei mentality would reconceive each of these seven and in so doing would be cooperating with many other trends pointing in the same directions.

The myth of a single person called the manager, for example, would be replaced by a view that accepted the managing that goes on everywhere in the organization, by everyone. The split between manager and managee, and the implicit imbalance in responsibility that accompanies it, would be altered in a newer view. This notion of everyone taking responsibility for the system as a whole has become widespread. The second myth, of a single freestanding organization, would be altered to a more embracing view that understood the ''organization'' as just a very fragile and temporary abstraction from the totality, not a monolith but more of a soap bubble, subject to and responsive to a vast range of influences. Wu-wei would seek to reduce the siege mentality that so many managers develop about their organizations. Control through a pyramidal chain of command, the third myth, would be replaced by a more democratic way of talking about power, and this is in fact what has been happening in Western organizations through the participative management movement. More broadly, society as a whole has seen a trend toward empowerment of the disenfranchised. This consciousness is widespread and cannot help but continue to influence organizations profoundly. Myth number four, the myth of the organization as pure instrument, would be replaced by an understanding of an organization as a field within which myriad purposes and processes play out. The irrelevance of culture, myth number five, would be replaced by an understanding of the "UCPs" of various organization members as part of the synergy that any course of action should seek. Wu-wei would be particularly conscious of our present tendency to ask organization members to suppress those parts of their UCP that don't fit with what the organization is asking of them. The sixth myth, that the primary output of the organization is a product, would be seen by wu-wei to be a futile attempt by the organization to formalize and standardize its activity and to delimit the nature of its relations with and responsibilities to its customers. Wu-wei would seek a heightened awareness of all the other things the organization is and does to generate its outputs and all the other forms of output it creates besides product packages. And finally, the seventh myth, that rational analysis is the chief means for understanding and directing the organization, would be replaced by a view of rational analysis that keeps it related to a philosophy of life that itself transcends rational analysis. This last myth requires considerably more discussion, and the next chapter is devoted to that. The problem is that if rational analysis reigns supreme, awareness and experience end up in fragments. But if rational analysis is to be made subordinate to something else, the question is how to do that without lapsing into antirationalism and dogma.

Beyond its contribution to transforming these various myths, there are a number of specific modern issues in management that wu-wei might have a refreshing view of. For example, about twenty-five years ago in Southern California, aerospace companies were beginning to talk about so-called matrix structures. But there has been hardly any innovation since World War II that has been more misunderstood than matrix structures. It is easy to describe the structural change from a bureaucratic chain of command. The problem, though, has been to clarify what a matrix structure means for the attitudes and actions of those living in it. Some have "muddled through" to an operating philosophy that works and that is very consistent with wu-wei ideas about thinking holistically and synergetically. But too many people never have figured out what the new structure means and so spend their time cursing the matrix and wishing for more clarity and order.

Those who have been able to make participative management and two-way communication work have tended to take a view of these practices that is consistent with wu-wei thinking. These ideas and practices bring the manager into quite a different relation with subordinates. Their energy and their ideas are invited into the manager's or leader's thinking. Too many managers don't realize that when you become truly participative, you get into a lot of uncomfortable conversations in which you hear things about the situation and about yourself that you may not like. Wu-wei awareness, of course, is not surprised by this.

In Chapter Four, I spoke of the need for "high-performing boundary spanning" in order to keep groups of high-performing systems or skunk works more or less in communication and coordination with each other. The wu-wei consciousness is essential for this linking work, I think, and it is also an example of how wu-wei need not be passive. Clearly, to keep a group of high-powered skunk works on track with each other is going to be hard work. The wu-wei attitudes of looking for synergy, of patience, of being accepting of emergent events, of never seeking to abstract oneself from the situation but instead embedding oneself in it, are all qualities that seem essential for effective performance.

"Management by wandering around" (Peters and Waterman, 1982) is basically an expression of wu-wei consciousness. It cannot be a management technique, though. Its essence is its spontaneity, its capacity to take an interest in whatever turns up, its willingness to match its agenda with the agendas it finds in the situations it wanders into. If it becomes a management technique, we will begin to talk about the better and worse ways to perform it. We will begin to discuss it in terms of "competency," and it will become the object of training programs and, ultimately, credit courses in management schools. All of this obviously will wreck it. Precious ideas for working in the world can get wrecked if they are used exploitatively for personal advantage. In some ways, that process is the history of management thought. Let us hope that it does not happen to this delightful notion of management by wandering around.

Does the "one-minute manager" (Blanchard and Johnson, 1982) have wu-wei consciousness? From all the jokes there have been about this concept, one's first reaction might be "no way." But in a curious sense, the one-minute-manager concept confronts us with the assumptions we make about what it takes to be effective and authentic in human systems. If the one-minute manager thinks that he or she can read a book and just start dealing skillfully and effectively with people, he or she, of course, is wrong, and the concept is an absurdity. But maybe there is something deeper here, not so much in the way the concept has been presented and discussed but in the way that it *might* be presented. I am thinking of the "flip" that is sometimes necessary to grasp a really new notion, the all-at-once insight that rearranges and reinterprets our understanding. The question is whether wu-wei consciousness is hard-won wisdom that is built up idea by idea, experience by experience, brick by brick. My hunch is that the process is different from this. Some background awareness of the possibility of wu-wei is needed, and that can accumulate by an ordinary learning process. But at some point a jump occurs, all at once, into this different frame of mind about everything. It might be that the one-minute manager has made that jump and really does see how to do with ease and economy things that the rest of us have to labor over. I don't think that it is very likely that the one-minute-manager as he or she has been written and talked about has the heightened awareness of wu-wei, but it's possible.

This chapter has argued really two things: First, there is a philosophy of life and of action expressed in the *Tao Te Ching* that is very relevant to the issues that leaders and managers in modern Western organizations face. Second, this philosophy can be found in scattered places in Western thinking, but the dominant mentality in splitting future from present, thought from action, and self from world is antithetical to the wu-wei mentality. I know of only one attempt to bring together the full array of Western ideas that are compatible with Asian philosophy (Siu, 1971). The scholarship involved is immense, but the effort is worth making so that the organizations of the entire world may benefit from both the Western genius in devising things for organizations to do and the Eastern realization that the meaning of all such capabilities can emerge only through the most careful and continuous contemplation.

Chapter 13

Management as
Snake Handling

In Chapter Three, I first introduced five broad categories of values that contain the ingredients for an organization's definition of effectiveness: the Economic, the Technological, the Communal, the Sociopolitical, and the Transcendental. I suggested that each category contains values and priorities that an organization must come to terms with: the Economic is concerned with acting to maintain viability in the environment; the Technological is focused on doing the work smoothly and well; the Communal focuses on developing and maintaining a feeling of community and mutual support in the organization; the Sociopolitical addresses the need to be and to be seen as a good citizen in the environment; and, finally, the Transcendental recognizes the need that everyone has to one degree or another to feel that the organization means something more than just what it does or just the money it makes.

I stated that no category can be totally ignored, for each will have one or more vociferous advocates both inside and outside the organization. The five categories of values have come up at various other points in these chapters. It is my position in this book that in the permanent white water of the modern world, organization leader-managers have to find ways of responding to the imperatives for the organization arising from these five categories. I think that in the longer run, the survival of today's organizations depends on doing so. As noted in Chapter Three, I also think that it makes no sense to talk about organizational excellence without developing an approach to the organization's quality in all five of these categories. Excellence must be considered as multidimensional.

However, as suggested in Chapter Twelve, we need to be careful not to make a quasi science out of the problem of reconciling the various strands and themes of these five categories. Since they always present themselves to an organization in a state of jumbled interdependence, and since human interests and advocacy skills are the media through which the values are offered, it means that we rationalize and formularize the process of considering these values at our peril. Basically, the process is human judgment exercised through human communication.

"Good judgment" is always on the lists one sees of what executives consider to be the essential qualities for organization leadership. I concur completely with that assessment, but I want to add one corollary quality that is less often mentioned—a quality, in fact, that I don't think I have ever seen mentioned as an essential and yet that follows directly if we are going to say that an executive needs "good judgment" to lead in defining and pursuing excellence among my five categories of values. This quality is the *ability to have faith in oneself and one's organization.* The organization cannot be managed by "science"; that is, we cannot logically determine what causes will produce what effects. Therefore, we need faith in our judgment, our intuition, our ability to understand ourselves and others, all in some broader environment. And further, this faith is not a blind unconsciousness of what is at stake, not a passive delegation of authority to fate, as it were. Rather, a mature faith is grounded in some broader, deeper view of humanity, of society, and of what we might call the more ultimate things. For some, the grounding is squarely in one of the world's religions; for others, it is a more personal, noninstitutional set of beliefs. Some ground their beliefs beyond the visible world, while others do not. The idea of God plays a role for some and not for others.

A moment's reflection will show, I think, that the crucial matter is the grounding of faith—the quality of it, the awareness that one is doing it, the connection of one's own ground to the searching that others have done over the centuries, and one's ability to let one's faith grow and mature through life and experience. Faith is personal, and I do not intend to advocate any particular mode or doctrine here. Rather, my key point here is the need for faith. In the face of all our half-conscious assumptions about how scientific management and leadership are, I wish to insist on the idea that we cannot banish the need for faith and on the implications of that idea. This chapter's title declares that point.

I thought it might be fun in this chapter to reflect on the need for faith as we act in organizations by imagining what it might be like to talk with five individuals from history whose work has profoundly shaped our thinking. Since I have five categories of values, I have tried to imagine a spokesperson for each, even though each person I have chosen is doubtless quite competent in all five areas.

For the Economic category, Adam Smith, who the *Encyclopaedia Britannica* says was dean of the faculty at the University of Glasgow, has consented to honor us with his presence. We are fortunate that Frederick Winslow Taylor is present to make available his vast knowledge of the rational design and conduct of production systems; he will be our expert for technology. Elton Mayo, the guiding spirit of the landmark Hawthorne research and first professor of human relations at the Harvard Business School, was my first choice to share his perspective on the Communal values, and he has graciously put himself at our disposal. I was less sure of who might be a good spokesperson for the Sociopolitical values, but I settled on John L. Lewis because he did so much to show the need for public accountability of corporations, and although he is primarily identified with unions, his insistence on the companies' responsibilities in the health and safety areas, his knowledge of the evils of company towns, and his influence in government make him a good spokesperson. The Transcendental dimension will be voiced by Ralph Waldo Emerson—there could really be no other choice. As one final note of introduction, I must say that except for

Mayo, I am little more than a casually informed layperson on each man's life and work. Their function in this essay is principally symbolic, and I realize that I risk distorting or trivializing each man's contribution, but I have decided to take the chance. I hope that it is not too indulgent of me to portray myself chairing a meeting of such a company. That is the most fanciful thing of all in this chapter.

Vaill: Gentlemen, thank you for agreeing to speak with me this evening.

Group: (Mumbles, mutters)

Vaill: Let me begin with a statement about why I have requested that we meet this evening. I do appreciate your gracious assistance and sincerely hope I have not caused you any inconvenience. Perhaps I can begin by explaining the title I have given our colloquy.

Lewis: I was wondering about that. Makes me think about the fellows you see back in the hollows in bib overalls and their hair slicked down with Wildroot, humming and swaying, swinging around some of the biggest old snakes you ever saw like they were so much old rope.

Vaill: Well, actually it was those practices I had in mind—for the purpose of a vivid analogy.

Smith: I am not familiar with the practices the gentleman describes. Please enlighten me.

Lewis: They think it is God's will whether they get bit!

Vaill: There is probably a lot of doctrine behind it, but all I want to do is suggest to some who may not think of themselves as handling actual snakes to consider that maybe they are handling metaphorical snakes that might be just as venomous. It is snake handling as an act of faith that I want to use as an analogy. I have asked you to come here not so much because I want you to lecture to me and my friends in your respective disciplines as because I am seeking your reactions to some thoughts of mine.

With the exception of you, Dr. Mayo, I do not possess the competence to hear a lecture from any of you beyond the most elementary level. But I think you may be able to help me with some matters I have been thinking about.

Each of you is a founding father within his area of interest. You probably did not think of yourselves that way at the time you were doing your work, but that is the way it has turned out. Having done some of the basic thinking and faced some of the dilemmas that attend the creation of any new body of ideas, I wish to test my understanding of the grounds of your fields. There have been changes since each of you worked, whether or not you feel they are improvements on your ideas. Still, I think the present foundations of the fields you represent are detectable in your original contributions.

As you know, I have a five-dimensional scheme for talking about the challenges faced by large organizations. Each of you is specially qualified to comment on at least one dimension, and most of you are highly competent in more than one; perhaps in all.

Taylor: I don't see what this has to do with snake handling.

Mayo: He is using a pure case from primitive society to illuminate something whose functional roots have become obscured by the formal overlay of the practices of industrialized society.

Vaill: That is a much more elaborate interpretation than I really intend. Perhaps I had better quickly say what my question to you is before any more confusion develops.

Taylor: Please do.

Vaill: I want to ask you how much faith is involved in the acceptance of the premises and major assertions of your respective fields. I want to ask you what you think of the idea that one who practices the principles of your respective fields does so in a faith that is as thorough and as profound as that of those people back up in the hollows with their snakes.

Emerson: Do you intend, sir, to include me in this inquiry you have undertaken?

Vaill: Yes.

Emerson: Then my contribution may be made with economy, unless my fellow respondents wish me to elaborate. My reply to your inquiry is simply to affirm your surmise. To be human is to be in a state of communion through faith with the Spirit.

Taylor: I didn't realize that this was going to be a religious discussion. I thought we were going to talk about management.

Vaill: Yes, that is my intent. I see what you mean, however, Dr. Emerson. For you, the mechanisms of faith are not the matters of possible debate that they might be for those of us who, for whatever reason, conceive of a secular realm in addition to a transcendent realm. I do think that my question applies to your fields of competence, but perhaps in a different sense than to the other fields. Could we hold further discussion of your particular subjects for a moment?

Emerson: Most assuredly.

Taylor: So now, as I understand it, you want to know how much one has to take on faith in order to practice the principles of our fields?

Vaill: Actually, I think a lot of faith *is* involved, and I want to know what you think of that suggestion.

Taylor: With all respect for you as the host, I must nonetheless say that I think the suggestion is preposterous. I don't mean that Scientific Management is perfect, or that some of our attempts at measurement and specification of the proper approach to the performance of a task are not faulty or capable of being improved upon. But it is still a long way from our fledgling science to outright faith, and I would resist any attempt to commingle the two.

Mayo: I would agree with my colleague, although, I suspect, for different reasons. I am not sure what Dean Smith's reaction might be owing to the somewhat less empirical nature of his field even to this day, but Taylor and I find ourselves in a rare state of agreement on this matter.

Lewis: Before I align myself with these two management consultants, I would like to know what you mean by faith. Taylor interprets it as religious, and I suppose most people do. But I gather you do not?

Vaill: Certainly in terms of my own upbringing, the primary context in which I have heard about faith is, as with the rest of you, a religious one. But as I have thought about the psychology of faith, I find myself coming to the conclusion that faith need not apply only to the acceptance of some particular set of religious principles. I don't see why that equation has to hold. I would rather decouple faith from religion and see what is left.

Mayo: One way to think about what is left is the idea of "assumptions." When you "act on faith" and when you "make an assumption," perhaps you are pretty much doing the same thing. Assumptions can be enormously powerful. It is not an exaggeration to say that the whole field of human relations in industry *exists* because of the mistaken assumptions made by those who would rationally design organizations and compel the individual human being's conformity to their prescriptions.

Vaill: Yes, I had considered the similarity between . . .

Taylor: If I might interrupt, could you elaborate, please, Dr. Mayo, on these "mistaken assumptions" you think were made in industry?

Mayo: I could, but I suspect that is not why our host has invited us here . . .

Taylor: . . . because if the suggestion is that the scientific principles for the analysis of work and the arrangement of improved manufacturing processes rest on mistaken assumptions, then I should like it demonstrated what those are!

Vaill: Well, I didn't really intend for you gentlemen to . . .

Lewis: Professor Mayo is right, you know, Taylor. Only thing is, he didn't go far enough. He thought he could get those managers to change their assumptions just by pointing them out to them. His problem is he didn't spend enough time with mine owners! If he had, he would have understood a little better what he is up against. They have a whole concept of what their rights are—and rights are what it is all about, aren't they?—which you are not going to change just by writing a book about it.

Taylor: The rational coordination of efforts and impulses is "what it's all about," as you say. It is as much in the worker's interests, however, as it is the owner's. I will compare my dedication to the working man's welfare to anyone's.

Vaill: My colleague Weisbord has just finished a major reevaluation of your contributions and I believe would agree [Weisbord, 1987, chaps. 1–2].

Taylor: I am in his debt.

Lewis: I suppose Weisbord is another management consultant.

Vaill: He is, but not one who is beholden to any narrow set of interests. (pause) Could we return to the question, please? I was starting to comment on Dr. Mayo's point about the relation between faith and assumptions. The same notion had occurred to me, and for some period of time I did equate the two ideas, but I have lately changed my mind about it . . .

Lewis: The owners are deucedly clever in my experience, and even with the best of intentions they can end up with you in their pocket.

Mayo: My dear Lewis, our host has asked us not to indulge our private passions this evening. You are convinced that there is no way that management—what I call your "owners"—can be invited to take a more balanced, humanistic view of their responsibilities. I have based my career on the idea that they can. You and Taylor can scoff if you like, but my trust is in the manager's innate capacity to act wisely as he acquires a progressively more valid grasp of the nature of the organization he is in charge of.

Taylor: I wasn't scoffing. In fact, I agree completely with you about the manager. Actually, we have Smith here to thank for our understanding of the manager's total commitment to whatever courses of action will best ensure the success of the enterprise given the circumstances in which it finds itself, eh, Smith?

Vaill: Dean Smith? Dean Smith!

Smith: Uh? Uh? Yes, why yes, I was just reflecting on the learned discourse engaged in by you, my worthy companions, and remembering the many evenings on which Hume and Berkeley and I would . . .

Vaill: We were wondering if you could comment on the intentions of the owners of enterprise as to their commitment to its welfare as opposed to the welfare of its members or of those in its immediate environs who might be affected by its conduct of its affairs.

Smith: There can be no question, although I might note in passing that the "opposition" you speak of is not the rule in my experience. But the first duty of the owner of the enterprise is to maintain and enhance the strength of the body.

Mayo: The *financial* strength. Yes?

Smith: What other kind of strength over the life of the enterprise is there? All assets that the enterprise might accumulate have no intrinsic worth to the owner, except as instruments to the increase of the wealth of the enterprise. This, writ large, is how an entire society of men benefits—through the mechanism of what I have called "the invisible hand" when all individual producers are acting to maximize their own wealth.

Lewis: Did you really . . . I mean, *do* you really *believe* that—that nothing the company owns or employs has any intrinsic worth except as a means to the ends of wealth?

Smith: You seem quite agitated, sir. Can nothing be more plain? For what other reason would a man enter into the conduct of enterprise if not for his own gain and that of his backers?

Mayo: I am willing for him to *enter* on the activity for reasons of financial gain, but his subsequent freedom becomes sharply curtailed by the limits of adaptability of those he employs. They are not infinitely flexible, as research has shown repeatedly. When the limits of their capacity to adapt are violated, the results are fatigue, hostility toward supervision, banding together in small informal groupings for protection, and in general obsessive-compulsive neurosis. Thus, the very institutions on which society relies for the creation of wealth produce conditions that are ultimately as costly to society as whatever wealth is created by productive activity.

Lewis: Mayo, old man! You sound more like a left-wing economist than the starry-eyed humanist I always thought you were. Well said!

Mayo: I am neither an economist nor a humanist. I am a *scientist*. My interest is in showing how our scientific knowledge of the human being, particularly the peculiar dynamics of the obsessive reverie to which men in industry are prone, requires a new approach to the management of institutions. Institutions should be conducted in conformance to scientific knowledge about human beings. The classical economics of Dean Smith, and the engineering principles developed by Fred Taylor, while impressive as systems of ideas, regrettably are based on invalid knowledge about the worker and hence cannot but produce dysfunctional effects.

Vaill: Would you agree, from a logical point of view, Dr. Mayo, that one's capacity to demonstrate the invalidity of another system does not by itself establish the validity of one's own?

Mayo: Is that what you have come to call feedback since I passed from the scene?

Vaill: To some extent, I suppose. It just seems to me that part of the appeal of the research and theory you launched is that they are so clearly concerned with the human being as we feel we know him or her. Our tendency might be to have more—if you will excuse the expression—faith in your work just because of its focus and its richness.

Mayo: I and my colleagues talked nondirectively to twenty thousand workers at the Hawthorne Works, so I know a little bit about when someone is not being quite candid. Are you suggesting that the studies of human behavior in organizations that I began and that have continued are accepted on *faith*?

Vaill: Yes, I'm afraid that I am—but that is not quite the criticism that you may think it is. It goes back to what I was starting to say a few minutes ago about the difference I think there may be between faith and assumptions. Maybe the two words do *literally* mean about the same thing, but practically, I think they have separate meanings and usages. I have devoted a whole essay to critiquing the "science story" we tell ourselves in this field [Vaill, 1985a, pp. 547–577]. It is relatively easy to show that our values run all through all our theories and research about human behavior in organizations. Our faith is in the rightness of those values of ours. Our readers—managers, students, other colleagues—have faith in *us;* indeed, the entire enterprise is a vast complex of faith. It is the same faith that competitors in the markets that Adam Smith here describes have to have in each other in order to sustain the structure of the market. Smith's theory of enterprise really describes the modes of behavior of oneself and one's competitors that can be trusted. Self-interest can be trusted, he says.

However, too often we forget that this proposition is an induction from experience that is not and cannot be decisive as a *scientific* result. It is accepted as true by many people, as are so many other generalizations about human beings' nature and behavior, not because it is scientifically or logically unassailable but because it has characteristics that qualify it for our trust. Among these characteristics are the quality of the data the idea is based on and the quality of the logic by which it is derived. But these only partially qualify an idea for our trust or faith, and, in fact, for many of us they are not even very high-priority matters, especially when the subject is the nature of humanity. We also use such criteria as whether the idea illuminates some practical question or difficulty we have, whether the idea accords with other things we have already placed our trust in, who is advocating the idea, how we think we will look to others if we adopt the idea, whether the idea elicits a good feeling in us.

Mayo: This itself is a theory of cognition.

Vaill: Of course.

Mayo: Can you prove it?

Vaill: If you mean can I offer a compelling argument to establish its validity, the answer is no, and the theory itself explains why I can't. No matter how hard I work, the trustworthiness of any theory is in the eye of the beholder. That is what the role of faith is all about. I like to reserve the idea of assumptions for the things an idea or theory itself takes for granted. Faith applies, for me, to the reaction of the "beholder," so to speak. The link between assumptions and faith is that if an idea or theory does make a lot of debatable assumptions, it is hard to place one's faith in it. If it doesn't make a lot of assumptions, or if the assumptions it makes are highly plausible, or if the assumptions it makes are invisible (whether deliberately obscured or not), *and* if the idea has practical appeal to us, then it is much easier to put our faith in it. I think that the theories and ideas that our modern managers use are theories and ideas that they do have faith in, but I am afraid too many of them have not stopped to think what this really means.

Taylor: Are you suggesting that we consciously obscured the assumptions on which our work is based?

Vaill: No, of course not, although I will say that we have drifted into a situation in the present day when it is possible to be very casual and sketchy about the assumptions one is making. But deliberate deception is not really the main problem, even in the highly commercialized system of teaching, consulting, and publishing we have today. The main problem is, in a way, insensitivity to the problem.

Smith: Could you give us an example that we might comment upon?

Vaill: Yes. In fact, I would like to give one that involves your field of economics, Dean Smith, but by extension the other fields as well. Then, if I might, I would like to pose one more broad problem—one that I hope Dr. Emerson here will find of interest—and then we may adjourn.

Lewis: Good, because my shade is being invoked at a conference over at the Mine Safety Academy in Beckley, West Virginia, and I should be there.

Vaill: We certainly shall honor that need. My first example deals with Dean Smith's comment of a few moments ago to the effect that the assets of the enterprise have no intrinsic worth to the owner except as instruments to increase wealth.

Lewis: I was wondering whether we were just going to let that crack go by.

Smith: "Crack?"

Emerson: An epithet. The utterance of a crackbrain.

Smith: A crackbrain, sir! Pray, wherein does my proposition merit such discommendation?

Vaill: The ease with which our feelings are stirred by the things we believe in is further evidence of the invisible foundation of faith on which our manifest reasons rest. Your proposition proposes that we have faith at two levels of action: the utilization of all the assets of the enterprise as instruments to its ends at the "local" level and the sum of all local action in the movements of the "invisible hand" at the societal level. Would you not say that you trust these two modes of action to continue on indefinitely?

Smith: Yes, unless constraining factors are introduced.

Vaill: Dr. Mayo suggested a moment ago that your system *produces* constraining factors by its very nature. But I wish to raise another question about it. Would it not be a prudent expectation that members of the enterprise would discover that they were valuable to it only as means to its ends?

Smith: Yes, they would perceive it.

Lewis: How could they miss it?

Vaill: And on discovering that the enterprise was being conducted according to a theory that valued them only as means to its ends, what would be their reaction?

Smith: They would have no reaction, for it would be their lot, and they would have been trained by society to accept their lot, indeed, to welcome it.

Vaill: Your theory rests on the members' acceptance of their lot?

Smith: Yes, for otherwise . . . (pauses).

Lewis: For otherwise they would proceed to make themselves less valuable to an enterprise that valued them only for what they considered to be a part, often a minor part, of themselves. They might even join a—horrors—union!

Vaill: If they did make themselves less valuable over a period of time, how could a manager be said to be pursuing the ends of maximizing wealth of the enterprise? Your theory leads him or her to conduct it in such a way that its human assets are moved to make themselves progressively less valuable to the organization.

Taylor: This is why people have to be told exactly what to do and be paid for it accordingly. The more completely the entire operations of the enterprise can be so engineered, the less it will be possible for anyone to conduct these depreciating activities. That's just a polite word for disloyalty and sabotage, by the way.

Vaill: Actually, I agree with you, Fred, although only with your logic and not with the *value* of engineering everything. But I do agree that if the broader frame is accepted, one way to deal with internal anomalies is to create control systems that prevent or reverse their effects. But note that this is another example of the way faith works—that having accepted the rightness of an overall philosophy and set of broad prescriptions—whether we understand them very well or not—we then are willing to evolve the lower systems and practices that will help to fulfill the broader faith.

Taylor: Are you suggesting that Scientific Management is merely a set of lower "systems and practices" for taking care of "anomalies"?

Vaill: After thinking about it, I can't convince myself that the system would ever have been invented had we not been intensely interested in shaping and controlling the human being as an instrument to the organization's ends. The faith in the value of the shaping had to precede the invention of the methods to do it. And of course, to this day, the invention of these methods proceeds on all fronts. One of its most recent manifestations is the invention of computer software that monitors, records, and comments on the efficiency of the person using the terminal in the real time of their action.

Taylor: That's *fantastic*!

Lewis: I would call it probably grievable.

Vaill: It depends on the frame in which you place your faith, doesn't it?

Mayo: I am not so sure. If a particular set of "systems and practices," as you call them, are producing unintended consequences, we then study in closer detail what is going on and develop more workable approaches. For example, we have shown repeatedly that if you talk to the people involved in the work, rather than scare them by filming them, putting a stopwatch on them, exhausting them with piecework incentive systems, they can tell you what sorts of changes need to be made in order for productivity to increase. If you permit the formation of small informal work groups rather than try to eradicate them by prohibiting talking and so forth, why, those small groups will reveal extraordinary capacity to perform the work at a high level of effectiveness and will develop high levels of satisfaction and commitment to the work, also.

Vaill: Yes, a latter-day application of your research is in the so-called skunk works, where even more than you ever thought groups could do is routinely being achieved. And on the shop floor, after years of stonewalling, managements are now spending millions of dollars a year to form small cohesive work teams that can take total responsibility for the product or service they produce. The work has many other interesting aspects, such as new gain-sharing plans to reward increased productivity and "employee assistance programs" to help people with problems in their personal lives. All this work is known collectively as quality-of-work-life experiments.

Mayo: That's *fantastic!*

Lewis: Some of this seems grievable, too.

Vaill: Once again, it depends on the frame you have faith in. And Dr. Mayo, I think you and Fred Taylor inhabit the same frame to a greater extent than either of you realizes. I do not hear you or your descendants arguing very much over the ends of the enterprise—only over the means, and the means, deriving from Smith's day, focus heavily on shaping the individual worker for loyal and predictable service to the organization.

Taylor: Wouldn't you say that is true of your own five-dimensional model of the values that the enterprise needs to reconcile— what were they?

Vaill: The Economic, Technological, Communal, Sociopolitical, and Transcendental.

Taylor: Yes. Don't those five stay within the frame, as you call it, of a desire for organizational effectiveness? Won't theories within these five exist just as much "within the faith," as it were?

Vaill: Well, I am not sure. I certainly don't think one's faith should be disturbed just for its own sake. But it seems to me that some of the "snakes" we have been casually handling—I like that phrase—"within the faith" are getting pretty troublesome. Many of the techniques we employ acquire a life of their own and end up not contributing what we thought they were going to contribute to the ends of the organization. Some are very wasteful. Some create more conflict than they resolve. Some contain serious ethical dilemmas. The faith in the rightness of the whole effort sustains us through these periods, or at least is supposed to. Some of these snakes have got pretty testy in the past couple of decades, and a lot of managers have been bitten. They put their trust in these elegant systems sold to them by their staff or by a consultant, and they frequently end up no closer to their strategic objective, plus now they have a whole host of subsidiary issues to deal with that accompany the installation of any new system. When bitten often enough, you may begin to lose faith in what it was that you thought would protect you. If we lose the wider faith that justifies the manager's efforts in the first place, and if we do not evolve another one to put in its place, all these systems that the staff and the consultants are pushing become ends in themselves.

Taylor: I saw that problem coming eighty years ago—the proliferation of staff experts, each one telling management something different.

Vaill: Each area of expertise is pressing back its own frontiers, tugging as it were at the core meaning of the organization. In economics, the trend to a service economy, the recent merger mania, as well as various global trends are profoundly changing the nature of the economic entity. In technology, it is the computer principally, but there are several other revolutions going on, too. In the communal area, multiculturalism and equal employment opportunity as well as new attempts to bridge work and family life are transforming what it is we are trying to be communal about. Global trends, particularly toward empowerment of the previously disenfranchised, are having a profound effect on the sociopolitical dimension. The paralysis of government and its inability to help organizations understand their sociopolitical responsibilities are another important trend. In the transcendental area, the crisis of the spirit is being talked about more and more widely, although the basic critique extends well back into the nineteenth century. In postwar America, Paul Tillich has been one of the most articulate spokespeople of the problem of meaning [Tillich, 1952]. Furthermore, all this work on the frontiers of various disciplines is going on with relatively little awareness of mutual effects and mutual implications. The only person who knows concretely how confused things are is the manager whose main task is still to try to get the organization to produce the goods and services that it is supposed to. It is this person—and there are hundreds of thousands of such individuals—who is the canary in the coal mine.

Emerson: The canary in the coal mine?

Smith: Do you still use canaries in coal mines?

Lewis: We would if it weren't for a few of us who wouldn't stand for it any longer. He refers, Dr. Emerson, to the practice of monitoring the concentration of methane gas with a canary. When it falls over, it is time to get out of the mine.

Emerson: Ah. So the suggestion is that this person called the manager may be experiencing higher and higher levels of gaseous confusion, which may be less detectable to those who reside in places where collisions of values, aspirations, and priorities are less in evidence?

Vaill: Yes. Those who live inside of the narrower assumptive frameworks have little idea how confused things are. The issues *within* their frameworks are complex and fascinating and provide all the challenge and variety one could want. One of the reasons I was interested in having you in this conversation, Dr. Emerson, was to get your advice on this problem of the loss of meaning and your thoughts about where we might look for renewal of our faith.

Emerson: I have been quite comfortable with the frequent professions of the significance of faith in this conversation. My way of expressing the relation of faith to assumptions is that the former contains the latter. It is the strength of our faith that makes it difficult for us to revise our assumptions, even when they are proved deficient. This is why devotees of Mr. Taylor and Professor Mayo can continue to deny the assumptions made by each other while holding to their own. Moreover, faith is not merely a thought *about* a matter. It would seem to be more of a merging of one's spirit with the thing one has faith in.

Vaill: A "merging of one's spirit"?

Emerson: Perhaps that image does not convey my meaning. It seems to me that one's consciousness of the thing one has faith in is fuller, more enfolding, and perhaps more taken for granted. To hold faith in something is to embrace it, not merely to think about it, certainly not to analyze it. This is why faith and doubt are such bitter enemies. Doubt comes to consciousness as faith wavers or is discredited, as we have been discussing with these "snakes" that managers are seeking to utilize.

Mayo: And this would mean that *anxiety* is doubt that is operating just below the level of awareness. Consciousness feels faith dissolving and doubt building but has nothing to put in its place—and becomes anxious.

Vaill: There is a mode of discourse I call "dialexia" that raises the expressions of doubts to the level of the main focus of thought and discussion. It is an endless search for a ground on which to stand, although, curiously, it serves to keep anxiety in check, because to participate in dialexic discussions is to think that something significant is being discussed. Dialexia has learned to criticize all grounds that lay claim to rationality and logical, scientific support. This leaves faith, however. In the context of our discussion, it would seem that a ground that dialexia cannot dismiss and discredit quite so easily is a faith of some kind. The faith our modern managers inherited has eroded, dialexia prevents anything from being put in its place, and thus, while acutely in need of renewed faith in the value of what they are doing, these managers find that they do not know how faith may arise again in their feelings.

Emerson: Over the centuries, men have created many objects of faith, some of which are remarkably durable but many of which are shoddy surrogates that blow away before the slightest breeze of adversity. The more complex and dangerous the world one is living in, the more resilient must be the faith, and the more durable yet infinitely yielding must be the object of the faith. It is an ageless problem.

Taylor: I knew it. This is going to be a discussion of religion.

Vaill: No, we will pursue the gentleman's image of faith in what is durable yet infinitely yielding some other time. I know that Mr. Lewis has to go and apparitionize at a meeting. So let me thank you all for coming. Perhaps we can do this again sometime.

Taylor: My pleasure.

Smith: A most pleasurable interlocution.

Vaill: Oh, and Dr. Mayo, I wonder whether you could stay behind for just a minute, please?

Mayo: How can I help you further?

Vaill: Well, actually, this is a little embarrassing, but since I am working on many of the same problems that occupied you, and since you went, well, *up there* at the end of your earthly so-journ, I was just wondering whether you could tell me whether you think I am . . . uh, that is, whether my work will get me . . . er, what I mean is, it's hard to know whether I'm on the right . . . that is . . .

Mayo: You're wondering whether, when your time comes, you will be joining me and the few other OB/OD experts that there are *up there*?

Vaill: Yes, that is my question.

Mayo: The rules are quite clear, my dear fellow, and it would not be possible for me to violate them. However, it is encouraged that the rules be explained in terms that each person can under-stand, so perhaps I could suggest something that will have mean-ing for you as one who has pursued a largely academic voca-tion during your life.

Vaill: I will appreciate anything you can tell me.

Mayo: Well, then: think of it as a tenure decision.

Chapter 14

The Requisites of
Visionary Leadership

"**A** becalmed sailor does not cease to believe in wind. He knows that it is there. It is fundamental, existential. He knows that he can seek it, but his seeking is within limits, and he accepts the limits, though he may curse them.

"The becalmed sailor does not cease to *seek* wind, either. He does things. He paddles. He watches the horizon. He listens to the marine radio. He trims and fine tunes. He hopes. He looks for wind and plays strategies about where he will find it.

"He does not assume that he can escape from his search. He does not assume that he will cease to be interested in it. He does not reflect on himself as a poor benighted soul who is inordinately dependent on wind. This is all out of his awareness. Someone else might see him engaged in a silly enterprise, but within the enterprise, there is no such thought as 'My search and hope for wind are basically a rather silly enterprise'" (Vaill, 1985d).

Some Preliminary Comments on Spirit

The little meditation on wind was written as I attempted to capture the meaning of my interest in organizational excellence and especially of my search for a better understanding of what fostering excellence involves. I was a little frustrated, and my mind went to the experience I have had many times of *knowing* that it (wind) is there and not gone for good, if only it will just show itself—soon! This chapter is about the quest, which in our various ways we are all on, for greater personal effectiveness as well as an improved understanding of what this means. As I have indicated repeatedly in preceding chapters, I think that the search for effectiveness, both in theory and in personal practice, has reached a crisis point in this world of permanent white water. Like my thoughts on the vital wind, though, my attitude is that the ingredients of effectiveness are not gone; they are just sometimes hard to keep track of amid all the turbulence. This chapter picks up a theme that has been mentioned several times already but has not been explored in any depth. This is the theme of "working spiritually smarter." Working spiritually smarter is offered as the most promising mode that we have for living and working in the permanent white water.

In Chapter Five, I mentioned the importance of a "credo" as a kind of personal guidance system for functioning amid paradoxes and absurdities. My own credo for the past three years has been "Helping men and women live and work purposefully and decently in the midst of seeming paradox and contradiction." As I have explored the meaning of this credo in my work with students, with colleagues, and with managers in organizations, I have more and more come to see that this credo demands of me that I work spiritually smarter. Furthermore, I am also discovering that the kind of help that is most needed by others is also aid in learning to work spiritually smarter.

In Chapter Thirteen, I portray Frederick Taylor backing away from discussing religion, and I intend to continue to back away from it in this chapter. I don't intend to say anything here that will violate anyone's religion, but I also don't intend to say anything that is about religion or that points toward religion. In fact, it is not an exaggeration to say that this chapter fails in its purpose if it sounds like a discussion of religion or of the need for religion. The real premise here is that our tendency to equate discussions of spirit with discussions of religion is a significant part of our problem as a society and as a profession of managers and management teachers and consultants. Religion has rendered the question of spirituality almost undiscussible except within a frame of doctrine and language that sound stilted and artificial to many in the world of work. For many of us, spirit is at best discussible only with great self-consciousness and diffidence, and that is a great tragedy.

A Way of Thinking About Spirit and Spirituality

"Spirituality" for me is the search for a deeper experience of the spirit of various kinds that one can feel stirring within. This stirring of spirit, however faint or disguised, is in all of us, for it is part—sometimes I think the main part—of what it is to be a human being. So the key things about the way I use the word *spirituality* are *search* and *stirring of spirit within*. I hope that this does not seem to be an eccentric or farfetched concept of spirituality. One thing about it that some may have noticed is that it is not clearly natural or supernatural. That is deliberate. In my own search, I am to the point of being pretty sure that the spirit that stirs within me as I can feel it is not purely natural. But I don't know exactly what else it is, or where it comes from, if it comes from anywhere. So I leave open for the moment the question of natural versus supernatural. Let us say for now that spirituality is either or both.

A second thing that I leave open for the moment is the question of the value of these stirrings of spirit within us. Unlike the issue of natural versus supernatural, though, this question cannot just be left up in the air. Some stirrings of spirit within us lead us toward what amount to "cheap thrills," as it were, while others do not. The main point of this chapter is that truly effective leadership has to get beyond catering to cheap thrills among its stakeholders, so obviously some way of thinking about what these cheap thrills are must be offered. Of course, what are "cheap thrills" for one person are "timeless expressions of the nobility of man" for another. This is probably why values are so hard to discuss; they are so relative. Still, would anyone deny that postwar Americans have been living in the middle of the greatest "glitzkrieg" in human history? There has to be a way of talking about all the energy we have put into what is relatively transitory or physically or psychologically harmful. I am not advocating doing *these* sorts of things with more spirit.

In my concept of spirituality sketched above, the ideas of "search" and "stirring within" are related. The more I search, the broader and richer the stirring of spirit in myself and also the more I can see spirit stirring in others. And the fuller my awarenes of my own and others' stirrings, the more the feeling of search, adventure, quest becomes real for me. Look at the variety of the stirrings of spirit as revealed in our everyday language. We use the expressions that follow because they *mean* something to us:

Spirited defense	Team spirit
Spirit of democracy	Spirit of inquiry
Lacking in spirit	Deeply spiritual
High (or low) spirits	Con spirito (musical marking)
Holiday spirit	Party spirit
Spirit of fair play	Spirit of the occasion
The human spirit	Evil spirits
Dispirited	School spirited
Spirited away	Mean spirited
Mind, body, and spirit	Spirit is willing/flesh is weak
Spirituals (songs)	Holy spirit
A few brave spirits	Blessed are the poor in spirit
Blithe spirit	The spirit, if not the letter
Company spirit	Public spirited

We need the concept of spirit, and there is no reason for it to make us nervous. The phrases quoted above are not merely conversational fluff—although I suppose it is possible for the meaning of the word to be debased, just as it is with any other word. The word is capturing something too important to us, though, for it to become terminally debased. It is built right into some of our words, such as *aspire, inspire, conspire, perspire, respire,* and *expire.*

What We Are Seeking

In most serious uses of the word *spirit,* we are reaching
for a word that captures our intuitive feeling of something that
pervades, energizes, weaves through, infuses, saturates some
person or action or thing or concept in our experience. As an
intuitive feeling for the character beyond what can be concretely
described, it is frustrating to many of us, particularly those who
have not spent much time trying to grasp the essence of these
intuitive feelings. Especially if one has an analytical, data-oriented mind, to speak of the spirit in things is exasperating. With
such a person, though, I would both accept the exasperation
and search in their interests and activities for the manifestations
of spirit that I am sure are there. In Chapter Six, for example,
I quote Michael Collins talking about what amounts to spirit
in fuel cells (Mailer, 1971, pp. 239–240). I don't know whether
Collins is a particularly romantically minded astronaut, but that
isn't the point. My experience is that there are things in each
person's experience that he or she needs an idea such as spirit
adequately to capture. The most tough-minded stockbroker
might talk about the current spirit among investors. The no-
nonsense top sergeant is comfortable with a notion of the spirit
in the ranks. The all-business surgeon is quite willing to grant
that a patient's spirits are a key factor in recovery. A relatively
famous mathematician once remarked to a class I was attend-
ing, as he finished off the proof of the fundamental theorem of
the calculus with a flourish, "There! When Newton saw that,
I'll bet it knocked him on his ass!" This exclamation is an expression of spirit in both Newton *and* the professor. Spirit is like
that; it begets itself.

We find the spiritual dimension in the concrete, in what
is palpable, whether another person, an activity, an idea, or
an institution. Our sensitivity to the spiritual aspect comes from
experience with the concrete phenomenon. As long as we keep
it at arm's length, treat it abstractly, as a member of a type or
a category, don't involve ourselves with it, we are able to ignore the spiritual part of it. It is easy to see why this is possible:

if spirit really does pervade and infuse, it is only the involvement
with the whole that reveals the presence of spirit everywhere in the
person or thing. To experience the whole, we must move in it
and with it, not stand back from it, for the more we stand back, the
more static and decomposable any phenomenon is. Ironically,
Western analytical thought thinks that this is *why* you stand
back—to enable observation "uncontaminated" by "subjective"
considerations, chief among which I suppose would be the belief
that something called "spirit" seems to pervade the phenomenon!

But there is a double irony. Owing to the fact that the
human being discovers spirit in what is experienced concretely
and fully, the same scientist or philosopher who argues for "objectivity," "abstraction," "clarity," "rigor" reveals in the very
passion of the argument a total devotion to the spirit of inquiry.
The more concretely the nature of inquiry is experienced, the
more one finds spirit there, too.

Rather than argue about the existence or nonexistence
of some abstract phenomenon called "spirit," let us reflect on
this: that human beings seem regularly, easily, unself-consciously,
and quite naturally to find spiritual dimensions in people and
things around them, including themselves. This has happened
in all of the "high-performing systems" I have investigated.
No one is shy in those organizations to talk about the spiritual
or mystical aspects of the team, the craft, the product or service, the persona of the leader, the history and the lore of the
activity, the meaning of being able to be a part of such a system.
Prior to the 1980s, this would have been perhaps a puzzling
statement, but all the case studies and other research results that
have come out about excellence and peak performance confirm
that both members and observers of excellent organizations consistently feel the spirit of the organization and the activity, and
that this feeling of spirit is an essential part of the meaning and
value that members and observers place on the activity.

Any single expression of the importance of spirit may be
casually dismissed as "subjective," I suppose. But it is not quite
as subjective for me to say, as a student of high-performing
systems, that spirit is found in their experience by individual
people everywhere.

The Loss of Spirit and the Search for Renewal

Unfortunately, the routine discovery of the spiritual aspects of our experience is not the whole story. There are other things going on inside us as well as around us that affect our ability to get in touch with the spiritual aspects of the people and things we encounter. Perhaps there have been other populations of people that had clear spiritual consciousness, or other ages when it was easy to discover and sustain it, but this world of permanent white water we are in does not seem to be such a place for most of us. The ongoing change described in Chapter One, the constant playing of a game one has never played before, the constant challenge of coping with the new and the different are not conditions that make the discovery of the spiritual dimension easy.

Almost as easily, it seems, as spirit flows into our experience of other people, activities, ideas, and institutions, spirit can flow out. It does not take much disturbance for many spiritual experiences to be spoiled. The power lawn mower under the church windows at the most solemn moment of the service is the classic example. We all know how intense our annoyance is when some unexpected interruption takes the spirit out of something. It can happen to works of art, to occasions where we hoped to enjoy family and friends, to celebrations that don't come off as planned, to pieces of equipment that break down on us, to people whose magic we count on having an off day, to vacations and other adventures we eagerly looked forward to; it can happen to any of the things in this world whose essence has come to have spiritual significance for us. No spiritual relationship is safe from potential disruption.

Given this state of affairs, it is possible to see what goes on in the typical organization in a rather different light. We have human beings naturally flowing toward spiritual relationships with the specific people and things they come into concrete contact with, and quite often we find *very* meaningful relationships forming. At the same time, we have a world of permanent white water where these relationships are constantly being disturbed or severed entirely. Because the search for spiritual relationship is natural in the person, we have a nonstop process of spiritual search, discovery, and loss going on. It is a "good news/bad news" joke on a macro scale: the good news is that spiritual discovery is everywhere available; the bad news is that it is nowhere secure.

It is also another one of those games no one ever told us we were going to have to learn how to play. There is very little in our culture that prepares us for an ongoing process of spiritual search, discovery, loss, and renewal. Yet that, it seems to me, is about what the experience of spirituality has to be in this world. Here, I think, we come to the real meaning and role of what we call faith. Faith is the feeling that spirit is present in a person, activity, or idea, even if for whatever reason one cannot experience that spirit directly.

Religion—a Brief Digression

Ours, of course, is hardly the first turbulent age, and for all we know, other ages have coped with more life-threatening uncertainty than we can imagine. Investing one's spiritual yearnings and energies in a religious faith has been a way that millions of humans have tried to overcome the agonies of this good news/bad news joke I have just described. The world tests religious faith, however, just as constantly and severely as it tests all other values and all other kinds of faith. Spiritual feelings and relationships grounded in religious faith seem no more immune from buffeting, from contradiction, and from temptation than spiritual feelings not infused with religious faith. To the person who has developed a faith in the god of religion, all the buffeting, contradiction, and temptation, of course, have a different meaning, but the disturbances are still felt. And of course, when something happens to such a person that cuts at the religious faith itself, as may have happened to many as a result of the transgressions of the TV evangelists, the spiritual loss is devastating.

I am taking a moment on the subject of religion because I simply want to note that embracing religious faith does not take away our problems and dilemmas. A religious faith may change the meaning of the permanent white water, but it does not do away with it. My own view is that the church exists not to make the world better but rather because the world doesn't get any better.

Spirituality in the Workplace

We naturally discover the spiritual aspects of the people and things that are close to us and that we become involved with. The world of permanent white water routinely disturbs and severs these relationships. Over a period of time, a feeling of what Tillich (1952) calls emptiness and meaninglessness develops. Our spiritual energy is not extinguished, but it is turned down low, at least while we are in the situations where the spiritual punishment has been most intense. If we let ourselves experience our spiritual aloneness, it often produces intense anxiety. We are not able to bring any inspiration to our work in such situations, and it is hard for us to take seriously anyone who tells us we ought to be more inspired.

Not that we don't want to be inspired, for most of us have discovered that inspired work is easy to do. We can sit up all night doing inspired work. There is always time for inspired work. Inspired work is approached eagerly and conducted lovingly. Inspired work is relatively unconcerned with whether anyone else thinks it is important (although, of course, inspired work likes a little applause now and then as much as any other kind of work). Inspired work has extraordinary momentum of its own and can tolerate distractions and interruptions that uninspired work will use as an excuse to pack up for the day.

It is hard in the environment of constant change to discover the spiritual possibilities of the work we do and of the people we do it with. This is why we have to learn to work spiritually smarter—because inspiration is so much harder to come by in the world of permanent white water. As discussed in Chapter One, the content of jobs in the postindustrial society is often fascinating, but the process of performing them is frequently agonizing, bedeviled as they are with organizational politics, budget squeezes, litigious stakeholders, pressure for short-term results, mechanistic performance criteria, and a host of other crazy-making factors.

Caught in this absurdity, we may opt for easy victories, for pleasures and indulgences that don't have much lasting meaning and value, but that at least seem to keep our minds off pain and loneliness for the moment. I have called these things "cheap thrills." Cheap thrills are attempts to achieve the effects of spiritual consciousness and relationships without having to endure the anxiety and the effort that spiritual growth requires. Cheap thrills may be the shallow pleasures of the "glitzkrieg society." They may be illegal or directly in violation of Judeo-Christian moral codes. In a way, these are the "easy" practices to condemn. We *know* they contain no spiritual nourishment. In these chapters, I have been concerned with some newer kinds of cheap thrills that may be more specific to the organizational world of permanent white water and not yet identified as spiritually empty practices.

The workaholic, technoholic, and powerholic modes of working smarter described in Chapter One are cheap thrills. Each seems to be doing something that is work related and constructive, but none of them is an inspired mode. It is a compulsive response to anxiety when a person does not choose one of these modes but instead goes automatically to it when the pressure is on. I want to underline the importance of the point about absence of inspiration in these modes. I have seen the weariness on the faces of those who attend executive development seminars and have felt their reluctance to complicate their lives any further with yet one more model of their situation or list of factors to consider. I have been briefed many times by managers about what is going on in their organizations and am continually struck by the nonstop preoccupation with power dynamics. The habit of working smarter by being more politically astute and clever has created a poisonous climate in thousands of offices. The destructive effect on people's spirits of an intensely political climate is a point that the advocates of more trust and openness have not often made. In my view, though, the crushing of spirit is the primary defect of political game playing.

Ignoring Satchmo's Paradox (Chapter Seven) gives us a cheap thrill. For an expert to ignore the fragility of the communication process and just plunge on with a recitation of his or her expertise is irresponsible. It preserves the form of communication but sacrifices the function. The experts who can hardly be bothered with the elementary questions they get are indulging themselves. Ironically, the layperson is being self-indulgent, too. The world is full of people who are sitting through classes, conferences, concerts, and conversations without understanding what they are hearing and not doing anything about it. They have an osmosis theory of learning—again, the form and not the function. Yet we know that when authentic communication occurs between teacher and student or expert and layperson, a true transmittal of spirit can occur. One of the more serious social tragedies of the modern age is the number of young people who can spend four or six or even eight years in a university without ever catching the true spirit of any subject. The primary cause is Satchmo's Paradox. I think that it is the experts and not the laypeople who are primarily at fault and who simply must learn to communicate their specialties more effectively.

Dialexia is a cheap thrill. Chapter Eleven makes my concern about it very clear. In terms of the present discussion, dialexia prevents the deep encounter with the concrete that is the essence of experiencing the spirit of anything. Dialexia stays abstract, loves concepts and models, loves "studies" that eviscerate the concrete phenomena. *Eviscerate* is a rather "purple" word, but it is exactly right. After giving the literal meaning of "disembowel," my dictionary says that *eviscerate* means "to deprive of vital content or force." Just so. That is what dialexia does, again, because it is so anxiety ridden itself that it cannot see how spirit avoidant it is. In dialexic meetings, there are no hugs, and there are no tears.

In Chapter Twelve, I mentioned in passing something called "enclavitis." This is another cheap thrill of the modern organization, and a very common one. Enclavitis is the pathology of the skunk works. It is the drawing in of energies, resources, and, indeed, spirit into an identifiable, controllable unit and then fighting off all influences that would destroy the unit's "integrity." Within the enclave, pride, fellowship, spirit, and constructive work flourish. The only problem is that the enclave is so inward turning that it may even be willing to sacrifice its responsibility to the larger whole in the interest of its integrity. I am quite aware of all the good things that do come out of skunk works. It is just that when I see the smugness that exists in some enclaves, I sense a cheap-thrill mentality just beneath the surface.

To conclude with a more general remark, the so-called seven deadly sins are not a bad framework with which to detect a cheap-thrill process that may be under way in an organization. Athos and Gabarro (1978) are the first management writers I know of to have suggested the utility of the seven deadly sins as an approach to understanding organizational dynamics.

As I have reflected on the seven deadly sins—pride, covetousness, lust, envy, gluttony, anger, and sloth—it has occurred to me that each is a perversion of an authentic need or objective. The authentic needs are part of what it means to be human and as such connect to the person's spiritual nature. But when the needs are pursued to excess, the spirituality goes out of them, and the search for cheap thrills is under way. For example, self-awareness and self-acceptance, if not grounded in spirit, can turn into pride. The friendliness and fellowship we feel toward others can degenerate into envy. Our desire for security and an improvement in our circumstances may become covetousness. Love and our desire for physical contact can become lust. Gluttony perverts our authentic need for nourishment, physical and mental. Anger is an expression of our right to defense and to justice carried to an extreme. And sloth, the age of the couch potato notwithstanding, takes too many liberties with our need for rest and replenishment.

It is a sobering exercise to take a look at life in the modern organization, including the life you and I are leading, and observe the seven deadly sins at work. Like all these cheap thrills I have been discussing, they are fallbacks, reluctant resolutions to pain that is almost intolerable. In the short run, these cheap thrills quell the anxiety that denial of our spiritual nature yields. In the long run? Well, we don't know. We have seen the spirit go out of whole institutions in our society, including *Fortune* 100 firms, government agencies, major universities, and whole professions. We have also seen spirit revived and renewed. As the final theme of this chapter, let us say a few things about that.

Spirituality and the Requisites
of Visionary Leadership

First of all, spiritual renewal is everybody's problem, not just the top team's, not just the CEO's. The "leadership" can come from anywhere. Some of the most significant leadership in human history has come from places that are the most unlikely, that any rational assessor of the odds would say had absolutely no chance of success. This is because rational assessors of odds often don't understand spirit. "Vision" that is not centered in a profound spirituality is nothing more than a "pictorial might-be" of an organization's future. It is the spirit within it that makes it live.

Second, it starts within the self, whoever I am and wherever I reside in the organization. I can't "go forth" with someone else's vision, someone else's technique, someone else's energy. This means that my own spiritual development has to be part and parcel of any vision I am trying to articulate for others. I must let my own spirit be dynamic and developing, including my periods of fear, sadness, and weariness, for these too are attributes of my spirit.

Third, I had best think of myself in spiritual terms as well as the psychological terms that twentieth-century society has taught me so well. I can find little spirit in terms such as *role model, participative leader, facilitator,* or *CEO.* My spirit recoils at doing anything to, for, or about the people around me in one minute. I can't follow a cookbook's five easy steps or someone's can't-miss method if what I am about has my spirit and that of others at stake—has "spiritual validity," so to speak. What metaphors and images are real for me as I move into my spiritual leadership? Am I a voyager, a knight, a quarterback, a chaplain, a father or mother, a servant?

Fourth, I think that all true leadership is indeed spiritual leadership, even if you hardly ever hear it put that flatly. The reason is that beyond everything else that can be said about it, leadership is concerned with bringing out the best in people. As such, one's best is tied intimately to one's deepest sense of oneself, to one's spirit. My leadership efforts must touch that in myself and in others.

Fifth, it is indeed a quest; that is, if I accept the definition of spirituality given earlier—the search for the stirrings of spirit in oneself. I can't be expected to have it all clear and together before I start. I discover spirit in myself and in others as I search. Living *is* the search.

Sixth, as I act this way more and more in my organization and in my life, it is going to bring me into some new and different relationships with people. It may cost me some friendships or even some income from my cheap-thrill days. I may have trouble at first recognizing the others in my organization who are trying to do what I am trying to do. I may be embarrassed as I realize that some of them have been up to the search for a lot longer than I have. And try as I may, there will be some whose spirit doesn't move me.

And finally, I do not conceive my search as a bringing of spiritual answers to others, for they have their own searches. What I bring to others are works and friendship enlivened with my spirit. I build outward from where I am, reconciling as I go whatever conflicts or mismatches in priorities or procedures may arise. The wider the circle grows, the more I discover, perhaps, that, to paraphrase George Washington, "the same spirit *does* animate the whole." And as this happens, not merely as speculation but as my concrete experience, I will see more clearly that spirit extends beyond any limits I can imagine.

References

Ackoff, R. L. *Redesigning the Future: A Systems Approach to Societal Problems.* New York: Wiley, 1974.

Allport, G. W. *Becoming: Basic Considerations for a Psychology of Personality.* New Haven, Conn.: Yale University Press, 1955.

Argyris, C. *Personality and Organization: The Conflict Between the System and the Individual.* New York: Harper & Row, 1957.

Argyris, C., and Schön, D. *Theory in Practice: Increasing Profes sional Effectiveness.* San Francisco: Jossey-Bass, 1974.

Athos, A. G., and Gabarro, J. J. *Interpersonal Behavior: Communicating and Understanding in Relationships.* Englewood Cliffs, N.J.: Prentice-Hall, 1978.

Auden, W. H. *The Age of Anxiety.* New York: Random House, 1947.

Barnard, C. I. *The Functions of the Executive.* Cambridge, Mass.: Harvard University Press, 1938.

Barrett, W. *The Illusion of Technique: A Search for Meaning in a Technological Civilization.* Garden City, N.Y.: Anchor Press–Doubleday, 1978.

Bartlett's Familiar Quotations. (14th ed.) Boston: Little, Brown, 1968.

Bennis, W., and Nanus, B. *Leaders: The Strategies for Taking Charge.* New York: Harper & Row, 1985.

Berger, P. L., and Luckmann, T. *The Social Construction of Reality.* Garden City, N.Y.: Doubleday–Anchor Books, 1967.

Blake, R. R., and Mouton, J. S. *The Managerial Grid.* Houston, Tex.: Gulf, 1964.

Blanchard, K., and Johnson, S. *The One-Minute Manager.* New York: AMACOM, 1982.

Bradford, D. L., and Cohen, A. R. *Managing for Excellence: The Guide to Developing High Performance in Contemporary Organizations.* New York: Wiley, 1984.

Chang, Chung-yuan. *Tao: A New Way of Thinking.* New York: Harper & Row, 1975.

Cleveland, H. *The Future Executive.* New York: Harper & Row, 1972.

Copeland, M. *And Mark an Era: The Story of the Harvard Business School.* Boston: Little, Brown, 1958.

Cornford, F. M. *Microcosmographica Academia.* (3rd ed.) Cambridge, England: Bowes & Bowes, 1933.

Cox, S. *Indirections.* New York: Viking Penguin, 1962.

Curtis, C. P. *A Commonplace Book.* New York: Simon & Schuster, 1957.

Denhardt, R. *In the Shadow of Organization.* Lawrence: Regents Press of Kansas, 1981.

Drucker, P. "Behind Japan's Success." *Harvard Business Review,* Jan.–Feb. 1981, pp. 83–90.

Emery, F. (ed.) *Systems Thinking.* New York: Penguin Books, 1969.

Fortune Editors. *Working Smarter: The Quest for Business Excellence.* New York: Penguin Books, 1984.

Gardner, J. W. *Excellence: Can We Be Equal and Excellent Too?* New York: Harper & Row, 1961.

Gleick, J. *Chaos: Making a New Science.* New York: Viking Penguin, 1987.

Hall, E. T. *The Silent Language.* New York: Doubleday–Anchor Books, 1973.

Harvey, J. B. "The Abilene Paradox." *Organizational Dynamics,* 1974, *3* (1), 63–80.

Harvey, J. B. *The Abilene Paradox and Other Meditations on Management.* Lexington, Mass.: Heath, 1988.

"What we are suggesting

in our society should cor

fulfillment of the individ

must, of course, have its

preoccupations, but over

else that it does, it should

this question posed by s

institution doing to foste

the individuals within it

(Gard

...that every institution
...ibute to the
...l. Every institution
...n purposes and
...d above everything
...e prepared to answer
...ety: 'What is the
...e development of

...r, 1961, p. 142)

Hofstede, G. "Motivation, Leadership, and Organization: Do American Management Theories Apply Abroad?" *Organizational Dynamics,* Summer 1980, pp. 42–63.

Kanter, R. *The Change Masters: Innovation for Productivity in the American Corporation.* New York: Simon & Schuster, 1983.

Kaplan, A. *In Pursuit of Wisdom.* Beverly Hills, Calif.: Glencoe Press, 1977.

Kelly, C. M. "The Interrelations of Ethics and Power in Today's Organizations." *Organizational Dynamics,* 1987, *16* (1), 4–18.

Kelly, C. M. *The Destructive Achiever.* Reading, Mass.: Addison-Wesley, 1988.

Koontz, H., and O'Donnell, C. *Principles of Management.* (3rd ed.) New York: McGraw-Hill, 1972.

Kroeger, O., and Thuesen, J. M. *Type Talk.* New York: Delacorte Press, 1988.

Kuhn, T. *The Structure of Scientific Revolutions.* Chicago: University of Chicago Press, 1962.

Lao Tzu. *Tao Te Ching.* (G.-F. Feng and J. English, trans.) New York: Random House, 1972. (Originally published 6th century B.C.)

Lasch, C. *The Culture of Narcissism.* New York: Warner Books, 1979.

Leavitt, H. J. "Unhuman Organizations." *Harvard Business Review,* 1962, *40* (4), 90–98.

Leavitt, H. J. *Managerial Psychology.* (4th ed.) Chicago: University of Chicago Press, 1978.

Lindbloom, C. E. "The Science of Muddling Through." In H. J. Leavitt and L. Pondy (eds.), *Readings in Managerial Psychology.* Chicago: University of Chicago Press, 1980.

Lombard, G.F.F. "Relativism in Organizations." *Harvard Business Review,* Mar.–Apr. 1971, pp. 55–65.

McGregor, D. *The Human Side of Enterprise.* New York: McGraw-Hill, 1960.

Magnet, M. "Managing by Mystique at Tandem Computers." *Fortune,* June 28, 1982, pp. 84–91.

Mailer, N. *Of a Fire on the Moon.* New York: New American Library–Signet Books, 1971a.

Mailer, N. *The Prisoner of Sex.* Boston: Little, Brown, 1971b.

Maslow, A. H. *Motivation and Personality*. New York: Harper & Row, 1954.

Merton, T. *The Seven Storey Mountain*. New York: Harcourt Brace Jovanovich, 1948.

Montagu, A. *Darwin, Competition, and Cooperation*. New York: Henry Schuman, 1952.

Myers, I. B. *Gifts Differing*. Palo Alto, Calif.: Consulting Psychologists Press, 1980.

Parkinson, C. N. *Parkinson's Law*. Boston: Houghton-Mifflin, 1957.

Peter, L., and Hull, R. *The Peter Principle: Why Things Always Go Wrong*. New York: William Morrow, 1969.

Peters, T. J. *Thriving on Chaos: Handbook for a Managerial Revolution*. New York: Knopf, 1987.

Peters, T. J., and Austin, N. *A Passion for Excellence: The Leadership Difference*. New York: Random House, 1985.

Peters, T. J., and Waterman, R. H. *In Search of Excellence: Lessons from America's Best-Run Companies*. New York: Harper & Row, 1982.

Phillips, A. "Proposal to Wrest More Current from Savage Leaves Angry Paddlers in Wake." *Washington Post*, Nov. 29, 1987, p. D6.

Popper, K. *Conjectures and Refutations: The Growth of Scientific Knowledge*. New York: Harper & Row, 1965.

Popper, K. *Popper Selections*. (D. Miller, ed.) Princeton, N.J.: Princeton University Press, 1985.

Potter, S. *The Complete Upmanship*. New York: Holt, Rinehart & Winston, 1971.

Raths, L. E., Harrison, M., and Simon, S. B. *Values and Teaching*. Westerville, Ohio: Merrill, 1966.

Roethlisberger, F. J. *Man-in-Organization: Essays of F. J. Roethlisberger*. Cambridge, Mass.: Harvard University Press, 1968.

Roethlisberger, F. J. *The Elusive Phenomena: An Autobiographical Account of My Work in Organizational Behavior at the Harvard Business School*. Boston: Division of Research, Harvard Business School, 1977.

Roethlisberger, F. J., and Dickson, W. J. *Management and the Worker*. Cambridge, Mass.: Harvard University Press, 1939.

Rogers, C. R. *On Becoming a Person*. Boston: Houghton Mifflin, 1961.

Scott, W. G., and Hart, D. K. *Organizational America*. Boston: Houghton Mifflin, 1979.

Simon, H. A. *The Sciences of the Artificial*. (2nd ed.) Cambridge, Mass.: MIT Press, 1981.

Simon, S. B., Howe, L. W., and Kirschenbaum, H. *Values Clarification: A Handbook of Practical Strategies for Teachers and Students*. New York: Hart, 1972.

Siu, R.G.H. *The Portable Dragon: The Western Man's Guide to the I Ching*. Cambridge, Mass.: MIT Press, 1971.

Siu, R.G.H. "Management and the Art of Chinese Baseball." In H. J. Leavitt and L. Pondy (eds.), *Readings in Managerial Psychology*. Chicago: University of Chicago Press, 1980.

Skinner, B. F. *About Behaviorism*. New York: Random House, 1976.

Slater, P. E. *The Pursuit of Loneliness: American Culture at the Breaking Point*. Boston: Beacon Press, 1970.

Tileston, M. *Daily Strength for Daily Needs*. New York: Putnam, 1934. (Originally published 1884.)

Tillich, P. *The Courage to Be*. New Haven, Conn.: Yale University Press, 1952.

Vaill, P. B. "Practice Theories in Organization Development." In J. Adams (ed.), *Theory and Method in Organization Development: An Evolutionary Process*. Alexandria, Va.: NTL Institute, 1974.

Vaill, P. B. "Management as a Performing Art." Commencement address, School of Government and Business Administration, George Washington University, May 1974. (Mimeographed.)

Vaill, P. B. "Cookbooks, Auctions, and Claptrap Cocoons." *Organizational Behavior Teaching Review*, 1979, *4* (1), 3-6.

Vaill, P. B. "The Purposing of High Performing Systems." *Organizational Dynamics*, Autumn 1982, pp. 23-39.

Vaill, P. B. "Process Wisdom for a New Age." In J. Adams (ed.), *Transforming Work*. Alexandria, Va.: Miles River Press, 1984.

Vaill, P. B. "Management as a Martial Art." *Organizational Behavior Teaching Review*, 1984-85, *9* (3), 96-97.

Vaill, P. B. "Integrating the Diverse Directions of the Behavioral Sciences." In R. Tannenbaum, N. Margulies, F. Massarik, and Associates, *Human Systems Development: New Perspectives on People and Organizations.* San Francisco: Jossey-Bass, 1985a.

Vaill, P. B. *The Layman's Lament: Learning to Not-Know.* Sunrise Seminar Audiotape Series. Alexandria, Va.: NTL Institute, 1985b.

Vaill, P. B. "O.D. as a Scientific Revolution." In D. D. Warrick (ed.), *Contemporary Organization Development: Current Thinking and Applications.* Glenview, Ill.: Scott, Foresman, 1985c.

Vaill, P. B. "A Personal Statement." *OD Practitioner,* 1985d, *17* (1), 15.

Vaill, P. B. "To Our Readers." *Organizational Dynamics,* 1987, *15* (4), 2–3.

Vaill, P. B. *Strategic Management Process Consulting.* Reading, Mass.: Addison-Wesley, forthcoming.

Waley, A. *The Way and Its Power: A Study of the Tao Te Ching and Its Place in Chinese Thought.* New York: Grove Press, 1958.

Watts, A. *Tao: The Watercourse Way.* New York: Random House, 1975.

Weick, K. E. "Careers as Eccentric Predicates." *Executive,* 1976a, *2* (2), 6–10.

Weick, K. E. "Educational Organizations as Loosely-Coupled Systems." *Administrative Science Quarterly,* 1976b, *21,* 1–19.

Weisbord, M. R. *Organizational Diagnosis: A Workbook of Theory and Practice.* Reading, Mass.: Addison-Wesley, 1978.

Weisbord, M. R. *Productive Workplaces: Organizing and Managing for Dignity, Meaning, and Community.* San Francisco: Jossey-Bass, 1987.

Whitehead, A. N. *Science in the Modern World.* New York: Free Press, 1967. (Originally published 1925.)

Whyte, W. H., Jr. *The Organization Man.* New York: Simon & Schuster, 1956.

Wilbur, K. *Eye to Eye: The Quest for the New Paradigm.* Garden City, N.Y.: Doubleday, 1983.

Zaner, R. *The Way of Phenomenology: Criticism as a Philosophical Discipline.* New York: Pegasus–Western, 1970.

Index

DEMCO